ALPINES

— THE —
ILLUSTRATED
DICTIONARY

ALPINES

— THE —
ILLUSTRATED
DICTIONARY

CLIVE INNES

Timber Press
Portland, Oregon

First published in the UK 1995 by Cassell, London

Text copyright © Clive Innes 1995
Photographs copyright © Clive Innes and Peter Stiles

First published in North America in 1995   635.9528
by Timber Press, Inc.
The Haseltine Building
133 S.W. Second Avenue, Suite 450
Portland, Oregon 97204, U.S.A.

1. Alpine garden plants
2. Rock gardens
I. T

ISBN 0–88192–290–0

Typeset by Typobatics
Printed and bound in Singapore by Kyodo Printing Co. Ltd

CONTENTS

ACKNOWLEDGEMENTS   6

INTRODUCTION   7

ILLUSTRATED A–Z OF SPECIES   11

GLOSSARY   188

INDEX OF SYNONYMS
   AND ALTERNATIVE NAMES   189

BIBLIOGRAPHY   191

PICTURE ACKNOWLEDGEMENTS   192

ACKNOWLEDGEMENTS

I must express my sincere thanks and appreciation to Harry Hay, one of the most experienced and knowledgeable plantsmen I have had the pleasure of knowing, especially in the realm of bulbous and similar plants, and I should also like to thank Lancelot Henslow, who has a keen interest in the plants of the Iberian Peninsula, both of whom have kindly helped with the photographs. The skilful photography of Peter Stiles is much in evidence in this work, and I am most grateful for his cooperation.

INTRODUCTION

When the opportunity arose to provide a fully illustrated record of alpine plants, I realized that I had a tremendous challenge on my hands! From the very outset, the immensity of the task was apparent. The primary question was what to include and – perhaps even more important – just what constituted an alpine plant. One's mind instinctively turns towards the Alps, that magnificent mountain range that dominates much of Italy, Switzerland and France and that, undoubtedly, gave rise to the use of the word 'alpine' to describe this group of plants. However, the plants we cherish and cultivate with such delight and devotion in our rock gardens and alpine houses are not confined to the numerous choice species that are native to this most beautiful, grandiose habitat. Nor, for that matter, are they plants whose natural habitat is confined to the other splendid and spectacular mountain ranges of Europe. There is no doubt that the term 'alpine' has long been controversial and is most likely to continue to be so for decades to come.

It should never be assumed that alpine plants are restricted to fairly low or medium altitudes. A number of plants can be observed even in snow zones. To see blue gentians pushing their heads through the snow is a sight never to be forgotten, but several other species, such as some saxifrages, primulas and even poppies, are to be seen displaying their colourful blooms as the snows melt away. The variety of plants that nature has ordained as being suitable for different elevations is almost unending, and travelling around the world, as I have had the opportunity and pleasure of doing, I would say that it is almost impossible to describe the huge range of plant material that can be discovered, from low to high altitudes, in other parts of the world – and most of these are species that will stimulate the interest of alpine plant enthusiasts.

Mountains and high, hilly country have always held a fascination for me. Looking back over many years of travel, I recall with constantly renewed excitement the discovery of lovely, often rare, and unusual plants in the mountainous region of Sierra Nevada, inland from San Francisco, and, further south in California, in the San Gabriel and San Bernardino ranges. Here were found relatively unknown *Sedum* species, miniature bulbous plants of the *Liliaceae*, such as *Calachortus*, frequently encountered growing in quite substantial numbers. Perhaps really outstanding and inescapable were the bright and vivid colours of several *Iris* species, including *I. hartwegii*, with flowers varying from pale to deep yellow and on to different shades of blue; the white, yellow and bluish shades of *I. innominata* and of *I. douglasiana*. Climbing high in the Chisos Mountains of Texas, the Chihuahan highlands, the Sierra Madre regions and further south, down to the Cordilleras of Oaxaca, Mexico, it was possible to see endless numbers of fascinating, truly alpine plants at both high and low altitudes. When I travelled across parts of South Africa, through the Drakensberg Mountains and through the seemingly endless, high, hilly country towards Namibia and southern Angola, a number of *Babiana* and *Romulea* were to be seen, together with several succulent plants that are well within the scope of the enthusiastic alpine plant collector.

New Zealand offered no end of intriguing plant life. This is a country well known for its extensive alpine plant life, and the high hills and mountains, especially those in South Island, still offer, I am certain, many high-altitude plants as yet unknown. Tasmania, an island of particular charm, is home to a number of lovely endemic species that are to be found in its several comparatively low mountainous regions, and some of these are to be found nowhere else in the wild. Happily, these native plants are successfully conserved in the Hobart Botanic Gardens.

So the story can continue to unfold. Just as memorable are the low-growing species of *Portulacaceae* and *Ascelpiadaceae*, not to forget the small bulbous plants of the *Liliaceae*, which are to be seen on the mountain slopes of Saudi Arabia, especially during the early months of the year, when weather conditions encourage growth and flowering. In the wholly different climate of St Vincent in the West Indies are a few species of *Campanulaceae*, especially *Lobelia*, while two or three species of *Selaginellaceae* are native to the volcanic mountain slopes of Soufrière and have, fortunately, survived extinction following the volcano's dramatic eruption in 1979. These, together with a host of desirable and keenly sought-after plants are native to several West Indian islands as well as to the mainland of South America, where, from the Andes, south to the high mountains of Patagonia, the realm of alpine plants extends, even to include several species of *Cactaceae* within the genera *Maihuenia*, *Pterocactus* and *Tephrocactus*, which form low-growing, mostly prostrate, spiny cushions.

So, back to Europe and all that that continent has to offer. I have lived in Spain in recent years, and I am constantly finding opportunities to explore the numerous hills and mountains that abound in almost every corner of the Iberian Peninsula, where plants can be seen in bloom throughout the year. The Pyrenees tend to compete with the Alps and the Apennines in the abundance of wild life and numerous varieties that can be found there. In many regions the miniature *Gynandriris sisyrinchium*, together with *Narcissus*, *Crocus*, *Colchicum*, *Tulip* and innumerable *Sedum* and similar succulent species, can frequently be located growing in close proximity to quite dense colonies of various species of choice terrestrial orchids. These, and so many other very desirable plants, are a never-ending source of pleasure for those willing – and able – to devote the time and energy to see nature at its best! Several of these plants are included within the pages that follow.

I make no apology for including bulbous and cormous species in this book – in fact, this was a deliberate decision as so many of these plants are true alpines. Similarly, several insectivorous species and ground orchids have been included, since these hold a great fascination for scores of plants-men – as they certainly do for me. My interest in these very different plants may astonish some readers, who are, perhaps, mindful of my reputation for being an enthusiast for cacti and succulents. Many of these plants are, however, well within the category of 'true alpines' and should not simply be regarded as plants of dry, desert areas, as so many people tend to assume. Many cacti and succulent plants flourish in a typical alpine environment. A great many of these, particularly cacti, are indigenous to the high zones of the Andes and other mountain ranges, often in forested areas. I have decided to include cacti with several other succulent plants, all of which may be regarded as true alpines, that are recorded with *Sedum*, *Sempervivum* and other genera of the *Crassulaceae*.

Many exceptionally fine works have been published on the subject of alpine plants, and it is my intention to augment and supplement these by describing different items, all of which may legitimately be considered alpines, thus broadening the scope of these extremely attractive plants. Those included in these pages are merely representative of the great many that it would have been possible to include but that would require many volumes to encompass.

The descriptions of the plants illustrated in this book include guidelines on cultivation, as well as an indication of habitat, habit of growth and any individual characteristics that are of especial interest. Although necessarily brief, I hope that these descriptions will be sufficient to ensure the successful culture of the species in question. Nevertheless, it seems prudent to enlarge on some of these features.

Where to plant and position a particular species is a matter of considerable importance. The fact is, of course, that many specimens encountered in the realm of alpines, which we endeavour to cultivate successfully, do not necessarily originate from identical climatic habitats and conditions. This is, of course, a factor that must be carefully considered from the outset – whether it should be placed in a shaded or sunny position; whether it is better to provide the protection of the alpine house; whether there is more or less guaranteed assurance of survival and success in the usually exposed location of the rock garden. Plants from low altitudes in warmer climates, such as the countries bordering the Mediterranean, are far less likely to prove totally hardy in more northerly European gardens, and these subjects are, in all probability, demanding of more sheltered positions. At the other extreme, those numerous species that grow wild at high altitudes or that are found in cool mountain pastures are likely to meet with disaster if set in a truly sun-baked, lowland garden. Equally, those plants from woodlands or forested areas definitely require protection from excessive heat and sun, and they should be carefully planted in a fairly shaded position where the soil will remain moist, even during the warmest months of the year.

The question of suitable soil raises a matter of much consequence. Unfortunately, no one soil mix has yet been produced to meet the needs of all alpine subjects. In general, by far the largest number of plants appears to flourish in a calcareous soil mix. There are, however, a great number that can be successfully grown only if set in an acid soil. These are aspects that must be taken into consideration, and, whenever a particular preference is demanded, this is included in the description of the individual species.

Watering is always an important subject. Very many alpines are succulent plants and, whether they are from open or shaded habitats, they tolerate less frequent watering – in fact, too much and too often is likely to encourage the foliage and the roots to rot. Those subjects located in the alpine house may need more careful attention in this respect and should be watered only when the soil becomes dry; during the winter months, they should receive little or even no water at all. Feeding these plants is advocated, but only two or three times a year, and then only during the growing and flowering season. Be selective when you buy a fertilizer. Although a general-purpose fertilizer, containing nitrogen and potash, can be useful, if possible you should try to obtain one that contains essential trace elements such as iron, magnesium, boron, manganese, copper and molybdenum. Fortunately, it is now possible to find proprietary fertilizers that contain some or even all of these ingredients. Some of these are offered in prepared liquid form; others as a soluble powder to be dissolved in water.

Propagation is an endlessly fascinating subject. Many of the most desirable species are rarely made available through commercial sources, at least as plants. It is, therefore, wise to endeavour to obtain seeds, and happily, very many are now obtainable from specialist seed merchants. When you are preparing to sow seed, select a suitable container, completely cover the base with a shallow layer of broken crocks or small gravel to prevent water-logging, and add a layer of seed compost to within 1 cm (½ in) of the top. Firm the compost well to create an even, level surface. If you are sowing very fine, small seed, it is better to cover the whole surface with a very thin layer of sharp, gritty sand before you carefully sprinkle the seeds on top. Do not cover them with more compost. Larger seed should be set on the surface of the compost, then covered with a layer of gritty sand, to about the same depth as the size of the seed. Lightly spray with tepid water, so that the compost is evenly moist, then place the container in a propagator – or even a sealed polythene bag – which should be placed in a partially shaded but warm location, preferably in a temperature of 10–20°C (50–68°F), according to the species, taking care to maintain the temperature throughout the germination period. Frequently germination takes only a matter of days, but sometimes weeks, or even months, can elapse before results are evident – so patience is also important. After germination, increase the light levels, while maintaining the temperature, then gradually acclimatize the seedlings as they develop, keeping the compost moist and airy, but out of draughts. Seedlings can be pricked out once they are large enough to be handled easily.

Many species can be propagated successfully by division or by stem or root cuttings. In general, this is best undertaken in spring or early summer. Division is a very satisfactory method, although the resulting plantlets need particular care until they are obviously established. Stem cuttings are best if the cut section is dipped in a hormone powder and left for a short while before being inserted in a prepared soil suitable to the requirements of the species. Alternatively, it can be put in a mixture of equal parts of washed, gritty sand and shredded peat. Keep in a shaded but warm position and, when rooting is apparent, plant out as necessary.

In conclusion, as far as is possible, current nomenclature has been adopted. In recent times name changes seem to occur far too often, and even Family titles have become involved in this 'name game', so that now one has to ask if a plant belongs to the *Compositeae* or the *Asteraceae*, to the *Liliaceae* or the *Alliaceae*. I hope that readers will be kindly disposed to the botanic status I have given. Where certain popular plant names have been changed, suitable synonyms have been recorded in the descriptions, and these are summarized in the Index of Synonyms and Alternative Names at the end of the book.

Clive Innes

ILLUSTRATED
A–Z OF SPECIES

Anchusa caespitosa

A

Abronia villosa var. aurita
NYCTAGINACEAE

A very sticky, hairy species, more or less prostrate but to about 30 cm (12 in) high, found in deserts in California and Arizona, USA. Many parts of the plant – stems, flowers and bracts – have this feature, the exception being the broadly oval leaves, borne on long trailing stems, 45 cm (18 in) long. Flowers, in spring, rose-red or pinkish-purple in umbels from leaf axils, subtended by lance-shaped bracts. A low-growing, trailing plant, needing full sun and a rich, very sandy, open soil. Propagate by division in summer or from seed, freshly gathered.

Acantholimon glumaceum
PLUMBAGINACEAE

A cushion-forming perennial plant found in the wild in Armenia and also known on Mount Ararat in Turkey. The cushions are formed of numerous dark green, needle-like leaves, each leaf about 2 cm (¾ in) long. Bright rose-pink flowers appear in summer, generally numerous, borne on slender spikes about 10 cm (4 in) long. Of very easy culture, requiring a bright, sunny position and a well-drained soil, in the open or in the alpine house. Propagate by division or from seed in spring.

Acantholimon hohenhackeri
PLUMBAGINACEAE

A species forming rather tight cushions, originating from central Asia. The dull greyish-green leaves, with spiny tips, are about 5 cm (2 in) long. Flowers, in summer, carried on long, leafless stems at intervals, 5 – 10 in number, clear lilac-pink with recurving petals and a prominent, protruding style. Needs a bright, sunny, but protected position and a well-draining, humus-enriched soil. Propagation is best achieved by soft wood cuttings in late spring. Seed only rarely set in cultivation.

Acanthus mollis
ACANTHACEAE

A robust plant, to about 60 cm (24 in) or more tall, found wild in rocky places in hills of southern Europe and north Africa. Leaves are large, the lower ones pinnately lobed and long-stalked, the upper ones smaller, the purplish bracts spiny. Flowers to 5 cm (2 in) long, white and purple-veined, borne in dense spikes in summer. Useful as a background plant in the rock garden, but needs bright light and a well-drained, fairly rich soil. Propagate from seed, sown in spring.

Achillea argentea
COMPOSITAE

(Because of reclassification this is now known as *Tanacetum argenteum*.) A mat-forming plant found in the wild in several parts of central and eastern Europe. The mats, often more than 30 cm (12 in) in diameter, are composed of numerous slender, almost thread-like, silver leaves. The flowers, too, are very small, pure white and carried on short stems, generally in summer. Needs a sunny position and flourishes in ordinary garden soil, if this is well drained. Propagate from seed or by division.

Aciphylla congesta
UMBELLIFERAE

A tufted perennial plant, native to South Island, New Zealand, and still an almost unknown species in cultivation. The dark green leaves form clusters, which seem to multiply quickly to large cushions to 60 cm (24 in) across. The thick, fleshy stem rises well about the foliage, with several rounded heads of white flowers, in early summer, formed into a globose, compact, terminal cluster. Needs an open position in bright sunlight, but accepts particularly low temperatures. Ordinary garden soil is suitable. Propagate by division or from seed in late summer.

Aciphylla traillii
UMBELLIFERAE

These are rather rare, hardy perennials as far as the genus is concerned. All originate from alpine regions of New Zealand and chiefly Stewart Island. This species is becoming known in Britain but is often wrongly named. A rosette-forming species, to 20 cm (8 in) across, the spreading leaves have thickened green midribs, which are enhanced by the prominent yellow margins. Bluish flowers are terminally borne in summer on long, erect stems. Needs moist, well-drained soil. Propagate by division or from seed. At present this must be considered an extreme rarity.

Adonis annua
RANUNCULACEAE

Commonly called pheasant's eye. An annual species found in moist meadows in southern Europe. Leaves are pale green, almost thread-like, spreading along the slender stems. Flowers, in late spring and early summer, bright scarlet with a prominent black centre, more or less cup-shaped, to 2.5 cm (1 in) across, with 5 – 8 petals. A decorative plant for the rock garden, needing a well-draining, slightly enriched soil in a sunny, sheltered site. Propagate by seed soon after harvesting, temperature about 12 °C (54 °F).

Adonis vernalis
RANUNCULACEAE

A tuft-forming hardy perennial from high mountainous regions of the Pyrenees and of southern and central Spain; also occurring in the Massif Central in France. Numerous small, almost scale-like leaves form quite substantial tufts, with brilliant yellow flowers borne on short stalks in early spring. Plants are not likely to exceed 30 cm (12 in) in height and are well suited to the alpine garden. A sunny position is advisable, and an enriched, open soil. Propagate from seed or by division in autumn.

Aeonium percarneum
CRASSULACEAE

A clump-forming, semi-succulent plant, originating from Gran Canaria, the Canary Islands, usually in high, hilly areas. Stems erect and freely branching, coated with a greyish rind and bearing terminal rosettes, to 12 cm (5 in) wide, of fleshy, green, slightly reddish suffused, oval leaves. Flowers pinkish, borne in a dense pyramidal, terminal inflorescence to about 30 cm (12 in) in length. Requires protection of alpine house for early summer flowering; needs a rich, porous soil. Propagate by cuttings or from seed.

Agapanthus praecox
ALLIACEAE

A tall-stemmed plant, native to more southern areas of South Africa, including Transkei. It has long, strap-like leaves 60 cm (24 in) or longer, invariably recurving to become almost prostrate. Flowers are borne in summer, in terminal umbels on stems 50 cm (20 in) or more long, white or blue, each flower to 7 cm (2¾ in) long and long-lasting. Reasonably hardy if placed in a bright, sunny, but sheltered position in the rock garden. Needs a well-drained, rich soil. Propagate from seed in spring.

Agapanthus walshii
ALLIACEAE

A clump-forming species, to 60 cm (24 in) or more tall when in flower. Native to Cape Province, in mountainous areas of the Caledon district of South Africa. Leaves long and strap-like, deciduous and basal. Flowers appear in summer, deep purplish-blue, tubular, pendent, 5 cm (2 in) or more long, borne terminally in a loose umbel. Not thoroughly hardy so best grown in the alpine house in a well-drained, humus-enriched soil, in full sun. Propagate from seed in spring, temperature 15 °C (59 °F).

Albuca canadensis
HYACINTHIACEAE

Possibly synonymous with *A. major*. A small, bulbous plant, found wild on mountain slopes in northerly parts of Cape Province, South Africa. Leaves very slender, to about 30 cm (12 in) long, all basal. Flowers in early summer, yellowish-green with a prominent dark green stripe on the outer surface of each segment, borne terminally on erect stems, each stem 40 cm (16 in) or more long. Needs alpine house culture and a rich, sandy soil. Propagate by seed.

Alchemilla mollis
ROSACEAE

A clump-forming plant, native to southeastern Europe, generally to 45 cm (18 in) tall when in flower. The bright bluish-green leaves are quite hairy, about 10 cm (4 in) in diameter, with dentate margins. The flower stem rises well above the basal leaves, and towards the apex small clusters of leaves are produced from which clusters of small, greenish-yellow flowers are produced on short spikes in summer. Ordinary garden soil and a sunny position meet its requirements. Propagate from seed, sown in spring.

Allium callimischon ssp. haemastictum
LILIACEAE

This is one of the forms of the dwarf-growing species that originates from the island of Crete. It rarely exceeds 10 – 15 cm (4 – 6 in) in height, and has fine, very slender green leaves only about 1 mm (1/16 in) wide, which appear in autumn, with the flower stalks apparent in spring. Flowers occur in autumn in an umbel to 3 cm (1¼ in) across, white with reddish spots, only a few to each umbel. A pleasing plant for a rockery area, where it requires a gritty but enriched, peaty, loamy soil. Propagate from seed or bulbils in spring.

Allium christophii
LILIACEAE

Syn. *A. albopilosum*. A particularly decorative species from many parts of central Asia. The rather large bulb produces slightly hairy, strap-shaped leaves to about 25 cm (10 in) in length. The extraordinarily large bloom is in the form of an umbel to 20 cm (8 in) in diameter on a stem to 50 cm (20 in) long and appears in early summer – each star-like, purplish-lilac flower 2 – 3 cm (¾ – 1¼ in) in diameter. These are often dried for indoor decoration in winter. Requires a sunny position, in well-drained soil. Propagate from seed, sown in early spring.

Allium karataviense
LILIACEAE

A most attractive and unusual species, native to central Asia and found mostly on rather loose limestone screes. Generally, each bulb has only 2 leaves, greyish-purple, more so on the under-surface, broadly elliptic, recurving, about 10 cm (4 in) wide. Flowers, in late spring, are borne on short stems in large umbels to 20 cm (8 in) in diameter, each star-like flower to 1.5 cm (⅝ in) wide, whitish, lilac or mauvish with a purplish central line on the petals. Grows well in open soil enriched with humus, in full sun. Propagate from seed or bulbils in late summer.

Allium mairei
LILIACEAE

A rather miniature species of clump-forming habit, originating from altitudes up to 5,000 m (16,500 ft) in Yunnan, China. Slender elongated leaves arise from rhizomatous rootstock at or near ground level. The inflorescence, in late summer, reaches to 15 cm (6 in) high, bearing a few-flowered, lax umbels, each pinkish or reddish-purple flower to 1 cm (½ in) wide with recurved petals. Needs a slightly gritty soil and slight shade to be sure of good growth, and will benefit from decomposed leaf mould being worked in around the rootstock. Propagate from seed or offsets in spring.

Allium mirum
LILIACEAE

An unusual plant, suited to an alpine house. It is native to Afghanistan, growing in rocky, mountainous country at an altitude of about 2,700 m (9,000 ft). Each bulb produces two greyish-purple leaves, about 12 cm (5 in) or more wide, at ground level. Flowers in summer, white to purplish, about 1 cm (½ in) in diameter, carried in a dense umbel 5 – 9 cm (2 – 3½ in) across, each papery petal having a dark stripe running centrally from tip to base. Needs a well-drained soil and a sunny position. Propagate by division or from offsets when replanting or from seed in spring.

Allium moly
LILIACEAE

A popular bulbous plant, which spreads freely, originating from mountainous areas in many parts of southern and southwestern Europe, mostly in wooded country. A robust plant, which offsets freely, it has many bluish-green leaves, somewhat sword-shaped, to 4 cm (1½ in) wide. The large umbel, to 6 cm (2½ in) in diameter, is spherical, with few or many bright, rich yellow flowers in midsummer, the stems about 30 cm (12 in) high. Ordinary garden soil meets its requirements, with a position in bright sun or partial shade. Propagate from seed or bulbils in spring.

Allium montanum
LILIACEAE

Syn. *A. senescens* ssp. *montanum*. A medium sized, thrift-like plant to about 30 cm (12 in) tall. It has stoloniferous rootstock with oval lobes, and is to be found growing wild in the Pyrenees, southern and eastern Spain and parts of central Portugal. Leaves basal, slender, to 4 mm (³⁄₁₆ in) wide, rounded on the underside. Flowers in summer, in a dense spherical head about 4 cm (1½ in) in diameter, the umbel borne on a stout stem, the small flowers pink to purple. Needs a fairly sunny position, and a porous, enriched soil. Propagate in autumn from seed or by division.

Allium narcissiflorum
LILIACEAE

A most beautiful miniature species, native to parts of Italy and France. The slender, bottle-shaped bulbs readily form compact clumps, becoming covered with fibrous tufts. Leaves are slender, 2 – 4 mm (⅛ – ³⁄₁₆ in) wide and bright green, sheathing only the lower part of the stem. Flowers appear in midsummer, usually 5 – 10 to a pendent umbel, rich red or purple, bell-shaped, each about 1 cm (½ in) long. Excellent plants for the alpine garden, adapting to ordinary soil. Propagate from seed or offsets in spring.

Allium neapolitanum
LILIACEAE

A bulbous plant, found wild in the Mediterranean region at low altitudes. Leaves, narrow, lance-shaped, keeled on the underside, form a basal rosette. Flowers white, star-like, to 2 cm (¾ in) across, borne in terminal umbels in late spring or early summer. A reasonably hardy plant needing a bright, sunny but sheltered position in a rock garden. The soil should be porous, composed of ordinary garden soil with fine grit and humus added. Propagate by offsets or from seed in spring.

Allium nevskianum
LILIACEAE

An exceptionally attractive species, which is still fairly unknown in cultivation. It is a native of low mountainous regions of central Asia, particularly in the area of the former USSR. The bulbs produce wide, fleshy leaves, which are more or less recurved and at ground level. In summer a large spherical umbel is borne on a short fleshy stalk, with many rose-pink flowers, the petals being very slender, almost feathery. Best suited to the alpine house, requiring an enriched porous soil. Propagate from seed in spring.

Allium nigrum
LILIACEAE

A medium sized bulbous species, native to southern Europe and through to parts of the Middle East. It is usually associated with rocky terrain that is dominantly alkaline. The oval bulb produces 2 – 3 broadly linear leaves, all basal, to 4 cm (1½ in) or more wide, which taper to a point. The many flowered umbel is 6 – 8 cm (2½ – 3 in) across, bearing white or, rarely, pale pink flowers with a blackish-brown eye and a green mid-vein on each petal, in early spring. Requires a sunny position, preferably in an alkaline soil. Propagate by division in autumn.

Allium oreophilum
LILIACEAE

Syn. *A. ostrowskianum*. A rather low-growing, bulbous plant to about 15 cm (6 in) tall, native to central Asia, Turkey and the Caucasus. Only 2 slender, greyish-green leaves appear, 3 – 8 mm (³⁄₁₆ – ⁷⁄₁₆ in) wide. A few reddish-purple flowers are borne in a hemispherical umbel to 4 cm (1½ in) in diameter, each flower about 1.5 cm (⅝ in) across, bell-shaped, at their best in mid-summer. Plants increase rapidly to form substantial clumps, requiring an enriched, fairly porous soil in a slightly shaded or sunny position. Propagate by division or from seed in spring.

Allium paniculatum
LILIACEAE

A bulbous plant of medium growth, found in the wild on fairly high ground throughout much of south, central and eastern Europe, mainly on stony hill sides. Leaves slender, hardly more than 3 mm (³⁄₁₆ in) wide, sheathing the lower part of the stem. Flowers appear from early summer to early autumn, in the form of a loose umbel about 5 cm (2 in) in diameter, bearing bell-shaped, often pendent pinkish or lilac flowers with darker veins. Ordinary garden soil is suitable, but best placed in slight shade. Propagate from offsets or seed in early spring.

Allium rosenbachianum
LILIACEAE

A fairly tall-growing species, 60 – 90 cm (24 – 36 in) in height, native to central Asia, especially northern Afghanistan, in stony, grassy areas at about 3,500 m (11,500 ft). The lanceolate leaves develop in clusters at ground level, with the tall, ribbed stems bearing a terminal umbel to 10 cm (4 in) in diameter containing numerous small, reddish-purple flowers in early summer. The flowers tend to shrivel quickly, leaving the stamens prominently protruding for several weeks. Likes a rich, open soil in an open, sunny position. Propagate from seed in early spring.

Allium roseum
LILIACEAE

A short to medium sized bulbous species, widely distributed in many parts of southern Europe and found growing at low altitudes, usually in grassy areas in slight shade. The more or less round bulb produces slender leaves, some very narrow, others to 1.5 cm (⅝ in) wide. Flowers are pale pink or almost whitish, borne in an umbel to 5 – 7 cm (2 – 2¾ in) in diameter, usually with many reddish bulbils, from late spring to early summer. Grow in sun or slight shade. It propagates freely from seed or bulbils in almost any garden soil.

Allium schoenoprasum
LILIACEAE

The chive of culinary use. A bulbous species of varying height, which groups readily. Native to many parts of Europe, being found on rocky slopes where moisture tends to abound. The cylindrical leaves are to 5 mm (¼ in) wide, several arising from a single bulb. The rounded or oval umbel of pale purple or lilac flowers is densely compact and appears during summer; a colourful addition to the alpine garden. Plant in a well-drained, sunny position in autumn, in ordinary garden soil. Propagate by division or from seed in spring.

Allium senescens
LILIACEAE

A bulbous plant found wild in many parts of Europe, usually in low mountainous regions in grassland. Plants are generally to about 20 cm (8 in) tall, with very slender, more or less erect, green leaves. Flowers are generally pale pink (deeper colouring is known), appearing in summer in densely flowered umbels to 4 cm (1½ in) in diameter. A popular clustering rock garden plant, needing sun and a permeable, slightly enriched soil. Propagation is easily achieved by division or from seed, sown in early spring.

Allium sphaerocephalon
LILIACEAE

A medium to tall bulbous plant found wild in scrub or rocky places in the Mediterranean region. Usually 2 – 6 semi-cylindrical leaves with grooved upper surfaces, sheathing the lower section of the stem. Flowers are deep purplish-red, rarely white, carried in a dense, globular, many flowered umbel to 4 cm (1½ in) in diameter in summer, the individual flowers being tubular with protruding stamens. It has proved to be quite hardy, so is useful for rock garden culture. Needs a fairly rich, porous soil. Propagate from seed in spring or after flowering.

Allium stellatum
LILIACEAE

A medium sized plant with bulbous rootstock found wild in North America (Mississippi). The leaves are very narrow and generally more or less prostrate, to about 20 cm (8 in) in length, bright green. Flowers appear in summer, small, pink and strongly scented, borne in dense umbels on slender stems 25 – 30 cm (10 – 12 in) long. Requires the sunniest and brightest position possible and a very porous, humus-enriched soil. Suitable for either rock garden or alpine house. Propagate from seed, newly ripened.

Allium subhirsutum
LILIACEAE

A bulbous species native to the Mediterranean region, where it flourishes at fairly low altitudes in sandy or rocky areas. It develops a slender stem to about 30 cm (12 in) tall, with several basal leaves, which invariably wither before flowering. Flowers pure white or pale pinkish, to about 1 cm (½ in) in diameter, borne in umbels 4 – 6 cm (1½ – 2½ in) across in late spring and early summer. A bright, sunny position is advised, and a very porous soil. Keep moist once growth is apparent. Propagate by seed in spring.

Allium subvillosum
LILIACEAE

A bulbous species, similar in many ways to *A. subhirsutum* but with more dense umbels, found wild in southern Spain and north Africa. Leaves linear and long-pointed, generally 3 in number, densely ciliate on the upper margins. Dense terminal clusters of stalked white flowers in early summer. It prefers a slightly shaded position, having grown in long grass in its habitat (as shown). A porous, gritty, slightly enriched soil is advised. Propagate from seed when fully ripened.

Allium triquetrum
LILIACEAE

A well-known bulbous plant originating from regions bordering the Mediterranean, on islands and the mainland. The slender leaves have a prominent keel, and these vary a great deal in length. The flower stem is 3 - cornered, bearing an umbel 3 – 4 cm (1¼ – 1½ in) across, with white flowers marked with a central green stripe on the petals, each bell-shaped flower about 1 cm (½ in) or little more long, in late spring and early summer. Prefers a moist position and partial shade; ordinary garden soil is suitable. Propagate from seed, freshly harvested.

Allium tuberosum
LILIACEAE

A freely flowering species originating from China and Japan and widely cultivated in many parts of Asia for its culinary value. The rather slender, sheathed bulb produces several fleshy leaves and stems to 50 cm (20 in) tall. Small umbels of open, star-like white flowers, each 1 cm (½ in) long, appear in late summer and early autumn. Plants tend to cluster freely, thriving in a bright, sunny position in the garden, readily adapting to ordinary garden soil but benefitting by the addition of decomposed leaf mould. Propagate from seed or by division in spring.

Allium victorialis
LILIACEAE

A clump-forming species arising from narrow, bottle-shaped bulbs, found in the wild on fairly high mountain slopes in central and more north-eastern regions of Europe. The leaves tend to be leathery, more or less lance-shaped, 3 – 6 cm (1¼ – 2½ in) wide. White flowers appear during the summer, borne in spherical umbels to about 4 cm (1½ in) in diameter, each flower remarkably star-shaped. Needs enriched, permeable soil and partial shade. Propagate by division or from seed in early spring.

Allium wallichii
LILIACEAE

A bulbous species found in Nepal in the temperate Himalayan region at an altitude of about 3,000 m (10,000 ft). Leaves basal, about 60 cm (24 in) or more long, 4 mm (³/₁₆ in) wide, with flat margins, narrowing to a pointed tip. Flowers appear in early summer, purplish-red, in a laxly flowered terminal cluster to 7 cm (2¾ in) in diameter, each flower carried on pedicels about 3 cm (1¼ in) long. A really bright position is essential, and a very porous, enriched soil. Suitable for rock garden culture. Propagate from freshly gathered seed.

Aloinopsis schooneesii
AIZOACEAE

A dwarf, tufted succulent species with tuberous rootstock, found wild in hilly country in the Willowmore district of Cape Province, South Africa. Each short stem has 8 – 10 small, bluish-green, spathulate leaves, with more or less rounded tips, to about 2.5 cm (1 in) long. Flowers in early summer, yellow to red and silky, to 1.5 cm (⅝ in) across. Best suited to alpine house culture in an enriched, open soil. Propagate from cuttings or seed.

Alophia drummondii
IRIDACEAE

A rare bulbous species with a basal cluster of 2 – 4 erect, iris-like leaves, each to 30 cm (12 in) or more long, originating from wooded areas from Louisiana to Texas, USA. Stem simple or laxly branched, bearing in summer dark, rich purple flowers about 4.5 cm (1¾ in) across, the inner petals smaller, dark purple with brown speckles near the base, about 1.5 cm (⅝ in) long, each spathe having 1 – 2 flowers. Essentially an alpine house subject, needing a rich, peaty, open soil, in a sunny site. Moisture necessary in the growing season. Propagate from seed in autumn.

Alstroemeria chilensis
ALSTROEMERIACEAE

A clump-forming species with a fleshy, spreading rootstock, originating from Chile. Leaves deciduous, very narrow, soft and usually limp, to about 15 cm (6 in) long. Flowers appear in summer, pink or red, marked with yellow, funnel-shaped, about 4 cm (1½ in) long, borne terminally on rather weak, slender, branching stems to about 45 cm (18 in) or more long. Only semi-hardy but, given reasonable protection, can survive cold winters – best in a sheltered rock garden. Needs a rich, open soil, which must be well-drained. Propagate from seed or by division.

Alstroemeria haemantha
ALSTROEMERIACEAE

A hardy, perennial, tuberous-rooted species, found on low mountain slopes in Chile. Leaves slender, lance-shaped, about 8 cm (3 in) in length, but frequently longer. Flowers, in summer, orange-red streaked reddish-brown, about 5 cm (2 in) long. Prefers a moisture-retentive, enriched soil in a sheltered but sunny site in the rock garden. Propagates readily from seed, freshly harvested.

Alyssum spinosum
CRUCIFERAE

Syn. *Ptilotrichum spinosum.* A small, dense, shrubby plant not exceeding 15 cm (6 in) in height, originating from southeastern Europe. It has short, wiry stems, bearing narrowly oblanceolate, small, greyish leaves. Flowers, in summer, are borne in short dense clusters, white or pale pink. A satisfactory plant for outdoor culture, in a sunny position and a well-drained, alkaline soil. Propagate from seed, sown in spring.

Alyssum wulfenianum
CRUCIFERAE

Commonly known as madwort. A mat-forming, sun-loving species native to the southeastern Alps. It produces silvery grey-green leaves, which embrace the trailing woody stems, oblong-obovate in shape and very small. Bright yellow flowers appear during spring and early summer in small racemes. Plants rarely more than 7 – 8 cm (2¾ – 3 in) high, spread indefinite. Suited to the rock garden in a sunny position. Propagate from seed or by division.

Anacamptis pyramidalis
ORCHIDACEAE

A short, tuberous-rooted orchid found wild in much of the Mediterranean region in grassy places at high or low altitudes. Leaves narrow oblong to narrow lance-shaped, pale green. Flowers appear in late spring and early summer, pink or purplish-pink, very occasionally white, each flower about 1 cm (½ in) long, borne in a dense, rounded pyramidal head. Tends to multiply freely in the wild to form substantial colonies. Needs bright light and a rather acid, permeable soil – it is also said to flourish in more calcareous soils. Propagate from seed.

Anacyclus pyrethrum var. depressus
COMPOSITAE

An attractive species found in the Atlas Mountains of Morocco. The elongating, fleshy rootstock produces many slender, prostrate stems, to about 15 cm (6 in), that have numerous greyish, fern-like leaves. Flowers appear during spring and summer, white, daisy-like, the underside of the petals being reddish. Plants require a bright, sunny position and a light, gritty but enriched compost – ideal in rock crevices. Can be propagated easily from seed, sown in early spring.

Anacyclus valentinus
COMPOSITAE

A clustering, fairly erect species originating from France and from central eastern and southern Spain, usually on low hill sides amid rocks. Grows to 30 – 45 cm (12 – 18 in) tall. Leaves very slender, encompassing the stems for much of their length. Yellow flowers borne terminally in summer on the branching stems, the globular heads composed of numerous ray-florets, short and erect. A sun-loving plant, requiring a light, sandy, gritty, loamy soil. Propagate from seed or by division.

Anagallis alternifolia
PRIMULACEAE

A fairly compact plant, found on high ground in many parts of South America and the West Indies. Bright green leaves tend to remain prostrate but tufted, and are alternate. Flowers, white or in shades of pink, are borne terminally on stems to 10 cm (4 in) long in summer. A sun-loving species more suited to the alpine house. A slightly acid soil is recommended, but this needs to be permeable. Propagate from seed in spring.

Anagallis monellii
PRIMULACEAE

A fairly low-growing, shrubby plant of rather tangled growth, native to southern Europe and north Africa, where it grows in open countryside. The erect or spreading stems bear elliptic green leaves set opposite or in whorls, about 1 cm (½ in) long. Flowers of brilliant blue in summer, about 1.5 cm (⅝ in) across, borne terminally on short stalks. Suited to the alpine house or a bright sunny position outside. Flourishes in ordinary garden soil. Propagate from seed in spring.

Anchusa caespitosa
BORAGINACEAE

A more or less prostrate species originating from Crete. The bristly, dark green, slender, narrow leaves develop a rosette form. Flowers, in summer, are borne in clusters, 5 – 10 cm (2 – 4 in) long, on very short stalks and are a clear, rich blue with a prominent white centre, which enhances the attractiveness of the bloom. Careful attention is essential for successful culture, particularly as far as watering is concerned – excessive watering can be disastrous. Full sun is necessary, and an open soil. Plant in spring or autumn. Propagate from seed, by division or by root cuttings in late spring.

Anchusa undulata ssp. hybrida
BORAGINACEAE

A biennial species found on dry hill sides in the Mediterranean region. Leaves elliptical, some basal, others clasping the stem, the latter unstalked. Flowers appear in late spring and early summer, dark blue or violet, bowl-shaped, the tube 8 mm (⁷⁄₁₆ in) long, the limb 5 mm (¼ in) with oval to lance-shaped bracts, terminally borne. A hardy plant, requiring ordinary garden soil with grit and decomposed leaf mould added – and sun-loving. Propagate from newly ripened seed, temperature 12°C (54°F).

Androsace carnea
PRIMULACEAE

An almost stemless species originating from both the Pyrenees and the Alps, growing at altitudes to about 3,000 m (10,000 ft). A tuft-forming plant with narrow, dark green leaves formed into compact basal rosettes to about 4 cm (1½ in) in diameter. Flowers, in early summer, are variable, either white or pink, borne in an umbel of 1 – 6 individual blooms, the stalks 5 cm (2 in) or more long. A fairly acid soil is best for good flowering, and a sunny position is advisable. Propagate from seed in spring.

Androsace ciliata
PRIMULACEAE

(Thought by some to be a form of *A. pubescens*.) A cushion-forming species of particular attraction, found in the Pyrenees. This dwarf perennial has somewhat small lanceolate green leaves, which are formed into rosettes little more than 2 cm (¾ in) in diameter, these gradually clustering. Flowers are borne singly on very short stems in early summer, deep rose-pink in colour and only 12 mm (⁹⁄₁₆ in) across, with quite a conspicuous yellow throat. An enriched porous soil is advised, and a position in the sun. Propagate from seed, sown in spring.

Androsace delavayi
PRIMULACEAE

A fairly large, rosette-forming species native to central China (Yunnan) and still very rare in cultivation. Small, wedge-shaped leaves of dark green are formed into very small, dome-like rosettes, which in due course develop into large cushions, 20 cm (8 in) or more in diameter. Flowers of pink or white appear in early summer, on stalks, 10 cm (4 in) long, just above the centres of the rosettes. An enriched soil is recommended, and a bright position in the alpine house is preferable. Propagate by division or from seed, in spring.

Androsace hedraeantha
PRIMULACEAE

A bright cushion-forming species, probably of central European origin, though this is uncertain. It is low-growing, rarely exceeding 3 – 4 cm (1¼ – 1½ in) in height, and is composed of several rosettes of narrowly oval, shiny leaves. Rather flat, pink flowers are produced in umbels of 5 – 10, in early to late spring. Great care is necessary to grow this species successfully. It prefers a slightly shaded position in a cool alpine house, demanding a porous, enriched soil and careful watering at all times. Propagate by division after flowering or from seed, freshly harvested.

Androsace hirtella
PRIMULACEAE

A large, cushion-forming species found at high altitudes in the central Pyrenees. The very small, green, slightly finely hairy leaves provide small rosettes, which multiply to produce large, somewhat rounded mounds, 15 – 18 cm (6 – 7½ in) in diameter. Flowers appear in early summer, singly or in pairs on very short stalks; the flowers are generally white, but pale pink is also recorded. Needs a bright position and an open, well-drained soil; more adaptable to alpine house culture. Propagate by division after flowering or from seed, freshly harvested.

Androsace lanuginosa
PRIMULACEAE

A popular trailing plant with spreading stems, native to the slopes of the northwestern Himalayas. The trailing stems have silvery green leaves about 2 cm (¾ in) long, almost totally coated with fine silky hairs. Flowers, from late summer to early autumn, rose to lavender pink with a reddish eye, borne in terminal umbels, each about 1 cm (½ in) in diameter. A remarkably fine alpine, appreciating slight shade, which is best planted among rocks on slightly sloping ground in ordinary garden soil. Propagate from seed.

Androsace limprichtii
PRIMULACEAE

Syn. *A. primuloides watkinsii, A. sarmentosa watkinsii*. A mat-forming species native to the Himalayas, spreading by means of stolons. Leaves oblanceolate, 4 – 7 cm (1½ – 2¾ in) long, finely hairy, appearing in summer; others, in winter, are very small and densely covered with white hairs. Pink flowers appear late in spring, on stems to 15 cm (6 in) long, subtended by linear bracts. Suited to alpine house culture in gritty, rich soil. Propagate by division after the flowers have faded.

Androsace muscoidea
PRIMULACEAE

An attractive small plant, to about 3 cm (1¼ in) high, found in the Himalayas (Kashmir) at an altitude of about 4,000 m (13,000 ft). It is mat-forming, composed of many small rosettes of green, finely hairy leaves, which tend not to become intensely compacted. Flowers, borne singly or 2 – 3 or more in clusters, are at their best from midsummer to mid-autumn and are white, later fading to a very pale pink. This plant remains quite a rarity and is best kept in an alpine house. A sunny position, a well-drained soil and careful watering are important.

Androsace obtusifolia
PRIMULACEAE

A low-growing, tufted species, found wild in the Alps and Apennines at altitudes to 3,500 m (11,500 ft) in screes and rocky areas. The spoon-shaped, hairy leaves form rosettes. Flowers about 8 mm (⁷⁄₁₆ in) across appear in summer, white or pale pink, solitary or in long-stemmed umbels. Needs a very bright sunny location, and a gritty, enriched, loamy soil. Careful watering at all times. Best suited for alpine house culture. Propagate by division in spring, temperature 15°C (59°F).

Androsace pubescens
PRIMULACEAE

A cushion-forming species composed of many rosettes densely compacted together, originating from the Pyrenees. Leaves are greenish-grey and finely hairy, but in general are not evergreen, withering in autumn. Flowers appear in early summer from the centre of each rosette, singly on stems mostly less than 5 mm (¼ in) long, usually white, although very pale pinkish shades may occur. A well-drained soil is important, and a position in bright sunlight; best grown in an alpine house. Propagate from seed, sown in spring.

Androsace pyrenaica x carnea
PRIMULACEAE

There are several excellent hybrids between these two species, both originating from the Pyrenees. Unfortunately, only one or two have been named. Leaves are formed into small rosettes, which develop into dome-like clusters, 15 cm (6 in) across. The flowers, 5 mm (¼ in) wide, appear in spring or early summer, in varying shades of pink or white. Alpine house culture is advisable; needs gritty soil and a position in sunlight. Propagate by division after flowering.

Androsace sarmentosa
PRIMULACEAE

An herbaceous perennial, native to areas of the eastern Himalayas on mountain slopes in stony ground, to altitudes of 4,000 m (13,000 ft). The basal leaves form something of a rosette and are more or less lance-shaped, obtuse, narrowing to a short petiole and hairy. Flowers, in early summer, pink or red, formed in a terminal umbel subtended by an involucre of rounded bracts, each bloom about 1.6 cm (⅝ in) across, with a yellow throat. Needs a sunny position and rich, permeable soil. Propagate from seed in spring.

Androsace sempervivoides
PRIMULACEAE

A mat-forming species with rosettes resembling those of *Sempervivum*. It is found in the wild in the Himalayas (Kashmir and Tibet). Each rosette, approximately 2 – 3 cm (¾ – 1½ in) across, is formed of bright green, oblong, leathery leaves; each rosette has stolons, which connect to other rosettes. Flowers appear in spring, produced in small umbels of 4 – 10 flattish pink flowers with reddish eyes, 5 – 6 mm (¼ – ⁵⁄₁₆ in) across. Needs a position in full sun, and a very gritty soil enriched with humus. Propagate from seed.

Androsace spinulifera
PRIMULACEAE

A fairly large species, which is clump-forming and is native to central China (Yunnan). Linear leaves, 5 – 7 cm (2 – 2¾ in) long, with a spiny tip, are formed into fairly erect rosettes. Flowers, in early summer, in umbels to 15 cm (6 in) in diameter borne on long stems, the flowers red or purplish, each about 12 mm (⁹⁄₁₆ in) in diameter. The leaves die in winter to leave a cone-shaped base ready for the next year's growth. A bright position is recommended, and enriched garden soil. Propagate by division or from seed in spring.

Androsace vandellii
PRIMULACEAE

Syn. *A. imbricata*. A cushion-forming evergreen perennial, to 6 cm (2½ in) high when in flower, which originates from the European Alps. A rather mound-forming plant, with rosettes composed of slender white or grey-felted leaves. Flowers, 5 mm (¼ in) wide, appear singly in spring, white and almost stemless. A plant for the alpine house. It is not tolerant of lime and needs protection from excessive watering during the winter rest. An open, enriched soil is recommended, and a fairly bright position. Propagate from seed in spring.

Androsace villosa
PRIMULACEAE

A mat- or low cushion-forming species found in rocky terrain in the Alps, the Pyrenees and other parts of northern and eastern Spain. The leaves are silvery green and hairy, forming rosettes to 8 mm (⁷⁄₁₆ in) across, which connect by wiry stolons. Flowers, in summer, are white or pink, in small umbels on scapes about 2.5 cm (1 in) long. Very much a rock garden plant, needing a gritty, slightly rich soil. Provide protection from excessive rain in winter. Propagate by division or from seed in spring.

Androsace villosa var. jacquemontii
PRIMULACEAE

A mat-forming plant composed of many rosettes of hairy, grey-green leaves about 5 mm (¼ in) long, originating from the Himalayan region. Flowers in summer, pinkish-purple, borne on red stems 3 – 5 cm (1¼ – 2 in) long. Best suited to alpine house culture, needing full sun and a well-drained, enriched soil. Plants are rarely more than 5 cm (2 in) high. Propagate by division in late summer or early spring, or from seed sown immediately after harvesting, temperature 15°C (59°F).

Andryala agardhii
COMPOSITAE

A somewhat shrubby, tufted plant, usually associated with rocky, stony territory on high mountains of the Sierra Nevada, southern Spain. Leaves are silvery, thick, lance-shaped to spathulate, and coated with fine, yellowish hairs, which are almost woolly. The stem leaves are more narrow to lance-shaped. Stems have terminal bright yellow flowers, about 2 cm (¾ in) in diameter, appearing in summer. A very gritty but enriched soil is necessary, and as sunny a place as possible. Propagate from seed in spring.

Anemone narcissiflora
RANUNCULACEAE

A clump-forming plant from central and southern Europe, also recorded in Asia and North America in mountainous country. A variable species, with stems ranging from 25 – 45 cm (10 – 18 in) or more in length. Leaves palmate, with 3 – 5 lobes, dark green and borne in tufts. Flowers appear in early to midsummer in loose umbels of 2 – 8, white or cream, often flushed pinkish-purple, each flower 3 – 4 cm (1¼ – 1½ in) across. Needs a sunny position and a gritty, enriched soil, which should be moist, especially in the growing season. Propagate from seed in spring.

Anemone nemorosa
RANUNCULACEAE

A species that includes well-known wild plants of Europe, commonly known as the wood anemone. A rhizomatous rootstock encourages the formation of large carpets of deeply incised, mid-green leaves. Flowers, 2 – 3 cm (¾ – 1¼ in) across, normally white with yellow stamens, freely produced in spring and early summer. 'Alba-plena' (as shown) is a double white form of particular charm. Other forms are known, often with different coloured flowers. Requires shade and a moist, rather acid soil. Propagate from seed in early spring.

Anemone obtusiloba
RANUNCULACEAE

A loosely tuft-forming plant, to about 5 cm (2 in) high when in flower, found in the Himalayas (Kashmir). A most attractive 'buttercup', with fairly loose tufts of green, hairy leaves, rather palm-like and distinctly lobed. Long, spreading, branching stems bear flat, circular flowers of long-lasting blue, white or cream in summer. Very much a sun-loving species, and for good results it is advisable to use a coarse, gritty but enriched soil. Propagates best from seed, sown in early spring.

Anigozanthos flavidus
HAEMODORACEAE

Commonly known as kangaroo paw. A clump-forming species, found wild in the Albany district of Western Australia. It has slender, strap-like, bright green leaves, smooth on both surfaces, arranged along the length of the stems. Flowers appear in summer, carried in long racemes on stems to 45 cm (18 in) or more long, usually yellowish-green, but often bright red, each about 3 – 4 cm (1¼ – 1½ in) long. Best suited to alpine house culture, needing a bright, sunny position and a rich, porous soil. Propagate by cuttings or from seed in spring.

Anomalesia cunonia
IRIDACEAE

A cormous species bearing zygomorphic flowers, found wild in Cape Province, South Africa. Leaves 15 – 30 cm (6 – 12 in) in length but deciduous. Flowers in summer, several appearing together on a branching stem 30 cm (12 in) or more long, the upper laterals shorter, forming wings, the lower segments 2 – 3 cm (¾ – 1¼ in) long, wholly bright red. A frost-free, sunny site is necessary, so best in the alpine house, set in a light sandy soil. Keep dry when dormant. Propagate by offsets or from seed.

Anomalostylus crateriformis
IRIDACEAE

A tall-growing, bulbous plant from low mountainous regions at altitudes of 500 m (1,600 ft) or more in Brazil (Rio Grande de Sol) and Paraguay. Leaves slender, striated, 60 – 70 cm (24 – 28 in) or more long and 1.8 cm (¹¹⁄₁₆ in) wide; a few cauline leaves 12 – 40 cm (5 – 16 in) long. Stem branched, bearing in early summer several solitary, bright yellow flowers in pedicels, the obovate segments sparsely puberulous, the outer 3.5 cm (1⅜ in) long, the inner 2.5 cm (1 in) and narrower. Needs open, rich soil and alpine house culture. Propagate from fresh seed.

Anomatheca laxa
IRIDACEAE

A deciduous, cormous, miniature species native to South Africa (Uitenhage) and northwards to Mozambique. Leaves basal, soft and slender, often overlapping the inflorescence. Flowers red, blue or white, about 2 cm (¾ in) or little more across, appearing at differing periods in summer and autumn. The zygomorphic character of the flower is a feature; the lower three segments have a dark reddish-purple blotch near the base. Needs the sunniest position possible and an enriched soil. Suitable for indoor or outdoor culture. Propagate from seed, freshly harvested.

Anthericum liliago
LILIACEAE

Known as St Bernard's lily. An attractive, clump-forming species with thick, fleshy rootstock, found in the wild from southern Europe through to Turkey. Narrow, greyish-green, fleshy leaves to 30 cm (12 in) long. Flowers, in early summer, borne in racemes on stems to 45 cm (18 in) long, each white star-like flower 3 – 5 cm (1¼ – 2 in) across, 20 or more in each raceme. Best in bright sun and enriched, permeable soil. Propagate from freshly harvested seed.

Antholyza namaquensis
IRIDACEAE

A cormous, rather short species to about 35 cm (14 in) high, found wild in sandy areas in Little Namaqualand, southern Africa. A rare plant. Plicate leaves to 35 cm (14 in) long. Stem, also to 35 cm (14 in) long, is densely villous, with a many flowered spike of bright red flowers, about 5 cm (2 in) long, borne in late spring. Essentially a subject for the alpine house; position in full sun in slightly enriched, sandy compost, minimum temperature 10°C (50°F). Propagate from fresh seed.

Antholyza ringens
IRIDACEAE

A cormous-rooted species from dry, open areas on hill sides in more southwestern regions of Cape Province, towards Clanwilliam, South Africa. Leaves rosulate, to about 25 cm (10 in) long, deeply pleated. Flower spike, in late spring, to about 45 cm (18 in) long with cluster of 4 – 10 deep scarlet, funnel-shaped flowers. Needs alpine house culture; grow in a rich, sandy soil in a sunny position. Propagate from newly ripened seed.

Anthyllis montana
LEGUMINOSAE

A variable species, native to many areas of eastern Europe and the southern Alps in particular. Typically it is a mat-forming plant composed of many small green leaves, 10 – 12 mm (½ – 9/16 in) long, covered with silvery hairs. Flowers appear in summer, borne on stems 10 cm (4 in) long, heads 2 cm (¾ in) wide, and are either rose-pink or, occasionally, white, produced in the form of rounded heads of numerous florets. A rather gritty, coarse soil suits it best, and it is better planted on a slightly sloping bed. Propagate from seed sown in spring.

Anthyllis tetraphylla
LEGUMINOSAE

A prostrate, annual species, native to many areas of southern Europe and northwest Africa, with a generally spreading habit. Leaves mostly divided into 5 leaflets, the uppermost one being larger. Flowers pale yellow, about 1 cm (½ in) long, borne solitary or in clusters, mostly in late spring. Will thrive in the rock garden, planted in ordinary but permeable soil. Propagate from seed gathered fresh from the swollen, bladder-like fruits.

Antirrhinum barrelieri
SCROPHULARIACEAE

A slender, erect-branched, often climbing perennial, found in hill side scrub in southern Europe. Leaves slender, lance-shaped, hairless, arranged along the length of the stem. Flowers appear on spikes in summer, rose-purple with white or yellow throat, 2 – 3 cm (¾ – 1¼ in) long, borne on flower stalks to 4 mm (3/16 in) long. It responds well to outdoor culture, so is best grown in the rock garden. Needs bright light and a gritty soil, enriched with rotted humus. Propagate from seed in spring.

Antirrhinum majus
SCROPHULARIACEAE

Commonly known as snapdragon. A fairly tall plant, to 45 cm (18 in) or more, native to low mountain slopes and rocky areas in southern Europe. Leaves lanceolate or oval, to 7 cm (2¾ in) long, variously arranged along the stem. Fragrant flowers, during summer, pink or reddish-purple, to 4.5 cm (1¾ in) long, with white or yellowish lip. Ideally suited to the rock garden, preferably grown as an annual, in ordinary garden soil. Propagate from fresh seed.

Aphyllanthes monspeliensis
LILIACEAE

The sole species of the genus, a tufted perennial native to warm hill sides in the Mediterranean region. Leaves bract-like, small, clustered around the base of the flowering stems. Flowering in late spring and early summer, the 6-petalled, pale to deeper blue flowers are about 2 – 2.5 cm (¾ – 1 in) across, borne terminally from the rush-like stems. Needs sun and well-drained soil. Propagate by division in spring.

Aquilegia chaplinei
RANUNCULACEAE

A fairly dense, clustering species found only in the Guadalupe Mountains, New Mexico, USA. The tripinnate, dark green leaves are thick and waxy. Flowers appear in summer, bright canary yellow, to about 7 cm (2¾ in) long, with medium to long spurs, on stems 30 cm (12 in) or more in length, the flowers often pointing upwards. Needs a fairly sunny position, and a humus-rich soil. Propagate by division in spring or from freshly harvested seed, temperature 15°C (59°F).

Aquilegia flabellata var. alba
RANUNCULACEAE

There is some controversy whether this is a botanically acceptable variety or of hybrid origin. A clump-forming perennial plant to about 25 cm (10 in) tall, found in the wild in scrubland and moist woodlands in Japan. A rhizomatous species with rounded, finely divided leaves, which are mostly basal. Stem leaves are quite short, ternate and stalkless. Flowers in early summer, generally 2 – 3 to each flowering stem, invariably downward-pointing, pure white. Needs good light and ordinary garden soil. Best propagated from seed.

Aquilegia scopulorum
RANUNCULACEAE

A dwarf columbine, rarely more than 7 cm (2¾ in) in height, which comes from the Rocky Mountains in North America. The glaucous blue-grey leaves with fringed edges are divided into 9 oval leaflets. The pale blue flowers with creamy-white centres and long spurs appear in summer; occasionally pinkish shades are produced. A hardy plant, which accepts very low temperatures; best in slight shade in an enriched, porous soil, preferably in a slightly sloping area. Propagate from newly ripened seed.

Aquilegia vulgaris
RANUNCULACEAE

The columbine. A fairly low-growing species except when in bloom, native to southern Europe, generally found in mountain pastures or shaded, rocky areas. Leaves bright green, ternately compound, carried on very slender, almost wiry stems. When in flower plants may attain 45 cm (18 in) in height. The flowers, which appear in summer, are mainly in violet shades, also rose-pink, crimson or white, 2.5 – 4 cm (1 – 1½ in) wide, with short, strongly hooked spurs. Needs a gritty soil, preferably enriched with leaf mould, in sun or shade. Propagate from seed in spring.

Arabis bryoides 'Olympica'
CRUCIFERAE

A densely tufted perennial species found in Greece and the Balkans. Leaves very small, more or less oval in shape, covered with very fine, soft hairs, providing very compact, basal clusters. Flowers appear in summer on short stems, just protruding above the foliage, white, about 8 mm (⁷⁄₁₆ in) in diameter, in racemes. This improved variety is best suited to alpine house culture; bright sun and porous soil are essential. Propagate from seed in spring.

Arabis ferdinandi-coburgi
CRUCIFERAE

A low, prostrate, mat-forming species originating
from Macedonia. Leaves narrow, lance-shaped,
green, pubescent, carried on long stalks, more or
less rosulate. (*A. ferdinandi-coburgi* 'Variegata',
shown here, has white and green leaves.) White
flowers in spring, each about 1 cm (½ in) across,
borne in racemes. Of easy culture, suited to the
rock garden, needing a bright, sunny site and
well-drained soil. Propagate by division or from
seed in early spring.

Arenaria grandiflora
CARYOPHYLLACEAE

A small, creeping plant, forming loose cushions,
native to dry, rocky areas of south Spain and
Portugal at altitudes of about 2,000 m (6,600 ft).
Leaves dark green, narrow, lance-shaped and
with pointed tips, 2 – 3 cm (¾ – 1¼ in) long.
Flowers appear in early summer, pure white,
solitary or 2 – 3 together, each about 1.5 cm (⅝ in)
across. A species for rock garden culture; needs a
moisture-retentive, enriched soil. Propagate from
ripened seed.

Arenaria tetraquetra 'Granatensis'
CARYOPHYLLACEAE

Syn. *A. tetraquetra amabilis*; sometimes referred to
as *A. nevadensis*. A perennial, densely cushion-
forming variety of the species, found in high
mountains in southern and eastern Spain,
including the Pyrenees. Minute leaves, rarely more
than 2 mm (⅛ in) long, are densely crowded in
quadrangular rosettes, these forming a hummock
to 15 cm (6 in) high. Flowers are white, appearing
just above the dense leafy stems in summer. Best
suited to alpine house culture; needs sun and a
very porous, humus-enriched soil. Propagate by
division.

Arisarum simorrhinum
ARACEAE

An alpine found in rocky habitats in southern and
eastern Spain and north-west Africa. It has a
tuberous rootstock with creeping rhizomes
forming groups of bright green, heart-shaped
leaves borne on stems about 10 cm (4 in) long.
Flowers appear in autumn and spring. A fleshy
stem bears a spathe 3–4 cm (1¼ –1½ in) long,
hairy externally, with a very swollen spadix with a
knob-like tip. Best planted in a humus-rich soil, set
in a south-facing but shaded position, in late
spring, when propagation by division can be
achieved.

Arisarum vulgare
ARACEAE

A tuberous-rooted perennial, which forms
patches, found wild in much of the Mediterranean
region of Spain and in Portugal. It has oval to
heart-shaped leaves of deep green, with even
darker spots and markings, borne on a 4 cm
(1½ in) long stem. The long-stalked inflorescence
bears a narrow spathe 4 – 5 cm (1½ – 2 in) in
length, green to dark brown, striped and speckled
in the lower part, hooded above, tubular below,
with a protruding green spadix, in spring and
autumn. Needs slight shade and enriched soil.
Propagate from offsets or freshly harvested seed.

Aristea biflora
IRIDACEAE

A rhizomatous species found in the wild in many
areas of Cape Province, South Africa. Plants
20 – 30 cm (8 – 12 in) tall, with leaves densely
rosulate, 5 – 10 cm (2 – 4 in) long, and usually a
single cauline leaf 7 cm (2¾ in) long. Flowers
appear in late autumn, generally in pairs, in
varying shades of blue or lilac with a whitish
throat, each flower segment about 2 cm (¾ in)
long. An attractive plant for the alpine house,
needing bright sunlight, a rich, permeable soil
and a minimum temperature of 13°C (55°F).
Propagate from seed or offsets.

Armeria alliacea
PLUMBAGINACEAE

A perennial species to about 45 cm (18 in) tall, growing in scrub or grasslands (as shown) in many parts of southern Europe. It has linear, lance-shaped leaves, 3 – 8 mm (³⁄₁₆ – ⁷⁄₁₆ in) wide, mostly basal, arising from a woody rootstock. Flowers appear in summer, borne on stems to 45 cm (18 in) or more long, deep pink, rarely white, heads about 2 cm (¾ in) across, subtended by brownish or reddish bracts, and a sheath below the flower head to 5 cm (2 in) long. Needs an enriched, porous soil and a sunny site in the rock garden. Propagate from seed in spring.

Armeria juniperifolia
PLUMBAGINACEAE

A cushion-forming, evergreen perennial, which, in the wild, frequents mountain pastures and rocky territory in Spain. Rosettes are composed of pointed, greyish leaves to 1.5 cm (⅝ in) long and 1 mm (¹⁄₁₆ in) wide, with ciliate margins. Flowers appear in late spring and early summer in loose heads to 1.5 cm (⅝ in) across, pale pink or purplish. Very much a sun-loving plant, which flourishes in a very porous, peaty, loamy soil; possibly best grown in an alpine house. Propagate by division or from seed.

Armeria maritima
PLUMBAGINACEAE

Commonly known as sea pink or thrift. This evergreen, clump-forming perennial plant is native to many parts of Europe and continues to prove very popular for the rock garden. Stems 5 – 30 cm (2 – 12 in) long. Leaves, 2 – 15 cm (¾ – 6 in) long, are dark green, narrow, almost grass-like. Flowers are variable – generally, round heads, 2.5 cm (1 in) across, of lilac-pink or white are carried on stiff, slender stems, at their best in summer. Thrives in ordinary garden soil, and given a bright, sunny position will flower in profusion. Propagate from seed, sown in spring.

Armeria maritima var. corsica
PLUMBAGINACEAE

A plant very similar in many respects to the species, but because of certain differences merits varietal status. Leaves are similar, but, if anything, slightly longer and more spreading. The principal difference is in the flowers, which are also summer-flowering but are a much deeper colour. Cultivation requirements are the same as for the species, but, because of its Corsican habitat, this will be better kept in an alpine house.

Arum pictum
ARACEAE

Commonly known as autumn arum. This is a quite extraordinary plant, found in several of the Mediterranean islands and in Italy. It has a tuberous rootstock, with thick, dark, shiny green, whitish-veined, arrow-shaped leaves, which appear at or just before flowering time. The dark purple spathe is to 25 cm (10 in) long; the similarly coloured spadix is cylindrical, narrow at the base, appearing in autumn. A somewhat shade-loving plant, requiring acid soil for successful culture. Propagate from offsets when dormant or from freshly harvested seed.

Asarina procumbens
SCROPHULARIACEAE

Sometimes known as creeping snapdragon. A creeping, trailing plant originating from shady, rocky areas in mountains in northeastern Spain, including the Pyrenees. Stems are very brittle and sticky, bearing reniform leaves with rounded lobes, palmately veined. Flowers appear in early summer, whitish-yellow, about 3 cm (1¼ in) or little more long, sometimes with pinkish lines. A bright, sunny position is essential, and a fairly rich, permeable soil. Seed, which is freely produced, can give successful results if sown newly harvested.

Asperula arcadiensis
RUBIACEAE

A hummock-forming, low-growing species from mountainous country in southern Greece. Broad, lance-shaped, grey-woolly leaves, about 1 cm (½ in) long, form tufts, which very quickly multiply. Flowers appear in spring to early summer, in terminal umbels, each about 1 cm (½ in) long, pink, with spreading lobes. Best kept in the alpine house, where it can enjoy good light and controlled watering. A porous soil is essential. Propagate by division or from seed in spring.

Asperula daphneola
RUBIACEAE

A dense, cushion-forming perennial species found in mountainous areas of Greece. The dark green, narrow leaves, 1.5 cm (⅝ in) or more long, are arranged in whorls. Flowers appear in summer, lilac-pink, each somewhat tubular in shape, with spreading corolla lobes about 7 mm (⅜ in) or more long, singly or in clusters. Best cultivated in an alpine house. A very gritty, humus-enriched soil is advised, and a position in a sunny site. Propagate by division or from seed in spring.

Asperula nitida var. puberula
RUBIACEAE

A tufted, densely hummock-forming species found in mountainous regions of central Greece. Leaves narrowly lance-shaped, slightly downy, to about 1.5 cm (⅝ in) long. Flowering throughout summer, the 4-petalled flowers are pinkish-purple, to 8 mm long, borne terminally, often in small clusters, overtopping the mass of whorled foliage. Best cultivated in an alpine house in a bright position, using a very porous, gritty, slightly enriched soil. Propagate by division or from seed in spring.

Asphodeline lutea
LILIACEAE

An attractive herbaceous perennial with a fleshy rootstock, found on rocky hill sides and mountain slopes in Italy, Sicily, the Balkans and Cyprus. Leaves linear, deep to bluish-green, 2 – 3 mm (⅛ – ³⁄₁₆ in) wide, embracing nearly the whole stem. Flowers appear in summer, yellow, 3 – 4 cm (1¼ – 1½ in) across, borne in dense racemes, each petal with a green centre vein. A useful plant for rock garden display, in a sunny, sheltered position. Soil should be sandy, enriched with humus. Propagate from seed or by division in spring.

Asphodelus albus
LILIACEAE

A tuberous-rooted plant found on dryish hill sides and mountains in areas bordering the Mediterranean. Leaves are slender, keeled and all basal 45 – 60 cm (18 – 24 in) long, 1 – 2 cm (½ – ¾ in) broad. Flowers appear in early summer on an erect, unbranched spike, white, rarely pinkish, about 3.5 cm (1⅜ in) wide, each petal with a brownish centre vein. Suited to rock garden culture in well-drained soil, and a bright, sunny, sheltered position. Propagate in spring either from seed or by division.

Astelia nervosa
LILIACEAE

A low-alpine species, native to New Zealand at altitudes to 1,500 m (5,000 ft), growing in moist, peaty areas of grassland. A tuft-forming plant, eventually forming clumps, with leaves 60 cm (24 in) or more long, pale green, with a silvery or hairy covering on the upper surface, the under-side even more silky-hairy. Reddish flowers in late summer, on short, fleshy stems, in racemes. Best suited to alpine house culture, positioned in sun or slight shade, in a rich, peaty, moisture-retentive soil. Propagate from seed or by division.

Astragalus glaux
LEGUMINOSAE

A robust, clump-forming perennial species, with many semi-erect branches, to about 30 cm (12 in) high, found wild in dry pastures in central and southern Spain. Branches are clothed with numerous pinnate leaves composed of 12 – 15 pairs of narrowly oblong leaflets, hairy on the underside. Flowers appear throughout summer, bright purple, about 1 cm (½ in) long, in terminal clusters on short stalks. Plants remain attractive after flowering, when the fruits form. Needs sun and an enriched, peaty soil; suitable for rock garden culture. Propagate from fresh seed.

Astragalus monspessulanus
LEGUMINOSAE

A low-growing, tufted, stemless, rather sprawling plant, native to high ground at altitudes to 2,500 m (8,200 ft) in the Alps, Pyrenees and Apennines. Leaflets dark green, oval or oblong, arranged in pairs. Flowers throughout summer, reddish-purple or purplish-violet, borne in terminal clusters, each to about 2 cm (¾ in) long. Suited to rock garden culture; needs a calcareous soil. Propagate from seed in spring.

Astragalus sieberi
LEGUMINOSAE

A rare, clump-forming shrublet 30 – 50 cm (12 – 20 in) high, found wild in semi-desert regions of Saudi Arabia. Stems are white-woolly, bearing long, greyish-green pinnate leaves divided into 30 or more leaflets 3 – 5 mm (³⁄₁₆ – ¼ in) long. Flowers appear in early summer, pale yellow, somewhat tubular in shape, 3 – 5 cm (1¼ – 2 in) long. Definitely a subject for alpine house culture, needing full sun and slight warmth. Soil must be very porous, primarily sandy, with thoroughly decomposed leaf mould added. Propagates easily from ripened seed, sown in spring.

Azorella trifurcata
UMBELLIFERAE

Syn. *Bolax glebaria* of gardens. An evergreen, perennial, low-growing species, native to the Falkland Islands. Hummock-forming, composed of tiny, hard, leathery green leaves, more or less oval in shape, set in rosettes, these becoming very congested, 30 cm (12 in) or more wide and 8 – 10 cm (3 – 4 in) high. Minute yellow flowers in summer in umbels in the centres of the rosettes. Suitable for an alpine house or the rock garden, needing a sunny site and very gritty, slightly alkaline soil. Propagate by division in spring.

Boykinia jamesii

B

Babiana nana var. confusa
IRIDACEAE

Very similar to var. nana (see next entry) and from similar habitats. Usually only 6 dark green leaves, 6 – 7 cm (2½ – 2¾ in) long, about 1 cm (½ in) wide. Flowers borne in late spring or very early summer, mauvish-blue, zygomorphic, funnel-shaped, each 3 – 4 cm (1¼ – 1½ in) long, the perianth tube curved, about 1 cm (½ in) wide near the throat. Needs a minimum temperature of 10 ℃ (50 ℉), so requires alpine house culture. Propagate from offsets or seed.

Babiana nana var. nana
IRIDACEAE

A dwarf, cormous plant, found wild in hilly country near to the coast in Cape Province, South Africa. Stem partly subterranean, to 10 cm (4 in) above ground. Leaves, 5 – 7 in number, 6 cm (2½ in) or more long, 1 cm (½ in) wide. Flowers appear in early summer, scented, variable colour – rose-pink or shades of blue – with a pale yellowish mark in centre of lower segments. Best in alpine house; needs rich, sandy soil. Propagate from seed, freshly harvested.

Babiana scabrifolia
IRIDACEAE

A species with tufted, spreading, fan-like leaves arising from a cormous rootstock, native to sandy flats and low mountain slopes in South Africa. Leaves more or less lanceolate, to 9 cm (3½ in) long, 2 cm (¾ in) wide, and a short, somewhat decumbent stem tipped with a spike of 4 – 8 flowers. Flowers appear in summer, pale blue to lilac with a perianth tube about 1.5 cm (⅝ in) long. Requires a sunny location in the alpine house. A porous but rich compost is needed; water freely in summer, allowing a dry rest once the leaves have withered. Propagate from seed, freshly harvested.

Babiana striata var. planifolia
IRIDACEAE

A cormous species, native to hilly country in Namaqualand, southern Africa. Lance-shaped leaves, usually 5 – 6 in number, to about 12 cm (5 in) long and 1.2 cm (⁹⁄₁₆ in) wide, often twisted at the tips and with slightly undulate margins. Flowers, borne in early summer or late autumn in a spike of several flowers, bilabiate, yellowish-green with mauvish edges to the segments, each flower to about 3 cm (1¼ in) long. Essentially a subject for the alpine house; needs sandy soil. Propagate from fresh seed.

Belamcanda chinensis
IRIDACEAE

A short, stout rhizomatous species, native to hilly country in China and Japan and naturalized in Malaysia. Sword-shaped leaves, bluish-green, to 50 cm (20 in) or more long. The erect stem, to 1 m (3ft) tall, carries a loose cluster of yellowish-orange flowers with red and purplish spots, about 7 cm (2¾ in) across. Flowers at their best in late summer. Suited to the rock garden, given partial shade and a humus-rich soil. Propagate by division or from seed in spring.

Bellevalia forniculata
LILIACEAE

A dwarf bulbous plant, 12 – 15 cm (5 – 6 in) tall, similar to *Muscari*, to which genus it was originally assigned. It originates from northern regions of Turkey, generally in moist alpine meadows. It has long, slender, channelled green leaves, which exceed the flower stem. Flowers appear in early summer, bright blue, rather tubular in shape, and pendent, carried in a short dense raceme. Very well suited to rock garden culture; needs a moisture-retentive, peaty, loamy soil. Propagate from seed, newly harvested.

Bellis rotundifolia var. caerulescens
COMPOSITAE

A low-growing, daisy-like plant, found wild in the Atlas Mountains in Morocco. It has oval, radical leaves carried on long stalks. Flowers are seen at their best in early summer, pale lavender blue, carried terminally on short stems, to 8 cm (3 in) long. A shade-loving plant, needing protection from varying weather conditions, so best given alpine house culture, but if grown in the rock garden in ordinary garden soil, shelter the plant well from inclement weather. Propagate from seed, sown in spring.

Bellium bellidiodes
COMPOSITAE

A fairly low-growing perennial species, found wild in eastern Spain, Sardinia and the Balearic Islands, tending to become clump-forming by means of fine stolons. Leaves elliptical, forming a basal rosette. Flowers appear in early summer, white or pale pink, with a bright yellow central disc, to about 1.5 cm (⅝ in) across, borne on slender stalks. Perhaps not fully hardy, but useful for the rock garden if provided with a warm, sunny, sheltered site. Requires a sandy, humus-enriched soil. Propagate from seed in spring.

Blackstonia perfoliata
GENTIANACEAE

Commonly known as yellow-wort. This attractive annual is native to the Mediterranean region at low and medium altitudes. It has oval leaves set opposite, the upper ones closely appressed round the stem, almost fused together. Flowers are in evidence throughout the summer, bright golden-yellow, to 1.5 cm (⅝ in) wide, singly or in terminal clusters. Needs bright light at all times. Easily propagated from fresh seed in a sandy, peaty soil.

Blandfordia punicea
LILIACEAE

An attractive and colourful plant, native to a rather restricted area of Tasmania, mostly on low mountain slopes. Leaves are many, arising from a thickened rootstock, varying in length to about 40 cm (16 in), and with serrated margins. Flowers are borne in late summer in a terminal raceme on elongating stems – each semi-pendent orange-red flower is about 4 cm (1½ in) in length. Needs a sunny, warm position, preferably on sloping ground in permeable soil. Propagate from freshly harvested seed.

Boophane disticha
AMARYLLIDACEAE

A huge bulbous species, found wild throughout South Africa, except the southwestern districts of Cape Province. The bulb is often to 20 cm (8 in) in diameter, with a very short stem that lengthens only after flowering, when long leaves appear to form a fan-shape about 60 cm (24 in) wide. Flowers appear in summer in a rounded head about 16 cm (6½ in) or more across, composed of numerous reddish stalks bearing short maroon flowers. For alpine house culture only, needing a very porous, enriched soil, dry and dormant in winter. Propagate from seed.

Borago officinalis
BORAGINACEAE

A fairly robust, low-growing plant, noted for its oil-rich seeds, native to much of the Mediterranean area. The oval leaves, 10 – 20 cm (4 – 8 in) long, dark green, crinkled and wavy-edged, initially form a rosette, and others clasp the hairy stems. Flowers are produced throughout much of the summer, on stems 20 – 40 cm (8 – 16 in) long, bright blue with a white throat, 2 cm (¾ in) across, the stems generally branching. Sun and well-drained soil are essential. Propagate from seed, freshly harvested.

Boykinia jamesii
SAXIFRAGACEAE

A carpet- or mat-forming species native to Pike's Head in Colorado, USA. The leaves, all stalked, are a rich, deep green, somewhat kidney-shaped, with prominent toothed edges. Flowers appear in early summer, borne in a rather dense raceme on spikes to 15 cm (6 in) long, deep bright red, occasionally in paler shades. Best in a bright, sunny position, sheltered from too severe weather. Needs a well-drained, peaty, enriched soil. Propagate from seed, sown immediately after harvesting.

Brachycome rigidula
COMPOSITAE

This bush plant, to 30 cm (12 in) high, is a perennial found wild in Tasmania and Australia on mountain slopes at altitudes to 1,800 m (6,000 ft). Leaves glossy, finely dissected, both basal and those embracing the many stems. Flowers appear in summer, the flower heads 2 – 3 cm (¾ – 1¼ in) wide with numerous bluish or lavender ray-florets. An excellent species for either rock garden or alpine house. Needs a sunny site and a well-drained, humus-enriched soil. Propagate by careful division or from seed.

Brassica balearica
CRUCIFERAE

A hairless, perennial subshrub, 30 – 40 cm (12 – 16 in) high, found wild in Majorca. Leaves bright green, forming a rosette, each leaf similar in shape to the oak leaf. Flowers appear in summer, about 2 cm (¾ in) long, yellow, in short racemes. Occasionally cultivated as an ornamental plant, but suited to rock garden culture. Needs bright sunlight and a rich, porous, calcareous soil. Propagate from seed, sown in autumn or early spring, temperature 12°C (54°F).

Bravoa geminiflora
AGAVACEAE

An unusual bulbous plant found in low mountainous areas in central Mexico. Leaves lanceolate, more or less basal, bluish-green, to about 30 cm (12 in) long, 2 cm (¾ in) wide. Inflorescence slender, leafy in the lower part, bearing a loose raceme of pinkish or yellow flowers in pairs, 6 – 7 mm (⁵⁄₁₆ – ³⁄₈ in) across, on a tube about 2.5 cm (1 in) in length, in midsummer. A plant more suited to alpine house culture, needing a very well-draining soil. Best to replant annually. Propagate from seed, sown freshly harvested.

Brimeura sp.
LILIACEAE

An unusual bulbous plant found in rocky areas of northern Spain and France. Leaves are slender, strap-like forming a basal cluster. Flowers appear in spring and early summer in a terminal cluster borne on slender stems about 20 cm (8 in) long, pale to bright blue. Similar to species of Scilla. Needs a bright, sunny position and a well-drained soil. Propagate from freshly harvested seed.

Bulbine mesembryanthoides
LILIACEAE

A short, fleshy-rooted, semi-succulent species, found wild on hill sides in Little Namaqualand, Cape Province, South Africa. It develops a partially subterranean caudex, from which emerge slightly tuberous roots. Leaves 1 – 2 in number, pale green, fleshy, to 1.8 cm (¹¹⁄₁₆ in) long, to 1 cm (½ in) thick, grey, pruinose. In summer, inflorescence to 15 cm (6 in) tall, bears 3 – 6 yellow flowers, about 1 cm (½ in) across. Requires alpine house culture in sandy soil. Propagate from seed.

Campanula arvatica

Calceolaria darwinii
SCROPHULARIACEAE

A hardy perennial species originating from the Straits of Magellan, Chile. A rhizomatous plant producing tufts of toothed, dark green, oblong leaves to 7 cm (2¾ in) long. Flowers appear in summer, borne solitary on stems about 10 cm (4 in) long, yellow with reddish speckling and a prominent white cross-bar across the pouch, about 3 cm (1¼ in) long. A sunny position is needed, and rich, open soil. Propagate from seed or cuttings or by division.

Calceolaria tenella
SCROPHULARIACEAE

A prostrate, creeping, mat-forming plant, native to Chile. Stems slender, trailing and rooting at ground level. Leaves bright green, broadly ovate, about 1 cm (½ in) long. The bright yellow flowers, in summer and autumn, 1 cm (½ in) or little more long, are borne in terminal clusters on stems about 10 cm (4 in) long. Useful for an alpine house or sheltered rock garden. Needs partial shade and a humus-rich, open soil. Propagate from seed in spring.

Calluna vulgaris 'H.E. Beale'
ERICACEAE

A most attractive cultivar of the parent, which originates from many parts of north Europe and the Azores, usually on high ground. A shrubby plant, to about 45 cm (18 in) high, with semi-erect stems and many short, somewhat scaly leaves. Flowers borne in autumn in slender, terminal racemes; double blooms, pale pinkish, bell-shaped, about 4 mm (³⁄₁₆ in) long. Ideal for the rock garden. Propagate from heel cuttings in late summer.

Calochortus uniflorus
LILIACEAE

A bulbous plant, which develops a prominently tufted basal growth, found wild in moist pastures in California and northwestern Oregon, USA. Flowers appear in early summer, erect, lilac, each inner petal marked with a dark spot in the centre, to 5 cm (2 in) across, borne terminally on long stems. It has proved useful for alpine house culture, but can also be grown in the rock garden, given a sunny, sheltered position on sloping ground and a slightly acid, permeable soil. Propagate by bulbils from the leaf axils or from seed.

Calyptridium umbellatum
PORTULACACEAE

Syn. *Spraguea multiceps, S. umbellata*. A prostrate species native to northwestern California, USA, found on high ground in the Cascade Mountains. Fleshy, evergreen leaves, often tinted with dull red, form small, flat rosettes, 5 – 8 cm (2 – 3 in) across, the ovate leaf blades narrowing sharply to short stalks. In summer flower stems radiate from the rosette, with terminal heads of pinkish bracts enclosing the very small, closely compacted, pinkish flowers. Suited to alpine house culture; needs a lime-free soil. Propagate from seed.

Campanula alpestris
CAMPANULACEAE

Syn. *C. allionii*. A useful alpine species, which tends to spread very freely. It originates from the French Alps, growing mainly in rocky areas or on scree. A rather variable plant, which develops close-set clumps. Leaves mostly linear and erect, green or silvery grey, to 5 cm (2 in) long. Flowers generally blue, more rarely white, appearing in early summer, quite large and bell-shaped, borne singly on stems to 7 cm (2¾ in) long. An enriched, porous soil and a sunny position are essential. Propagate by division.

Campanula arvatica
CAMPANULACEAE

A mat-forming plant, which is found growing among rocks on mountain slopes in northern Spain. It has trailing, leafy stems; the leaves are bright green, rather small, with smooth or notched margins. Flowers, in summer, are borne on stems about 7 cm (2¾ in) long, star-shaped, bright violet-blue, with widespread, wide lance-shaped petals. There is also a white form. A fine species for the rock garden; best in a gritty, enriched soil. Propagate from seed or by division.

Campanula betulifolia
CAMPANULACEAE

A tufted species of more recent introduction and well suited to the alpine house. It originates from Armenia, where it grows on hill sides, often on scree. Leaves rather wedge-shaped with prominently pointed tips, inclined to have a drooping habit. Flowers mostly in loose clusters, white or pale pinkish, bell-shaped, on slender stems to 7 cm (2¾ in) long, at their best in summer. Can be propagated from seed, sown in spring and transplanted as soon as the seedlings can be handled easily; ordinary soil is sufficient.

Campanula carpatica
CAMPANULACEAE

A truly useful trailing plant, native to the Carpathian Mountains but only rarely available; however, hybrids and forms can be obtained. Leaves are slightly heart-shaped, glossy green, long-stalked, forming quite dense tufts. Flowers vary in colour, shades of blue and purple to paler colouring, even white, open, bell-shaped, on stems to 15 cm (6 in) long in midsummer. Best grown in a warm position in full sun, in a sandy, loamy, enriched soil. Easily propagated from seed.

Campanula cochleariifolia
CAMPANULACEAE

Syn. *C. pusilla*. A most variable plant, recorded in the European Alps and the Pyrenees at high and low altitudes. A spreading, low-growing species, forming large clusters by means of underground runners. The small, bright green leaves are rounded, rather heart-shaped, on short stalks. Short, branching stems, to 7 cm (2¾ in) long, bear partially drooping, bell-shaped flowers in varying shades of blue in summer and early autumn. Thrives in rich, porous soil in a fairly sunny position; is easily propagated by division or from seed in spring.

Campanula elatinoides
CAMPANULACEAE

A freely flowering species, to 8 cm (3 in) high, found in some parts of the Italian Alps, usually in quite rocky areas. Leaves of greyish-green form spreading clusters, with lengthy stems bedecked with smooth or slightly hairy alternate leaves. From the leaf axils, open, purplish-blue flowers with a whitish throat are borne singly or in small clusters in summer. Best planted among rocks on slightly sloping ground in a rather alkaline soil. Propagate from seed in spring.

Campanula formanekiana
CAMPANULACEAE

This is a monocarpic species found growing in rock crevices in different areas of eastern Europe, particularly in Greece and Macedonia. Greyish-green leaves initially form a rosette; later many leafy stems, 30 cm (12 in) or more in length, emerge, with large, bell-shaped, white flowers appearing singly from the leaf axils, mainly in early to midsummer. Grow in well-drained soil in a sunny position. Being monocarpic, plants tend to die back after flowering, but are easily propagated from the ripened seed.

Campanula fragilis
CAMPANULACEAE

A fairly low-growing plant, rarely more than 15 cm (6 in) high, native to the Italian Alps. It has a rather woody rootstock from which emerge quite dense clusters of glistening green, serrated-edged leaves on long stalks. Stems are more or less prostrate, branched, bearing open blue flowers in summer. Plants require an alkaline soil, preferably set among rocks in a bright, sunny position, or in an alpine house. Propagate from seed in early spring.

Campanula herzegovinensis
CAMPANULACEAE

(Sometimes available as *C. hercegovina*.) A low-growing, bush-like, spreading plant, found in Bosnia-Herzegovina on fairly low mountain slopes among limestone rocks. Stems are quite short, with numerous green leaves with crenate edges in a dense arrangement. Flowers appear in summer, lilac-blue, on stalks about 10 cm (4 in) long, star-like when fully open. There is also a form 'Nana', which is about 5 cm (2 in) high and more free-flowering. A sunny position is advised, and a soil with limestone chippings added. Propagate by division or from seed.

Campanula hispanica
CAMPANULACEAE

A slender, stoloniferous species found on hill sides in central, northern and eastern Spain, also in the Pyrenees. It has exceedingly narrow upper leaves, almost thread-like, those at the base more or less rounded and toothed. Flowers in early summer in branched clusters, small, deep rich blue, to 1.5 cm (⅝ in) long, on long stalks. Very suitable for rock garden culture, needing a sunny site and porous, slightly calcareous soil. Propagate by division or from seed, sown in early spring, temperature 12 °C (54 °F).

Campanula portenschlagiana
CAMPANULACEAE

A wide, clump-forming species found wild in the Balkan region. The green leaves are ovate or rounded-heart-shaped with toothed margins. Flowers appear in summer and autumn, carried on semi-prostrate stems to 15 cm (6 in) long, lilac-blue, about 2 cm (¾ in) long. Needs sun or slight shade, a porous, humus-enriched, gritty soil and, in colder areas, winter protection. Propagate by division in spring or after flowering or from seed, freshly harvested, minimum temperature 12 °C (54 °F).

Campanula raineri
CAMPANULACEAE

A plant with a woody rootstock, found growing in limestone rock crevices in the Italian Alps and in Switzerland. Dark green, somewhat ashy-grey, leaves appear at almost ground level in tufts. Large, bell-shaped flowers of rich blue are borne singly or in pairs, on erect, leafy stems to 8 cm (3 in) long in summer. A most desirable plant; this and its sometimes white-flowered form are not difficult to grow if given a permeable, alkaline soil and a bright, sunny position. Propagate from freshly harvested seed, sown in sandy soil.

Campanula trachelium
CAMPANULACEAE

A tall, bushy, clump-forming species, with stems 50 – 70 cm (20 – 28 in) or more long, found in the wild at low to medium altitudes in southern Europe, north Africa and Siberia. Dark green leaves, broad, rather heart-shaped, are rough surfaced and toothed. Flowers, in summer and autumn, are deep purplish-blue, 2.5 – 3.5 cm (1 – 1⅜ in) long, decidedly bell-shaped and borne in leafy racemes. Suited to the rock garden; needs well-drained soil. Propagate from cuttings or seed.

Campanula waldsteiniana
CAMPANULACEAE

A low-growing, clump-forming species, originating from high ground in Dalmatia and Croatia. The small, dark green leaves form a dense mass, almost cushion-shaped, the leaves being almost stemless. In late summer and early autumn numerous bluish-violet flowers with a paler throat appear on stems 7 – 10 cm (2¾ – 4 in) long, very star-like, often almost hiding the foliage. Needs a very sunny location, preferably on slightly sloping ground among rocks, and a very gritty, enriched soil. Propagate from freshly harvested seed, sown in sandy soil.

Campanula zoysii
CAMPANULACEAE

A tufted perennial with very slender stolons, which spread freely to produce clumps, to 6 cm (2½ in) high, native to the Alpine regions of Italy and Austria, in calcareous soil. Leaves glossy green, the lower more or less rounded on short stalks, the upper linear. Flowers are freely produced in midsummer, basically bell-shaped, swollen towards the base, then constricted and enlarging to a 5-projectioned tip, shades of blue or violet. Plants wither in winter, but new growth forms in spring. A porous soil is essential. Propagate from freshly ripened seed.

Caralluma europaea
ASCLEPIADACEAE

A low, spreading succulent plant, found wild in dry, rocky areas on low mountain slopes and hilly country in southern Spain and north Africa. Stems 4-angled, curved, greyish-green, 1.5 cm (⅝ in) or more thick. Scale-like leaves develop but fall quickly. Flowers, borne in terminal clusters in early summer, are greenish-yellow with purplish-brown, transverse bands, about 1.5 cm (⅝ in) wide. Needs alpine house culture in gritty soil. Propagate from cuttings or seed.

Carduncellus caeruleus
COMPOSITAE

An attractive perennial thistle, to about 45 cm (18 in) tall, found at low to high altitudes in many parts of southern Europe. Leaves generally pinnately lobed and toothed. Flowers appear in summer, blue heads, later turning pinkish, to 3 cm (1¼ in) across, subtended by leaf-like bracts. When first in bloom it is a very pleasing plant for the rock garden; thrives in ordinary garden soil. Propagate from seed, freshly harvested.

Carduncellus pinnatus
COMPOSITAE

A very attractive rosette-forming species from parts of north Africa, also known on Sicily. It is very low-growing, with leaves spread at ground level, to 18 cm (7½ in) or more; the pinnate leaves have prominent spines at the tips of leaf segments. Flowers are formed in early summer in a dense head arising from the centre of the rosette – the pinkish-blue florets have very slender segments. A dry, warm, sunny position is advisable and an open soil. Propagate from seed, sown in early spring.

Carduncellus rhaponticoides
COMPOSITAE

A large rosette-forming plant originating from Algeria and Morocco, and particularly abundant in the Atlas Mountains. A series of lanceolate or slender spathulate green leaves with reddish midrib provides a large, flat rosette, 15 – 20 cm (6 – 8 in) in diameter. The thistle-like head of purplish or pinkish-blue flowers arises in the centre of the rosette, stemless, to over 4 cm (1½ in) in diameter and height, appearing in early summer. Needs a dry, sunny position, and ordinary garden soil. Propagate from seed, sown in early spring.

Carlina acaulis
COMPOSITAE

A perennial, low-growing, variable species, wide-spread in the Pyrenees and also known elsewhere. One of the less vicious thistles, the leaves are more or less hairy, widely spreading and deeply lobed with spiny teeth, formed into a flat rosette. Flowers solitary, 10 – 15 cm (4 – 6 in) across, outer bracts yellowish-white, inner bracts yellowish, florets yellow or white, either stemless or with very short stem, throughout summer. Needs full sun and calcareous soil. Propagate from seed, sown when newly ripened.

Carmichaelia enysii
LEGUMINOSAE

A hummock-forming plant to 24 cm (9½ in) in diameter, native to New Zealand. Leaves develop a dense formation, and as they fall are immediately replaced by interlacing, bright green, flattish branches. Racemes of 1 – 3 flowers, purple with deeper veins, each about 5 mm (¼ in) long, appear in summer. Hardly more than 5 cm (2 in) high, this is a proven alpine for outdoor culture, requiring a rich, permeable soil and a sunny position. Propagate from heeled cuttings in late summer or from seed in spring.

Carpanthera pomeridiana
AIZOACEAE

A tufted, succulent species found wild in south and southwestern regions of South Africa. It has spathulate-lanceolate leaves, 4 – 10 cm (1½ – 2¾ in) long and 2.5 cm (1 in) wide, the margins minute ciliate. Flowers appear in summer, light golden yellow, 4–7 cm (1½ – 2¾ in) in diameter, on pedicels 3 – 10 cm (1¼ – 4 in) in length, with numerous linear-acute petals. An unusual mesembryanthemum for the alpine house, requiring bright sun and a soil mix of equal parts loam, peat and sharp sand. Propagate from seed, newly ripened.

Carpobrotus acinaceiformis
AIZOACEAE

A quickly spreading, succulent plant originating from Cape Province, South Africa, but naturalized in many parts of Europe. The thick, fleshy branches have sabre-like leaves, 9 – 10 cm (3½ – 4 in) long, broadly keeled, 8 – 10 mm (⁷⁄₁₆ – ½ in) thick, greyish-green. Flowers open about midday during summer, rich carmine-purple, 4 – 5 cm (1½ – 2 in) in diameter. Needs a sunny position with winter protection, so best kept in the alpine house, although in ordinary garden soil. Propagate by stem cuttings in spring.

Carpobrotus edulis
AIZOACEAE

This widely spreading, low-growing species is native to Cape Province, South Africa, but is now naturalized in other areas of Africa, Asia and Europe. Branches are angular in shape and spread freely, bearing uniformly angled, bright green leaves, about 11 cm (4½ in) long, 12 mm (⁹⁄₁₆ in) thick, rather incurving, the keel finely serrate. Flowers, in summer, open at midday, yellow to purplish, about 10 cm (4 in) in diameter. Best for alpine house culture, but in ordinary garden soil. Propagate by cuttings in spring.

Catananche caerulea
COMPOSITAE

A slender-stemmed perennial species found in dry meadows and rocky areas of southern Europe. Leaves mostly basal, linear, sometimes toothed, stem leaves only very few. Flowers appear in summer, the flower heads blue, to 3.5 cm (1⅜ in) across, borne solitary, the spreading ray-florets and papery swollen involucral bracts making this unique in the genus. Needs a sunny site and well-drained, slightly enriched soil; perhaps best suited to an alpine house. Propagate from seed, sown in spring.

Catananche caespitosa
COMPOSITAE

A fairly rare rosette-forming species, 12 – 15 cm (5 – 6 in) high, originating from the Atlas Mountains in Morocco. The rosettes are composed of several long, linear, greyish-green leaves with pointed tips. The bright yellow flowers are carried on short stems in spring, and are fairly long-lasting. Best suited to alpine house culture, requiring bright light and a very open, enriched soil. Propagate from seed, freshly harvested.

Cautleya robusta
SCITAMINAE

An unusual and rare species, found in the wild at altitudes of about 1,800 m (6,000 ft) in the Himalayas (Sikkim). The dark green leaves, to 30 cm (12 in) long and 7 cm (2¾ in) wide, are produced along the stem. The peduncled flower spike, about 20 cm (8 in) long, carries reddish bracts, 2 cm (¾ in) long, and yellow flowers in early summer. Requires a cool position in the alpine house or, if planted outdoors, winter protection. Propagate from the pinkish seeds, planted in enriched, permeable soil.

Centaurea pullata
COMPOSITAE

A low-growing, rarely branching species found on scree in southern Europe and north Africa. It has stems of varying lengths, to about 30 cm (12 in) high, bearing large, pale rose, purplish-pink (rarely white) flowers terminally with narrow, lance-shaped leaves subtending, each flower 5 – 6 cm (2 – 2½ in) across. Basal leaves rough, hairy, often forming a basal rosette. Bright sun and a fairly rich, open soil will encourage summer flowers. Propagate from freshly harvested seed.

Centaurea rhapontica
COMPOSITAE

A species of knapweed, with stems 30 cm (12 in) or more long, found in the wild in many areas of southern Europe, often on quite high, hilly terrain. The large, rather oval leaves, white-woolly on the undersurface, are mainly concentrated towards the base of the stems. Flowers appear in summer, purplish flower heads 5 – 10 cm (2 – 4 in) or more across, subtended by rather jagged, brownish bracts. Can be grown in ordinary soil in the rock garden. Propagate from seed.

Centaurea simplicicaulis
COMPOSITAE

A rhizomatous species originating from Turkey. Leaves dark green, white on the undersurface and hairy, pinnate with wide segments, mainly resting on the ground. Flowers are in evidence in summer, rose-pink to mauve, in heads 3 – 4 cm (1¼ – 1½ in) wide, borne on unbranched stems 15 – 20 cm (6 – 8 in) or more long. A very fine hardy plant for the rock garden, requiring a bright, sunny position and open, enriched soil. Propagate from seed, sown in early spring.

Centaurea toletana
COMPOSITAE

An unusual, thistle-like species, found in mountainous country in central and southern Spain, generally in the protection of low bushes and scrub. Leaves basal, greyish-green, much divided and woolly-hairy on the undersurface. Flowers appear in summer, each head about 3 cm (1¼ in) in diameter and composed of numerous yellow florets – the shiny bracts form a cone-like structure from which the flower arises. Suited to rock garden culture in normal soil. Propagate from seed.

Centaurium erythraea
GENTIANACEAE

A medium sized, biennial species, native to low and medium altitudes in southern Europe. Stem erect with more or less oval, dull green leaves, the lower ones always forming a rosette. Flowers pinkish to purplish, about 1 cm (½ in) or a little more in diameter, borne in early summer in terminal, flat-topped clusters. Can be grown in a sheltered rock garden in slightly calcareous soil. Propagate from seed, freshly harvested.

Cephalanthera longifolia
ORCHIDACEAE

A rhizomatous rootstock, providing an erect, attractive orchid found wild in many parts of southern and eastern Europe and north Africa, in shaded rocky areas in woods. Leaves few or several, mainly lanceolate and long-pointed. Flowers in a loose or fairly dense pyramidal cluster of 5 – 16, white with yellowish-orange markings in the lip, the lip 1 cm (½ in) long, petals and sepals similar. A hardy, deciduous plant to 60 cm (24 in) tall, gradually withering after summer flowering. Suited to a shady rock garden. Propagate by division, using a chalky loam.

Cephalophyllum regale
AIZOACEAE

A wide-spreading, semi-prostrate succulent plant, found on low hills in Little Namaqualand, Cape Province, South Africa. The elongate stems, with internodes, about 2 cm (¾ in) long. Dark green leaves, densely spotted, long, tapering, truncate above, to 9 cm (3½ in) long and 8 mm (⁷⁄₁₆ in) wide and thick. Flowers appear in summer, purple-pink, about 5 cm (2 in) in diameter. Best grown in the protection of the alpine house; needs rich, permeable soil. Propagate from cuttings or seed.

Chasmatophyllum musculinum
AIZOACEAE

A dense mat-forming, succulent species with prostrate stems, originating from mountainous and hilly country in many parts of southwestern Africa and the Orange Free State, South Africa. Greyish-green leaves, semi-cylindrical, to 2 cm (¾ in) long, with a slightly rough surface. Flowers appear in summer, bright yellow and about 1.5 cm (⅝ in) in diameter. Requires alpine house culture in a rich, porous soil. Propagate from cuttings or seed.

Cheilanthes vellea
PTERIDOPHYTA

A tufted fern found wild in western and central Mediterranean regions, including Cyprus, in dry, calcareous, rocky areas. Leaves linear-lanceolate in outline, about 25 cm (10 in) long, coated completely on both upper and undersurfaces with yellowish hairs; the leaves persistent, carried on yellowish-brown stalks. This provides an excellent, attractive plant for pot culture in an alpine house, requiring a slightly calcareous, free-draining soil. Propagate from spores as ripened.

Chiastophyllum oppositifolium
CRASSULACEAE

Syn. *Cotyledon oppositifolia*. A dense, mat-forming succulent species originating from the Caucasus. The fleshy, rounded leaves are dark green with crenate margins, borne on stems, each leaf 5 – 10 cm (2 – 4 in) long and arranged opposite. Tiny, 5-petalled, golden-yellow flowers, closely compacted together, appear in late spring and summer in branched racemes to 15 cm (6 in) tall. Needs a very open soil and partial shade. Propagate in spring, by stem cuttings or division.

Chionodoxa luciliae
LILIACEAE

A small bulbous species found wild in western Turkey on mountain sides to an altitude of about 2,000 m (6,600 ft). Leaves basal, usually only 2 – 3, soft, lance-shaped. Flowers appear in early summer, pale lilac-blue, about 2 cm (¾ in) in diameter with a large white centre, borne in a lax raceme on stems to about 20 cm (8 in) tall. A suitable pot plant for the alpine house, or it may be planted in a rock garden. Needs a well-drained, slightly enriched soil, in a sunny position. Propagate from seed, in autumn or spring.

Chionodoxa sardensis
LILIACEAE

A spring-flowering bulbous plant native to mountainous regions of Turkey. Generally of low growth, rarely exceeding 15 cm (6 in) in height. Leaves, channelled and linear, are 10 – 15 cm (4 – 6 in) long. Flowers of rich, clear blue are borne in clusters in spring, each flower about 1.5 cm (⅝ in) long, with quite a prominent white eye. A fairly open setting in ordinary garden soil is advisable, preferably where there is good drainage. Planting and division are best undertaken in late summer or early autumn.

Chrysanthemum coccineum 'Kelway's Glorious'
COMPOSITAE

Syn. *Pyrethrum roseum* 'Kelway's Glorious', *Tanacetum coccineum* 'Kelway's Glorious'. A perennial, clump-forming plant, to 50 cm (20 in) or more tall, from southwest Asia. Leaves generally bipinnate, divided into slender leaflets, deep green in colour. Flowers in early summer, borne in terminal heads about 7.5 cm (2⅞ in) wide, with numerous rich scarlet rays and a brilliant yellow disc. A porous, but moisture-retentive, enriched soil is essential, and a sunny site. Propagate by division in spring or autumn.

Chrysanthemum coronarium var. discolor
COMPOSITAE

A particularly attractive, bushy perennial, to 80 cm (32 in) tall, found in the wild at varying altitudes in Europe. Stems are branched and leafy, the leaves twice cut into sharply toothed, lanceolate lobes. Flowers appear during spring and summer, the heads about 6 cm (2½ in) across, the ray-florets yellow and partly white, the disc yellow. Suitable for the rock garden in normal garden soil. Propagate from seed.

Chrysanthemum frutescens
COMPOSITAE

Syn. *Argyranthemum frutescens*. A bushy, half-hardy species, usually about 60 cm (24 in) high and wide, found wild on rocky hill sides in the Canary Islands. Leaves often rather fleshy, either simple or bipinnate. Flowers, mainly during spring and summer, with heads to 3 cm (1¼ in) across, ray-florets white, disc yellow. If afforded some protection, will thrive in the rock garden; otherwise grow in the alpine house in a slightly enriched soil. Propagate from seed.

Chrysanthemum hosmariense
COMPOSITAE

Syn. *Rhodanthemum hosmariense*. A perennial species, tuft-forming with more or less semi-prostrate stems, found wild in Morocco. Leaves greyish-green, coated with silky hairs, either singly or twice trifid. Flowers are in evidence from autumn to early spring, white, daisy-like, about 4 cm (1½ in) in diameter, with many white rays and a golden-yellow disc. A bright, sunny position will encourage growth and flowering; needs a well-drained, gritty, rich soil. Propagates easily from fresh seed, sown soon after harvesting.

Chrysanthemum leucanthemum
COMPOSITAE

Syn. *Leucanthemum vulgare*. Commonly known as the ox-eye daisy. Very much a European species, making bushy plants 45 cm (18 in) or more high. Leaves more or less obovate with crenate margins, stem with leaves more often lobed, bearing flowers about 4 cm (1½ in) in diameter, white rays and bright yellow disc, in spring and early summer. Needs a bright, sunny position and a free-drained, slightly enriched soil. Propagate by division in autumn or from seed sown in spring, temperature 15 °C (59 °F).

Cichorium intybus
COMPOSITAE

Commonly known as chicory. A fairly tall, perennial herb, with many intricate, green branches, found wild in grassy habitats in southern Europe. Leaves vary, basal ones toothed, upper ones lanceolate and clasping the stem. Flowers appear in summer, bright blue, to about 4 cm (1½ in) wide, borne on leafy spikes. Needs an enriched, permeable soil and a sunny position in the rock garden or alpine house. Propagate from seed in spring.

Cipura paludosa
IRIDACEAE

An unusual bulbous species found wild in moist regions of Mexico through to southern Brazil and in the West Indies. Leaves, all basal, 1 – 3, generally overtopping the inflorescence. Flowers appear in late summer and early autumn, pale blue or white, 2 – 4 cm (¾ – 1½ in) in diameter, produced in succession. Requires warmth at all times, so best kept in an alpine house. Needs a fairly rich, porous soil, and preferably a winter temperature of 10 °C (50 °F), when plants should be allowed to dry completely. Propagate from seed, which is freely produced.

Cirsium vulgare
COMPOSITAE

A most variable biennial species, 45 cm (18 in) or more tall, sometimes to over 1 m (3 ft), found wild at various altitudes to 750 m (2,500 ft) in southern Europe. Leaves lanceolate, pinnately lobed, with prominently spined margins, to about 5 cm (2 in) long. Flowers, borne in summer in a terminal panicle, reddish-purple, about 4 cm (1½ in) in diameter. Can adapt to rock garden culture, given an open, slightly enriched soil. Propagate from seed.

Cistus palhinhae
CISTACEAE

Syn. *C. ladanifer latifolius*. A compact, shrubby plant to about 50 cm (20 in) tall, growing wild in southwestern Portugal. Leaves extremely sticky, oblanceolate to spathulate, 2 – 6 cm (¾ – 2½ in) long. Flowers in midsummer, pure white, 7 – 10 cm (2¾ – 4 in) across, borne solitary and terminally on short, spindly branches. Needs a well-drained soil and a sheltered, sunny position. Suited to rock garden culture. Propagate by heel cuttings in late summer or from seed sown in spring, temperature 15 – 18 °C (59 – 64 °F).

Cistus psilosepalus
CISTACEAE

An evergreen, low-growing, shrubby plant, to about 40 cm (16 in) tall, originating from south-western Spain and Portugal. It develops a rather dense covering of oblong, dark green leaves to about 6 cm (2½ in) long. Flowers appear in early summer, pure white, 4 – 6 cm (1½ – 2½ in) across, with a brilliant yellow centre, borne on quite slender stalks. Fairly hardy if planted in a sunny, sheltered area and in a rich, porous soil. Propagate by cuttings in summer, or from seed in winter.

Claytonia nivalis
PORTULACACEAE

A low-growing, rosette-forming species, native to mountainous areas of northwest America. Leaves are linear, somewhat fleshy, dark green, forming tufted rosettes. Flowers in late spring and early summer, deep rose-red, carried on very short stems to 5 cm (2 in) long. Best suited to alpine house culture, needing a bright, sunny position and totally lime-free, open soil. Propagate from seed, freshly harvested.

Clematis alpina
RANUNCULACEAE

A deciduous, climbing plant, originating from mountainous regions of north and central Europe. Stems to about 2 m (almost 7ft) can spread and climb, bearing coarsely toothed, dark green leaflets to 5 cm (2 in) long. Flowers in spring, pendent, widely bell-shaped, solitary, violet, to about 4 cm (1½ in) long. A useful and colourful alpine subject. Needs humus-rich soil. Propagate by stem cuttings in late summer.

Colchicum autumnale var. album
LILIACEAE

This unusual variety, found in many parts of Europe, comes into bloom in late summer and lasts until well into autumn. The flowers, white with petals to about 5 cm (2 in) long, appear before the leaves; several flowers can appear from each bulb. The glossy green leaves are to be seen in late winter, usually in an erect cluster, often to 3 cm (12 in) long. Bulbs should be planted 7 – 8 cm (2¾ – 3 in) deep in a shaded position that remains fairly moist, late summer being the best period. Propagate from seed, freshly harvested.

Colchicum bivonae
LILIACEAE

A cormous-rooted species, found wild in Italy, Greece and Turkey in pine woods at altitudes of about 500 m (1,600 ft). Leaves, to 25 cm (10 in) long and 4 cm (1½ in) wide, appear in spring. Flowers tend to vary in shape, but are rose-pink in colour. Suited to the rock garden or alpine house; needs a bright position and well-drained, fairly rich soil. Propagate by cormlets, removed during dormancy, or from seed, freshly harvested.

Colchicum boissieri
LILIACEAE

This species has a rhizome-like, cormous rootstock and is found wild in Greece, at altitudes of about 1,500 m (5,000 ft) in the Taygetos Mountains. Leaves, produced after flowering, are very short and narrow. Flowers are clear rich pink, the perianth tube 2 – 4 cm (¾ – 1½ in) long, the individual segments about 4 cm (1½ in), in early autumn. Because of its late flowering and leafing it is best considered a subject for an alpine house, needing an open, fairly rich soil. Propagate from freshly ripened seed.

Colchicum cupanii
LILIACEAE

A low-growing cormous species widely distributed in the southeastern Mediterranean region. The green leaves are linear-lanceolate, to 15 cm (6 in) long, usually only 2 in number. Flowers appear in autumn, solitary or several together, pale pinkish-purple, to 2 cm (¾ in) across, with dark purplish anthers. A sunny position is best, and a well-drained, fertile soil; ideal for the rock garden. Propagate by division of corms during dormancy.

Colchicum 'Lilac Wonder'
LILIACEAE

A hybrid developed in the Netherlands by cross-pollination between *C. speciosum* and *C. bivonae*, both of which originate in Asia. Leaves are produced soon after the flowering period. Flowers, in autumn, rose-pink and borne on stems 10 cm (4 in) or more long, the flower lobes about 5 cm (2 in) long. Suitable for either the rock garden or the alpine house; needs well-drained, slightly enriched soil in a sunny position. Propagate from cormlets, removed during dormancy.

Colchicum peloponnesiacum
LILIACEAE

A low-growing, perennial, cormous species, found in rocky areas of southern Greece (Peloponnese). Plants rarely exceed 5 cm (2 in) in height, with 3 – 5 very narrow leaves, 4 – 6 in (1½ – 2½ in) long. Flowers mainly in autumn, pale pinkish-mauve, about 2.5 cm (1 in) in diameter, the tepals to 3 cm (1¼ in) long, 1 cm (½ in) wide. Suited to the rock garden; plant in good garden loam about 15 cm (6 in) deep. Propagate from seed sown soon after ripening.

Colchicum speciosum var. album
LILIACEAE

A most decorative cormous plant, found wild in Iran and the Caucasus. Leaves 4 – 6 in number, to 40 cm (16 in) long, glossy green. Flowers, in autumn, with a long, fleshy tube, pure white, the lobes 6 – 8 cm (2½ – 3 in) long. Can be grown in rock garden or in alpine house, but does best in a sunny position; well-drained soil is essential. Propagate from cormlets, removed during dormancy.

Colchicum 'Water Lily'
LILIACEAE

This is considered to be a hybrid of *C. autumnale* 'Pleniflorum', the parent plant being native to Europe. A cormous-rooted plant, with leaves 15 cm (6 in) or more long. Flowers appear in autumn, rose-lilac, fully double and freely produced, each about 5 cm (2 in) across. Very suitable for the rock garden; needs a well-drained soil and, preferably, a sunny position. Propagate from cormlets, removed during dormancy.

Conicosia capensis
AIZOACEAE

A fairly low-growing, spreading succulent species, native to high ground in South Africa. Stems to about 15 cm (6 in) long. Leaves dark green, compressed-trigonous, to 40 cm (16 in) long. Flowers appear in mid- to late summer, yellowish, each bloom 7 – 8 cm (2¾ – 3 in) across. Needs winter protection, so is best grown in the alpine house in humus-enriched, permeable soil. Propagate from freshly harvested seed.

Consolida orientalis
RANUNCULACEAE

A medium to tall, slightly sticky, annual species, found in the wild at low and high altitudes in much of southern Europe. Bright green leaves divided into slender segments to about 5 cm (2 in) long. Flowers, purplish-violet, 2 cm (¾ in) or more long, borne in loose or dense terminal racemes in early summer, the spur about 1 cm (½ in) long. Well suited to rock garden culture in ordinary garden soil. Propagate from seed in spring.

Consolida pubescens
RANUNCULACEAE

A rather hairy, annual species, native to many areas of southern Europe at low and quite high altitudes. Stems 45 cm (18 in) or a little more long, with linear-lobed, thread-like leaves. Flowers vary in colour – pale blue or pinkish-white – about 2 cm (¾ in) long, borne in panicles in early summer. Can be grown in the rock garden in a humus-rich, permeable soil. Propagate from seed, freshly harvested.

Convolvulus althaeoides
CONVOLVULACEAE

A low-growing, scrambling species of prostrate habit, native to many parts of southern Europe, mostly in fairly dry areas on low hill sides. Leaves are covered in short hairs, deep green, varying in shape, with prominent crenations. Flowers appear in late spring and early summer and are pale purplish-pink in colour, 2 – 3 cm (¾ – 1¼ in) in diameter, borne on long stalks. Tends to become invasive but is, nevertheless, useful in the rock garden. Needs a sandy soil, in a sunny position or in slight shade. Propagate from seed or by division in spring.

Convolvulus boissieri
CONVOLVULACEAE

A beautiful, dense, cushion-forming plant native to some of the higher mountain areas of southern Spain. The leaves are quite small, oval in shape, rather folded and have a silvery effect over basically green leaves – the silvery effect being the result of a covering of shining silvery white hairs. Flowers are almost stalkless, 2 – 3 cm (¾ – 1¼ in) in diameter, rosy-white in colour, appearing in early summer. A fairly sunny position and a permeable soil, preferably with added humus, are required. Propagate from seed in spring.

Convolvulus elegantissimus
CONVOLVULACEAE

Syn. *C. altheoides* ssp. *tenuissimus*. This is a scrambling and climbing species, which frequents bushy areas on dry hill sides from north Africa and Italy to Turkey. Both stems and leaves are densely coated with silvery hairs; the leaves are variable, the lower somewhat heart-shaped, the upper being cut into fine, narrow linear lobes. Flowers appear in early summer, solitary, purplish-pink, about 4 cm (1½ in) in diameter on longish stalks. Will thrive in any garden soil in a fairly sunny position. Propagate from seed, sown in early spring.

Convolvulus lineatus
CONVOLVULACEAE

A somewhat variable plant, especially as far as flower colour is concerned. It comes from southern Europe and is associated with rocky areas, where it forms clusters. Leaves are green with silvery appressed hairs, linear in shape and smooth edged. Flowers in deep pinkish shades (rarely white), to 3 cm (1¼ in) in diameter, single or several together on long stalks, in late spring or early summer. Suited to the alpine house or a warm place in the rock garden. Ordinary garden soil is suitable. Propagate from seed or cuttings.

Convolvulus sabatius
CONVOLVULACEAE

Syn. *C. mauritanicus*. A vigorous, trailing or climbing species of perennial growth arising from a woody rootstock, originating from Italy, Sicily and northwest Africa. Stems, to 3 m (10 ft) long, are bedecked with soft, rounded, green leaves, which are softly hairy. Flowers, 2 cm (¾ in) wide, are produced in early to midsummer, either singly or 2 – 3 together, in varying shades of blue or pinkish-purple. Suitable as a background plant in either rockery or alpine house. Needs a sunny position and a permeable soil with humus added. Propagate from seed or cuttings in spring.

Coris monspeliensis
PRIMULACEAE

A stiff, woody-based species found wild in fairly sandy regions on hill sides near the Mediterranean coastline. Stems to 25 cm (10 in) long, more or less erect. Leaves small, narrow, tough and hairless, usually spiny at the base, dull greyish-green. Flowers appear in early summer, pinkish-lilac with reddish-purple sepals, each flower 2-lipped. Best suited to alpine house culture; needs a very open, sandy, humus-enriched soil. Propagate from newly ripened seed.

Corydalis aitchisonii
FUMARIACEAE

A tuberous-rooted species native to eastern Iran and Afghanistan at altitudes to about 2,200 m (7,200 ft) in moist, rocky areas. The somewhat spherical tuber produces ternate leaves of bluish-grey-green, with very oval or rounded lobes. Flowers golden-yellow, 3 – 4 cm (1¼ – 1½ in) long, the lower petal reflexed, carried on stems scarcely 10 cm (4 in) long in late spring. Best suited to the alpine house, where it can be developed as a pot plant in porous, humus-enriched soil. Propagate by division or from fresh seed.

Corydalis ambigua
FUMARIACEAE

A globular, tuberous-rooted species originating from Japan, bearing many single stems to 30 cm (12 in) long. The mostly bipinnate green leaves are divided into leaflets 2 – 3 cm (¾ – 1¼ in) long, which are somewhat rounded in shape. The stems carry terminal racemes of several bluish-purple flowers, each 1.5 – 2.5 cm (⅝ – 1 in) long, in spring. Needs sun or partial shade and a porous but moisture-retentive soil. Propagate by division or from offsets in autumn.

Corydalis caucasica var. alba
FUMARIACEAE

Syn. *C. malkensis*. A slender, tuberous-rooted species found wild in the Caucasus, where it is widespread. Leaves pinnately cut into 3 – 5 linear-lanceolate leaflets. Flowers appear in late spring or early summer, in a lax raceme on stems to 15 cm (6 in) long, creamy white, about 2.5 cm (1 in) long, the lower petal expanded to 1 cm (1½ in) wide. A hardy plant, suited to rock garden culture, but has a preference for partial shade and a sandy, peaty soil. Propagate from newly ripened seed.

Corydalis cheilanthifolia
FUMARIACEAE

A particularly attractive species found wild in China. The fern-like leaves are about 15 cm (6 in), long, bipinnate, deep green, but bronze-tinted if grown in bright light. Flowers yellow, on stems to 30 cm (12 in) long, in dense racemes about 1 cm (½ in) long, throughout summer and into early autumn. A bright, sunny position is recommended, and an enriched, slightly moisture-retentive, porous soil. Propagate by division or from seed, freshly harvested, in autumn.

Corydalis nobilis
FUMARIACEAE

An impressive species with a thick, fleshy root-stock, originating from Siberia. The greenish leaves are deeply divided into several leaflets. Flowers are 4-petalled, yellow with orange tips, borne on 30 cm (12 in) stems in a rounded raceme in late spring and summer. A really bright, sunny position is advisable, and a partially moisture-retentive, enriched soil. Propagate from seed, freshly harvested.

Corydalis ochroleuca
FUMARIACEAE

A densely tufted plant, native to parts of Italy and the Balkan region. The spreading leaves are bipinnate or tripinnate, glaucous on both surfaces. Flowers about 2 cm (¾ in) long, tubular, cream with yellow tips to the petals, somewhat pendulous, borne in early summer on stems overtopping the foliage. A bright site is recommended and a porous, rich, moisture-retentive soil. Propagate from seed, freshly harvested.

Corydalis wilsonii
FUMARIACEAE

An erect, compact and very attractive species originating from China. Leaves glaucous, bipinnate, finely divided to appear almost fern-like. Bright yellow flowers in early summer, about 2 cm (¾ in) long, borne terminally on erect stems about 30 cm (12 in) long; several flowers in a raceme. Best kept in an alpine house to ensure continuity of growth; needs well-drained but moisture-retentive soil. Propagate by division or from freshly ripened seed.

Cotula atrata
COMPOSITAE

A densely mat-forming species native to South Island, New Zealand. The fleshy green leaves, generally suffused purplish-brown, are about 3 cm (1¼ in) long, bipinnate, set alternately along the fleshy stems. Flowers may occur in spring or summer, the rounded heads to 2 cm (¾ in) across, dark crimson with numerous whitish stigmas. Grow in moisture-retentive, rich soil, in sun. Propagate from seed or by division in early spring.

Crassula orbicularis
CRASSULACEAE

A rosette-forming, freely offsetting, succulent species, found in the wild on hill sides along much of southern parts of South Africa, through to Natal. Pale greyish-green leaves obovate, 3 – 6 cm (1¼ – 2½ in) long, densely arranged to form multiple rosettes. Flowers borne in summer in branched terminal clusters; each flower very small, whitish-yellow, occasionally reddish. Alpine house culture is advised; needs a rich, gritty soil. Propagate by division.

Crassula socialis
CRASSULACEAE

A tufted, often mat-forming succulent plant, found in the wild in hilly country in southeast Cape Province, South Africa. The small, oval-triangular, dark green leaves, about 6 mm (⁵⁄₁₆ in) long and wide, form rosettes, eventually making very dense cushions. White flowers are borne in summer in dense, terminal umbels on stems to 12 cm (5 in) long. Best grown in the alpine house in an enriched, porous soil. Propagate by division or from seed.

Crocosmia paniculata
IRIDACEAE

A tall-growing species, to over 1 m (3ft) high when in flower, native to moist areas at altitudes of 1,500 – 1,750 m (5,000 – 5,700 ft) in Natal and eastern parts of Transvaal, South Africa. Leaves form flattish tufts, to 1 m (3ft) long, 6 cm (2½ in) wide, bright green and tapering at tips and base. Inflorescence branched, each with many orange-red flowers; each flower tubular, funnel-shaped, to 3.5 cm (1⅜ in) long, borne mainly in midsummer. Thrives in the rock garden, given a slightly sheltered position and rich soil. Propagate from offsets or seed.

Crocus ancyrensis
IRIDACEAE

A cormous species originating from central Turkey at altitudes to 2,500 m (8,200 ft). The corm has a netted tunic, producing 3 – 4 slender leaves. Flowers appear in late winter and early spring, deep orange-yellow, about 7 cm (2¾ in) long, the outer segments often slightly brownish externally, the anthers yellow, the style yellow to deep orange. Needs a rather bright position and a well-drained soil. Propagate from seed, immediately it is ripe.

Crocus baytopiorum
IRIDACEAE

A cormous plant found wild in rocky areas of southwest Turkey, invariably in woodland. It has 3 bright, shiny green leaves, usually about 15 cm (6 in) long, appearing at about the same time as the flowers, maybe only very small at first but gradually developing fully. Flowers, in late spring, are pale purplish, opening to 4 – 6 cm (1½ – 2½ in) across, with yellow anthers. Probably best kept in an alpine house; however, given a bright, sunny and sheltered position, can be planted in a rock garden in ordinary garden soil. Propagate from seed as soon as it is harvested.

Crocus chrysanthus
IRIDACEAE

A popular cormous plant, to 15 cm (6 in) tall, found in many areas of southeastern Europe (Bulgaria, Greece, Turkey and so forth). Leaves appear at the same time as the flowers, during winter. Flowers pale to deep yellow or orange, the outer segments veined violet externally. Because of its early flowering, this is best suited to alpine house culture. Needs a bright position, and a slightly gritty but enriched soil. Allow the soil to dry out during the period of dormancy. Propagate from seed, freshly harvested.

Crocus chrysanthus 'E.P. Bowles'
IRIDACEAE

This is one of several excellent hybrids produced by cross-pollination between *C. chrysanthus* and *C. biflorus*. The corms provide 3 – 4 or more rather greyish-green leaves, appearing more or less at the same time as the flowers. Flowers appear from late winter almost up to late spring – each about 8 cm (3 in) long, a deep, almost glossy yellow and prominently feathered. Ideal for the rock garden in normal garden soil. Propagate by removal of offsets when dormant.

Crocus cvijicii
IRIDACEAE

A rather rare species, to 15 cm (6 in) tall, with a cormous rootstock, found wild in Macedonia on mountains near the snow-line. Leaves only 2 – 3, short, invariably almost prostrate on the ground. Flowers appear in spring, bright, shiny yellow, more or less cup-shaped, with yellow style. Can be considered sufficiently hardy for the rock garden, set in a well-drained soil. Propagate from seed, sown soon after harvesting.

Crocus korolkowii
IRIDACEAE

A rather robust plant, to 8 – 10 cm (3 – 4 in) tall, with a cormous rootstock, found wild in hills and rocky mountain slopes and fields in northern Afghanistan at altitudes to 3,000 m (10,000 ft) or more. Leaves greyish-green, several appearing at the same time as the flowers. Flowers appear in winter and spring, deep yellow with brownish lines and markings externally. Completely hardy, so well suited to rock garden culture, planted in a moisture-retentive, open, fairly rich soil. Propagate from seed in late spring.

Crocus kotschyanus
IRIDACEAE

Syn. *C. zonatus*. A cormous species, 10 – 12 cm (4 – 5 in) tall, originating from Turkey, Syria, Lebanon and Iraq at altitudes to 2,000 m (6,600 ft). The somewhat angular leaves appear after the flowers. Flowers pale to rose-lilac and lined with darker shades; throat white or yellowish with 2 small orange dots at the base of each segment. Flowering commences in late summer and extends into autumn. As bright a position as possible will encourage good flowering. Needs a porous, enriched soil. Keep more or less dry during dormancy. Propagate from seed, freshly harvested.

Crocus laevigatus var. fontenayi
IRIDACEAE

This is a cormous plant, 6 – 10 cm (2½ – 4 in) tall, native to many parts of Greece. Leaves appear with or before the flowers, 3 – 8 in number, to 3 mm (³⁄₁₆ in) wide, dark green on the inner surface. The scented flowers appear from autumn to early winter, rose-lilac, feathered violet-buff externally, usually 1 – 3 to a corm. Leaves wither after flowering after having elongated slightly, then the seed capsule emerges to ripen. Needs a sheltered, though bright, site in the rock garden in enriched garden soil. Propagate from seed as soon as it is ripe.

Crocus minimus
IRIDACEAE

A cormous species with leaves and flowers appearing at the same time, found on the wild hill sides to altitudes of 1,500 m (5,000 ft) in Corsica and Sardinia. Leaves are very slender and narrow, tending to be widespreading. When in flower, plants 5 – 6 cm (2 – 2½ in) tall. Flowers in winter to mid-spring, deep lavender, inner petals bluish, outer segments purplish externally. A white form is also recognized. Requires as bright a position as possible and a slightly enriched, porous soil. Suitable for a protected rock garden. Propagate from seed, freshly harvested.

Crocus nudiflorus
IRIDACEAE

An attractive cormous species that develops stolons, resulting in small clumps being formed. It occurs in moist meadows to altitudes of 1,600 m (5,300 ft) or more in northeast Spain and south-west France. The 3 – 4 green leaves, 2 – 4 mm (⅛ – ³⁄₁₆ in) wide, appear after flowering. Flowers in late summer and early autumn, in shades of purple with white to lilac throat, the tepals to 6 cm (2½ in) long. Can be grown successfully in grassy areas, where it will multiply freely; also a splendid plant for the rock garden, where it will grow in ordinary soil. Propagate from newly ripened seed.

Crocus speciosus 'Artabir'
IRIDACEAE

The parent plant is a cormous-rooted species, native to western Turkey to Iran and neighbouring areas. Leaves, usually 3 – 4 in number, broad and dark green. Flowers appear in autumn or spring, bright purple, the segments deep purple veined, 10 – 12 cm (4 – 5 in) across. Useful plant for an open rock garden; need rich, well-drained soil. Propagate by division of cormlets at planting time.

Crocus vernus
IRIDACEAE

A species variable in flower colour, resulting in two subspecies. *C. vernus* ssp. *vernus* has mostly purple flowers; ssp. *albiflorus* (shown here and on page 53) has white blooms and is more frequently encountered in meadows in the Alps and parts of central Europe. Leaves 2 – 4 to a corm, 4 – 8 mm (³⁄₁₆ – ⁷⁄₁₆ in) wide, becoming visible as the flowers appear. Flowers 3 – 5 cm (1¼ – 2 in) long, coming into bloom in late spring and early summer. Can be grown successfully in a bright or slightly shaded position in ordinary garden soil.

Crocus vernus ssp. albiflorus
IRIDACEAE

A low-growing, cormous plant to 12 cm (5 in) high, found in the wild in the Alps and Pyrenees at altitudes of about 2,500 m (8,200 ft) in meadows or on grassy slopes. Leaves narrowly linear, dark green, whitish veined, usually apparent at flowering time. Flowers, in spring, pure white, 7 cm (2¾ in) wide, with rich orange style and stamens. An ideal rock garden subject; needs well-drained, slightly enriched soil. Propagate from cormlets or from fresh seed.

Cyathodes fraseri
EPACRIDACEAE

A low-growing, rather prickly, shrubby plant with wiry branches to about 15 cm (6 in) tall, native to New Zealand at altitudes to 1,600 m (5,300 ft) in fairly dry grassland. The creeping subterranean stems encourage large clusters. Leaves deep green, sharply pointed, erect, in dense formation around the stems. Flowers in autumn are small, white, tubular, tipped with 5 bearded lobes. Best kept in an alpine house; needs a well-drained, gritty, enriched soil and a sunny site. Propagate from seed or by division in spring.

Cyanotis lanata
COMMELINACEAE

Syn. *C. somaliensis*. A dwarf species, to about 30 cm (12 in) high, native to low mountainous areas of tropical Africa. Branches from base and slightly woolly. Leaves are linear, succulent, hairy, to 6 cm (2½ in) long. Flowers appear in summer in terminal clusters, purple, pink and occasionally white with pink border, with hairy filaments. Needs alpine house culture in a humus-rich, open soil. Propagate from seed or by division.

Cyclamen cilicium var. intaminatum
PRIMULACEAE

Syn. *C. intaminatum*. A fairly low-growing plant, found wild at altitudes of about 1,000 m (3,300 ft) in pine woods in southern and western Turkey. It has a flattened, rounded tuber, with dark green somewhat rounded leaves. When in flower plant is to 12 cm (5 in) tall. Flowers are carried on very slender, spreading stems, solitary, very pale pinkish-white, in late spring or autumn. A plant of easy culture if grown in a rather dry rock garden, in sun or partial shade, in an enriched but stony soil. Propagate from seed when newly ripened.

Cyclamen coum
PRIMULACEAE

Basically a garden plant, also known as *C. vernum* and as *C. orbiculatum*. Native to the eastern Mediterranean region, it has plain green leaves, fairly glossy, with a deeper marking along the centre of each orbicular leaf. Flowers, to about 10 cm (4 in) high, appear in late winter and spring, pale to deep purplish-pink, dark spotted at the base – but most variable! A fully hardy plant for a bright position in the rock garden; needs a humus-rich soil. Propagate from seed when ripe, or in spring.

Cyclamen coum var. caucasicum
PRIMULACEAE

One of the variable forms of *C. coum*, found growing in more easterly regions of Turkey. Leaves are prominently heart-shaped, glossy green, deeper coloured towards the centre. Flowers are fairly deep pink and definitely larger than the type. In all other respects it is similar to the species, requiring the same cultural conditions and having the same flowering season. Can be grown successfully in a shaded rock garden, in porous leafy soil. Propagate from freshly ripened seed.

Cyclamen creticum
PRIMULACEAE

A species with a prominent flattened tuber, native to Crete. Leaves heart-shaped, dark green, white-spotted, reddish on the undersurface, the margins roughly toothed. Flowers in spring, 1.5 – 2.5 cm (⅝ – 1 in) long, white or pinkish and scented. At its best in a shaded position, so possibly best suited to the alpine house. Plants need to be only very slightly moist during dormancy; water more frequently when growth appears. An enriched, peat-based soil is advisable. Propagate from seed, freshly harvested.

Cyclamen hederifolium
PRIMULACEAE

Syn. *C. neopolitanum*. Known commonly as sow-bread. Plants with a flattened, rather tough corm, forming tufts, native to Italy through to western Turkey. Leaves variable, narrow to broadly ovate, with many or few silvery markings, usually deeply lobed. Plants to 12 cm (5 in) tall when in flower. Flowers in early autumn, borne on slightly fleshy stems, solitary and terminally, in varying shades of pink, red, mauve or sometimes white. A peaty, enriched soil is advised and a partially shaded location. Propagate from seed, freshly harvested, temperature 15 °C (59 °F).

Cyclamen persicum
PRIMULACEAE

A most variable and, to some extent, not under-stood species, which originated from the eastern Mediterranean region. A rounded tuber coated with a rough, somewhat corky skin, with several very fleshy roots emerging. Leaves vary in almost every respect, particularly in shape and markings. To 12 cm (5 in) tall when in flower. Flowers appear in spring, white to shades of pink, often fragrant. Needs only partial shade and a very enriched, peaty soil. Propagate from seed.

Cyclamen pseudo-ibericum
PRIMULACEAE

A globular, slightly flattened tuberous plant, 10 – 15 cm (4 – 6 in) high, originating from Turkey and neighbouring areas. The dark green, heart-shaped leaves are pointed, with silvery marbling, reddish on the underside. The reddish-purple or magenta flowers, in early spring, have a brown blotch on each petal and a whitish line around the top of the corolla tube. Partial shade is recommended, and a rich, fertile soil. Propagate from fresh seed.

Cymbalaria muralis
SCROPHULARIACEAE

Syn. *Linaria cymbalaria*. A trailing, tufted plant found wild in the Balkans, Crete and the Aegean islands. Leaves almost round, with 5 – 9 lobes, arranged alternately on long stalks. Flowers appear in summer on slender stalks, pale lilac to violet, to 1.5 cm (⅝ in) long with a 3 mm (³⁄₁₆ in) long spur. A pleasing subject for an alpine house, needing an enriched, permeable soil and a position in sun or slight shade. Propagate from freshly harvested seed, sown in a sand-and-peat mix.

Cynara scolymus
COMPOSITAE

Commonly known as the globe artichoke. A colourful plant, growing in abundance in many parts of the Mediterranean region to 1.5 m (5ft) or more tall. Leaves bright green, pinnately lobed and smooth-edged. Although young flower heads are cooked and eaten as vegetables, the flower is particularly attractive – reddish-purple, 4 – 6 cm (1½ – 2½ in) in diameter and appearing in summer. Needs alpine house conditions and normal soil. Propagate from fresh seeds.

Cynoglossum cherifolium
BORAGINACEAE

A rather short, biennial species, to about 30 cm
(12 in) tall, native to open, stony areas at varying
altitudes in southern Europe. Stems felted.
Lanceolate, stalkless leaves slightly undulating
and grey-felted on both surfaces. Flowers, in late
spring and early summer, are reddish-purple,
about 5 mm (¼ in) wide, borne in terminal cymes.
Best grown in the alpine house in enriched, gritty
soil. Propagate from seed.

Cynoglossum creticum
BORAGINACEAE

A robust biennial species found growing wild
throughout much of the Mediterranean region,
usually in moist areas near streams. Leaves are
densely hairy, more or less oblong in shape, with
pointed tips, often embracing the very hairy stem.
Flowers are borne terminally, in summer, on the
elongating stems, deep blue with net-like purplish
veining, each about 9 mm (⁷⁄₁₆ in) wide. Fairly
hardy, so is useful for the rock garden; needs well-
drained soil and a sunny site. Propagate from seed
in spring.

Cypella lapidosa
IRIDACEAE

An attractive, bulbous species, native to fairly
high, hilly country in Argentina (Corrientes Santo
Tome). Plants to about 30 cm (12 in) tall when in
flower. Basal leaves only to 2 cm (¾ in) long;
cauline leaves slender, about 12 cm (5 in) long,
3 mm (³⁄₁₆ in) wide. Flowers appear in early
summer, yellow to orange with reddish-brown
markings on the petals, 5 – 6 cm (2 – 2½ in) across.
Can be grown in the rock garden given a sheltered
place, but needs winter protection. Propagate from
seed, freshly harvested.

Cypripedium calceolus
ORCHIDACEAE

Commonly known as the lady's slipper orchid.
A rhizomatous perennial species, to about 50 cm
(25 in) tall, found wild in many parts of Europe in
calcareous soil on mountain slopes in wooded
areas: also found in North America. Leaves, 3–6
in number, ribbed, to 20 cm (8 in) long. Flowers, in
late spring and summer, have greenish-yellow to
purplish brown sepals, bright yellow lip to 3 cm
(1¼ in) long. Needs partial shade and calcareous
soil. Propagate by division in spring.

Cytisus x beanii
LEGUMINOSAE

A hybrid of C. ardoinii x C. purgans, produced by
accident at Kew Gardens, London. A deciduous,
shrubby plant, about 30 cm (12 in) or more tall,
often of semi-prostrate habit with simple, linear,
green leaves about 1 cm (½ in) long. Flowering
mid- to late spring, in thick clusters of about
3 deep golden-yellow blooms. Suitable for rock
garden culture in a compost such as John Innes
No. 2. Propagate by stem cuttings with heel
in summer.

Cytisus scoparius var. maritimus
LEGUMINOSAE

Syn. C. scoparius var. prostratus. A prostrate, hardy,
deciduous, bushy plant from southern and central
Europe. Leaves usually trifoliate, with leaflets to
1.5 cm (⅝ in) long, more or less oval in shape.
Flowers appear in late spring, brilliant yellow, to
2.5 cm (1 in) long, singly or in pairs, densely
covering the plant. Needs a sunny site and a
well-drained, enriched soil. Propagate by heeled
cuttings in summer.

Dianthus brachyanthus

D

Dactylorhiza romana
ORCHIDACEAE

A short, perennial orchid, found wild in grassy
areas on hill sides and dry, rocky slopes in the
Pyrenees and in similar terrain. Leaves, up to 10
in number, are clear green, forming a dense, basal
rosette; stem leaves fewer and smaller. Flowers, in
early summer, are yellow or reddish-purple with
yellowish base to the lip, borne in a cylindrical
spike. Lip 3-lobed, about 7 mm (⅜ in) long. A
useful garden or alpine house subject; needs
humus-rich, open soil. Propagate from seed.

Dactylorhiza sambucina
ORCHIDACEAE

A fairly low-growing perennial orchid to about
30 cm (12 in) tall when in bloom. Found in many
parts of Europe, from south to north, including
Britain. It produces 4 – 5 green leaves, which
cluster towards the base of the plant; the upper
leaves are rather more slender and reach the
flowers, which appear in early summer in dense,
oval spikes, generally reddish-purple with a
purplish lip, or yellow with purple-spotted lip. A
partially shaded position is preferable and an
enriched peat, loam soil. Propagate from seed,
freshly harvested.

Daphne alpina
THYMELAEACEAE

Syn. *D. candida*. A deciduous, bushy plant native
to central and southern Europe, to 45 cm (18 in)
tall. Leaves lance-shaped, to 4.5 cm (1¾ in) long,
invariably clustered towards the tips of the stems.
Flowers appear in late spring and early summer,
in terminal heads, each flower about 8 mm (⁷⁄₁₆ in)
long, fragrant, pure white, followed by downy
reddish berries. A sunny position in the rock
garden is advisable and a porous, slightly alkaline
soil. Propagate by heeled cuttings in late summer.

Daphne arbuscula
THYMELAEACEAE

A small, bushy shrub originating from the
Carpathian Mountains of central and eastern
Europe. An evergreen perennial to 20 cm (8 in) tall,
with dark green, narrowly lanceolate leaves, about
2 cm (¾ in) or a little more long. Flowers appear in
early summer, in terminal heads of 3 – 8 deep
rose-pink flowers, each about 1.5 cm (⅝ in) long,
tubular in shape and fragrant. A sunny position is
essential and a slightly moisture-retentive,
enriched soil. Propagate by stem cuttings or from
seed in autumn.

Daphne cneorum 'Eximia'
THYMELAEACEAE

An improved form of the popular garland flower,
native to southern central Europe and into southwest Russia. An evergreen, decumbent plant,
rarely more than 15 cm (6 in) tall, but widely
spreading, with dark green, oblanceolate leaves
about 2.5 cm (1 in) long. Borne in terminal clusters
in early summer, the bright rose-red flowers, about
1.5 cm (⅝ in) long, are tubular in shape and
fragrant. Needs sun and a rich, porous soil.
Propagate by layering of long stems or from stem
cuttings in late summer.

Daphne gnidium
THYMELAEACEAE

An erect, tall-growing, almost hairless shrubby
plant, native to much of the Mediterranean region.
Leaves bluish-green, evergreen, thick, narrowly
lance-shaped, 3 – 4 cm (1¼ – 1½ in) long, covered
with numerous white spots. Flowers in summer,
white and scented, each flower 4 – 6 mm
(³⁄₁₆ – ⁵⁄₁₆ in) long, borne in terminal clusters on
leafy stems 60 cm (24 in) or more long. Needs a
bright, sunny position and a slightly alkaline soil.
Propagate from freshly harvested seed.

Daphne jasminea
THYMELAEACEAE

An erect, bushy shrub to about 45 cm (18 in) tall, native to Greece – and also a more prostrate form, which may be better considered an alpine! The latter develops mats of woody stems, coated with small, narrowly obovate, bluish-grey leaves. Flowers, in early summer, are fragrant, tubular, creamy white, often reddish externally, carried in few-flowered clusters. For alpine house culture, where a very open, gritty, but enriched soil is essential, and a position in full sun. Propagate by cuttings in summer or from freshly harvested seed.

Daphne mezereum
THYMELAEACEAE

A deciduous, bushy species found in Europe and Asia, varying in size and in flower colour. The rather grey-green, oblanceolate leaves, 5 – 9 cm (2 – 3½ in) long, appearing in the early spring, are arranged opposite along the long stems. In spring the fragrant, purplish-red flowers in small clusters adorn and wreath the stems, almost hiding what new foliage has developed. Suitable for rock garden culture only when young; requires enriched garden soil. Propagate from cuttings in summer.

Datura stramonium
SOLANACEAE

A medium sized plant, native to Central and South America but naturalized in the Iberian Peninsula, invariably in hilly areas. Leaves oval to elliptic, lobed and toothed. Flowers appear in summer, generally white, funnel-shaped, to about 10 cm (4 in) long, followed by spiny, egg-shaped fruits, about 1.5 cm (⅝ in) long. A poisonous plant. Needs a sunny position in the alpine house and open, enriched soil. Propagate from seed, freshly harvested.

Degenia velebitica
CRUCIFERAE

A cushion-forming species found wild in a very restricted area in the Velebit Mountains, Croatia. Many slender, greyish-green leaves, 3 – 5 cm (1¼ – 2 in) long, form neat rosettes, coated with fine silvery hairs. Flowers appear in summer, golden-yellow, 3-lobed, carried on very short stems. This is still considered a rarity, needing careful attention, so is best placed in an alpine house, in a bright, sunny position. Needs an open, fertile soil. Propagate by cuttings or from seed.

Delosperma ashtonii
AIZOACEAE

A tuberous-rooted, clustering species, native to high, hilly country in Transvaal, Natal and Orange Free State, South Africa. The elongating, thick branches bear narrow, lanceolate leaves, about 4 cm (1½ in) long, 2 mm (⅛ in) wide and 4 mm (³⁄₁₆ in) thick, fleshy and succulent. Flowers, in late spring and early summer, are daisy-like, purplish-pink and about 4.5 cm (1¾ in) across. Best kept in the alpine house. Propagate from stem cuttings or fresh seed.

Delphinium muscosum
RANUNCULACEAE

A dwarf-growing species found in the Himalayas (Bhutan). A tufted, bushy plant, to about 15 cm (6 in) tall, clothed with hairy, deeply linear-lobed green leaves. Flowers appear in summer, in varying shades of blue, hairy, borne solitary, about 3 cm (1¼ in) in diameter, on long stalks. Needs alpine house conditions, moisture-retentive, enriched but rather porous soil and sun. Propagate by cuttings in spring, when new growth is apparent.

Deutzia gracilis 'Nikko'
PHILADELPHACEAE

A cultivar of a Japanese species. Leaves long, slender-pointed, lanceolate, to about 7 cm (2¾ in) long, forming quite a dense mass of spreading foliage to about 75 cm (30 in) in diameter; the leaves, however, are deciduous. Flowers, pure white in upright clusters, are in evidence in late spring and early summer. A hardy plant, needing the sunniest position possible and a well-drained soil enriched with leaf mould. Propagate by soft wood cuttings in summer.

Dianthus brachyanthus
CARYOPHYLLACEAE

A most variable plant, whose nomenclature still remains in confusion. It is native to Spain, found at varying altitudes in both southern and central regions. It forms fairly compact hummocks of narrow, dark green leaves, and flowers appear in early summer, bright pink, 3 – 4 cm (1¼ – 1½ in) in diameter, carried on stiff stems, 15 cm (6 in) long, just overtopping the foliage. Does best in sun or partial shade and seems to prefer a lime-based soil. Propagate by division in spring.

Dianthus brachyanthus var. alpinus
CARYOPHYLLACEAE

Syn. *D. alpinus*. A mat-forming plant with deep green, narrow, somewhat strap-shaped leaves, originating from the European Alps. The oblanceolate, glossy leaves are very prominent and more or less compacted together. Flowers are borne on stems about 10 cm (4 in) long in summer, usually solitary, varying in shades of reddish-purple, growing paler with age, to 4 cm (1½ in) wide. Needs a partially alkaline soil and an open, sunny position. Propagate from stem cuttings or by division.

Dianthus glacialis
CARYOPHYLLACEAE

A short, rhizomatous plant forming low tufts, found at different altitudes in the eastern Alps, often in somewhat acid soil. The dark green leaves are set opposite, obtuse, glossy and blunt-tipped, often longer than the flowering stems. Flowers appear in summer, solitary, about 2 cm (¾ in) in diameter, reddish-pink with whitish throat. Needs a sunny position and a permeable soil, enriched with leaf mould. Propagate by division in spring.

Dianthus monspessulanus
CARYOPHYLLACEAE

A tufted species found in stony, alpine pasture in southern Europe throughout much of the Mediterranean region. Leaves extremely narrow, dark green, set opposite on the flowering stems. Flowers, in summer, are borne solitary, fragrant, with deeply fringed petals of lavender pink to (rarely) white, on stems to 30 cm (12 in) long. Best cultivated in partial shade, in an open, enriched soil. Propagate by division in spring.

Dianthus sylvestris
CARYOPHYLLACEAE

A low-growing perennial, native to low mountainous terrain in many parts of southern Europe. The long, slender, somewhat wiry green leaves tend to form a rather untidy mass, which remains persistently semi-prostrate. The rose-pink flowers appear in early to midsummer, these having slightly notched petals and in all measure about 2 cm (¾ in) across. A slightly sandy soil is advised, with regular watering throughout the year, and a sunny or partially shaded position. Propagate from seed or by division.

Dichelostemma volubile
LILIACEAE

A bulbous species found wild in California on low mountain ranges; being of climbing habit it quickly penetrates low-growing scrub. Leaves are long and slender, and mostly trail on the ground. Flowers appear in summer, in large terminal umbels – often 20 or more together – these are bright pink, somewhat bell-shaped, displaying themselves to advantage on stems that can, at least in the wild, reach 60 cm (24 in) or more in length. Bulbs need to be planted deep for outdoor culture in enriched, moisture-retentive soil. Propagate from offsets.

Dietes grandiflora
IRIDACEAE

A rhizomatous species, native to grasslands at quite high altitudes in Natal and eastern Cape Province, South Africa. Leaves dark green, 60 – 90 cm (24 – 36 in) long, forming a basal, fan-like rosette. Flowers appear in early summer, whitish and pale mauve, with orange and brownish marks near the base of the petals, 6 – 9 cm (2½ – 3½ in) wide. Only half-hardy, so is best kept in the alpine house in normal soil. Propagate by division or from seed.

Dionysia aretioides
PRIMULACEAE

A cushion-forming species found in the Elburz Mountains of Iran. The cushions are composed of numerous rosettes of tiny, softly hairy leaves, slightly toothed on the upper edge. Flowers, in spring, are almost stemless, primrose-like, scented, golden-yellow, about 1 cm (½ in) across. A plant best suited to alpine house culture, grown in a porous, slightly calcareous soil. Propagate by division or from seed sown in a similar soil in spring.

Dionysia curviflora
PRIMULACEAE

A densely cushion-forming species, to 15 cm (6 in) across, found wild in southern Iran. Leaves are greyish-green, carried on very short stems, making a close mass because the leaves tend to overlap each other. Flowers appear in spring, pinkish with a yellow eye, borne singly on each of the many shoots. Suited to alpine house culture, requiring a rich, permeable soil mix of peat, loam and gritty sand in equal parts. Propagate by division or from newly harvested seed.

Dionysia tapetodes
PRIMULACEAE

A variable cushion-forming species, to 15 cm (6 in) or more across, found wild in mountainous regions of Afghanistan, Iran and bordering countries. Leaves greyish-green, very small and overlapping, borne on short stems. Flowers appear in spring, yellow, tubular with 5 spreading petals, on short scapes. Not thoroughly hardy, so best kept in an alpine house, in a moisture-retentive, humus-enriched soil with a few limestone chippings added. Propagate by division or from seed.

Dodecatheon hendersonii
PRIMULACEAE

A tufted, perennial, rosette-forming species, native to North America. The narrowly spathulate leaves, to 15 cm (6 in) long, form a basal rosette. Flowers appear during summer in any array of colours – violet, lavender or white, yellow or maroon at the base – borne in umbels on leafless stems about 30 cm (12 in) long. A rich, moisture-retentive soil is needed, and a position in partial shade. Propagate from seed, newly harvested.

Dorotheanthus bellidiformis
AIZOACEAE

Syn. *Cleretum bellidiformis*, *Mesembryanthemum criniflorum*. Commonly known as the Livingstone daisy. There are many colour forms of this plant, which originates from South Africa. Leaves vary in length, but are always rough and fleshy, 3 – 7 cm (1¼ – 2¾ in) long, up to 1 cm (½ in) wide. Flowers appear in summer; the yellow form is more unusual, 3 – 4 cm (1¼ – 1½ in) across, often tinged with orange. Grow from seed sown in early spring, temperature 18°C (64°F), and plant out in a sunny position, in slightly enriched, open soil, once the seedlings are 6 – 8 cm (2½ – 3 in) high.

Douglasia nivalis
PRIMULACEAE

A loosely tufted plant, forming clumps to about 30 cm (12 in) across, found in the wild in British Columbia, Canada. Leaves narrowly spathulate, slightly hairy. Flowers appear in late spring and early summer, pink, carried in heads of 3 – 6 small blooms on short, hairy stems. Well suited to alpine house culture, needing sun and a porous, gritty soil enriched with humus. Propagate by division or from seed in late summer.

Douglasia vitaliana
PRIMULACEAE

A cushion-forming species found in many areas of Europe, including the Alps and the Apennines. The linear to lanceolate leaves, to about 1 cm (½ in) long, form small rosettes of greyish-green. Flowers in spring and summer, borne solitary, yellow, about 1 cm (½ in) wide and fragrant. Much care is needed for successful results; possibly best kept in an alpine house. Propagate by division or from seed, always using an enriched, permeable soil.

Draba bruniifolia
CRUCIFERAE

A loose-tufted plant originating from a region extending from the Caucasus to Turkey. The pale green, very slender, linear leaves, about 5 mm (¼ in) long, have hairy margins and remain ever-green. Flowers appear in spring, golden-yellow, 5 mm (¼ in) or slightly more in diameter, in racemes 5 – 10 cm (2 – 4 in) long. A sunny position is advisable, preferably on partially sloping ground, and in a very porous, humus-rich soil. Propagate by division in late summer or from seed in spring.

Draba bryoides var. imbricata
CRUCIFERAE

A dwarf, cushion-forming plant from the Caucasus, the cushions consisting of numerous dark green leaves in dense clusters to almost ground level, these not exceeding 5 cm (2 in) in diameter. Flowers are bright golden-yellow, appearing in terminal clusters on slender stems in April. Ideal for a rock garden; needs an enriched, sandy compost. Planting or division are best carried out in early spring – seed generally germinates freely.

Draba polytricha
CRUCIFERAE

A densely tufted, cushion-forming plant native to eastern Europe and Turkey. Light green leaves, about 5 mm (¼ in) long, narrowly obovate in shape and with white hairs on margins, form neat rosettes. Spring brings a display of numerous heads of bright, golden-yellow flowers, each about 5 mm (¼ in) wide, carried on short stems about 5 cm (2 in) long. Best in an alpine house, in a sunny position and in a very permeable, fairly rich soil. Propagate by division in spring.

Draba rosularis
CRUCIFERAE

A more unusual tufted species found wild in Turkey, having greyish-green, narrowly elliptic leaves to about 2 cm (¾ in) in length, covered with bright silvery hairs. Flowers, in spring or early summer, are bright yellow, in terminal clusters, on stems to 10 cm (4 in) long, each flower about 5 mm (¼ in) across. Best cultivated in a sunny position in an alpine house in rich, porous soil. Propagate by division in autumn or from seed in spring.

Dracocephalum ruyschiana var. speciosum
LABIATAE

Syn. *D. argunense*. An attractive plant for the rock garden, originating from northeastern Asia. A clump-forming perennial with stems 40 – 60 cm (16 – 24 in) tall. Leaves narrowly lanceolate, 5 – 8 cm (2 – 3 in) or more long, dull green, smooth-edged. Flowers bluish-purple, sometimes deeper shades, or pink or white, tubular and prominently 2-lipped, at their best in summer. A sunny position is recommended and an enriched soil. Propagate by division or cuttings in spring.

Dryas drummondii
ROSACEAE

A mat-forming, rather shrubby plant, very similar to *D. octopetala*, and native to North America. It has stout stems, which bear small, leathery, rather wedge-shaped, dark green leaves with crenate margins, white tomentose on the undersurface. Flowers appear in summer, creamy white or yellow, solitary, tending to bend downwards and not opening fully, about 2.5 cm (1 in) wide. An extremely hardy plant, accepting quite low temperatures. Very satisfactory for the rock garden, needing sun and a porous, enriched soil. Propagate from seed, freshly harvested.

Dryas octopetala
ROSACEAE

A small, woody evergreen, with many creeping branches forming large, leafy mats, from mountainous regions in central and northern Europe, the Caucasus and North America. Leaves ovate, green with crenate margins, white mealy on the undersurface. Flowers, white, to 4 cm (1½ in) across, borne singly from the tips of the stalks. A pleasing alpine, rarely more than 16 cm (6½ in) high. Needs a fairly sunny position and prefers a slightly calcareous soil mix. Propagate from seed, sown in late autumn or early spring.

Dryas x suendermannii
ROSACEAE

A hybrid of *D. drummondii* x *D. octopetala*, both parents originating from high altitudes in North America. The slightly glossy green leaves are about 2 cm (¾ in) long, with crenate margins. Flowers appear in summer, yellow in bud, but opening to white, usually slightly pendent, on short stems. Needs full sun and a porous, gritty, alkaline soil. Propagate by heel cuttings in early autumn or from newly ripened seed.

Edraianthus dinaricus

E

Echeveria lindsayana
CRASSULACEAE

A glabrous rosette-forming species thought to have originated in Mexico, through this is still uncertain. Rosettes gradually become caespitose; they are formed from obovate to oblong leaves, 5 – 9 cm (2 – 3½ in) long, 3 – 4 cm (1¼ – 1½ in) broad. Flowers appear in early summer, borne on an inflorescence to 50 cm (20 in) tall, pink and deep orange-yellow. One of the choicest of the genus, an attractive plant for the alpine house. A permeable, gritty, fertile soil is essential and a sunny position. Propagate by division of rosettes in autumn.

Echeveria multicaulis
CRASSULACEAE

A low-growing, rosette-forming succulent plant found wild in Guerrero, Mexico, on mountain slopes. Leaves broadly spathulate-obovate, dark green with reddened margins, 2 – 3 cm (¾ – 1¼ in) long, to 2 cm (¾ in) wide, producing an attractive basal rosette. Racemes of reddish flowers, each 1 – 1.5 cm (½ – ⅝ in) long, are borne in summer on stems 30 cm (12 in) or more long. Essentially a plant for the alpine house, a soil of equal parts loam, peat and gritty sand with humus added. Propagate by division of rosettes or from seed in spring.

Echeveria pilosa
CRASSULACEAE

A fairly short, rosette-forming, succulent plant, native to hilly country in Mexico (Puebla). A short-stemmed, branching species. White-felted leaves, 7 – 8 cm (2¾ – 3 in) long, 3 cm (1¼ in) wide, form a compact, lax rosette, the white hairs very apparent. In early summer inflorescence to 30 cm (12 in) tall, leafy, bears a terminal cluster of orange-red flowers, each about 1 cm (½ in) long. Best kept in the alpine house in a humus-rich, permeable soil. Propagate from cuttings.

Echeveria setosa
CRASSULACEAE

A rosette-forming succulent species found growing wild in Puebla, Mexico, generally on low mountain slopes. The rosette is densely leafy, more or less spherical, the leaves more or less spathulate, ovate above, 7 – 8 cm (2¾ – 3 in) long, both surfaces coated with fine white bristles. Flowers appear in summer, reddish-yellow, carried terminally on stems about 30 cm (12 in) long. Ideally suited to alpine house culture, requiring a well-drained, gritty soil enriched with humus. Propagate by division in early spring.

Echium plantagineum
BORAGINACEAE

Syn. *E. lycopsis*. A soft, erect, biennial species originating from sandy areas in the Mediterranean region. Leaves oval or lanceolate, prominently veined, the upper leaves embracing the stem, stalkless. Flowers, in summer, reddish at first, then changing to deep blue or shades of violet and purple, to 3 cm (1¼ in) long, funnel-shaped, with many fine, soft hairs. Can be grown success-fully in the rock garden; needs an enriched, very sandy soil. Propagate from fresh seed in sandy soil, temperature 15°C (59°F).

Edraianthus dalmaticus
CAMPANULACEAE

Possibly synonymous with *E. caudatus*. A low-growing species native to the Balkan region. The narrow basal leaves, 3 – 5 cm (1¼ – 2 in) long, make a rosette. It has stems about 15 cm (6 in) long, erect, bearing clusters of 4 – 10 bluish-violet flowers, about 2 cm (¾ in) long, bell-shaped, in summer. Alpine house culture is advisable; needs a sunny location and sharply draining soil. Propagate from seed, sown in spring.

Edraianthus dinaricus
CAMPANULACEAE

A hummock-forming plant originating from the Balkans. Leaves 2.5 – 3.5 cm (1 – 1⅜ in) long form clumps of narrow-leaved rosettes. Flowers, borne on short stems to 6 cm (2½ in) long, appearing in summer. A sunny site is recommended and a very open, permeable soil. Best grown in an alpine house. Propagate from seed, sown in spring.

Eleutherine bulbosa
IRIDACEAE

An unusual bulbous plant, found wild at altitudes of 600 m (2,000 ft) and over in Central and South America; also in the West Indies. Plants 30 – 60 cm (12 – 24 in) tall, with 3 – 4 prominently veined elliptic leaves. Inflorescence, with 4 – 10 flowers, branched, with leaf-like bracts at each branch. Flowers, borne in early summer in cultivation, white, about 3 cm (1¼ in) across, with equal, obovate segments. A subject for the alpine house; needs rich, open soil. Propagate from fresh seed.

Elisena longipetala
AMARYLLIDACEAE

A choice bulbous species originating from around Lima, Peru. Leaves long, shiny and strap-like, 30 – 45 cm (12 – 18 in) long, all basal. Flowers, borne on a stem about equalling the leaves, are pure white, often 15 cm (6 in) or more across, with a funnel-shaped corona, and appear in early summer in cultivation. Best grown under glass, the bulbs planted deep in a very rich, open soil with decomposed leaf mould added. Propagate from newly ripened seed, temperature 15 °C (59 °F).

Empodium namaquensis
HYPOXIDACEAE

A bulbous-rooted plant found wild in remote areas of Namaqualand in southern Africa. Leaves about 15 cm (6 in) long, decidedly pleated, appearing before or with the flowers. Flowers borne in summer on stems 10 – 45 cm (4 – 18 in) long, pale yellow, with widely spreading segments and prominent style and stamens. Needs alpine house culture and a bright, sunny position at all times. A porous, slightly gritty, but rich soil will encourage flowering. Propagate from seed, sown immediately it is harvested.

Epilobium crassum
ONAGRACEAE

A creeping, prostrate species native to low mountainous areas of New Zealand. The stems, to 15 cm (6 in) long, root at ground level, bearing fleshy, more or less erect, glossy green leaves, reddish on the undersurface. Flowers, pink or white, to 1 cm (½ in) across, appear in summer from near the apex of the stems. A bright, sunny position is important, and moist soil. Propagate from seed or by division, from autumn to spring.

Epimedium diphyllum
BERBERIDACEAE

A dwarf herbaceous perennial, rarely more than 15 cm (6 in) high, originating from Japan. The green leaves are bifoliate, providing a pleasing background to the rather unusual white flowers, which appear during spring – pendent, 4-petalled, without spurs, borne in loose panicles. Best grown in partial shade and in a humus-enriched soil. Propagate by division in spring or autumn, or from seed when it is fully ripe.

Erica herbacea
ERICACEAE

Syn. *E. carnea*. Commonly known as mountain heath. This is a low-growing, semi-erect, clump-forming species, to 25 cm (10 in) high, found in many parts of central Europe, in mountainous country. Linear leaves, about 6 mm (⁵⁄₁₆ in) long, are dark green. Flowers, borne in dense racemes in early spring, often late winter, are pinkish-red, to about 6 mm (⁵⁄₁₆ in) long. Suitable for the rock garden in ordinary or slightly calcareous soil. Propagate from seed in spring.

Erigeron borealis
COMPOSITAE

Possibly synonymous with *E. alpinus*. A tufted plant found in the Alps, Pyrenees and Apennines, and possibly in Britain, too. Stems about 20 cm (8 in) long, bearing a few leaves. Basal leaves are softly hairy, spathulate, to 8 cm (3 in) long. Flowers are borne in late summer, solitary or in a few-flowered cluster, each 2 – 3 cm (¾ – 1¼ in) wide, purplish-pink rays, yellow-centred. A sunny site is advised, and a truly open, gritty soil. Propagate by division or from seed in spring.

Erigeron compositus
COMPOSITAE

Syn. *E. multifidus*. A tufted, low-growing species found in northern parts of the western USA, through to Alaska. Stems to 15 cm (6 in) long, with hairy, lobed leaves 2 – 6 cm (¾ – 2½ in) long borne on long stalks. Flowers appear during spring and summer, each to 3 cm (1¼ in) across, with white to blue or even purplish rays, on 7 – 8 cm (2¾ – 3 in) long stalks. Needs a sunny setting and a very permeable, fertile soil. Propagate by division or from seed in spring.

Erigeron pinnatisectus
COMPOSITAE

A tufted plant with very attractive foliage, originating from the Rocky Mountains of north-west America. It rarely exceeds 15 cm (6 in) in height, with fern-like, much dissected, greyish-green leaves. Flowers, large, deep mauve, daisy-like, in spring and summer, each borne terminally and enhancing the fascinating appearance of the plant. A good, bright, sunny site is advisable, and an enriched, porous soil. Propagate by division or from seed in spring.

Erigeron speciosus
COMPOSITAE

A clump-forming plant with branching stems, about 45 cm (18 in) high, native to northern parts of western America (California and Oregon). The basal leaves are more or less lanceolate, ciliate, to 10 cm (4 in) long. Flower heads have 2 – 10 individual blooms, each 5 cm (2 in) across, in shades varying from lilac to rather deep purple, appearing in summer. Needs an enriched soil and sun. Suited to rock garden culture. Propagate by division or from seed.

Erinacea anthyllis
LEGUMINOSAE

Syn. *E. pungens*. This is a stiff, clump-forming, shrubby plant to 30 cm (12 in) high, native to Spain, the Pyrenees and north Africa. The hummock-like appearance, formed from stiff, spine-tipped branchlets, the younger growth green and soft with silvery hairs. Leaves oblanceolate, quickly falling, only 5 mm (¼ in) long. The blue-violet, pea-like flowers, to 1.8 cm (¹¹⁄₁₆ in) long, are carried in terminal racemes in late spring and summer. Needs sun and well-drained soil. Propagate from heel cuttings in summer.

Erinus alpinus
SCROPHULARIACEAE

The sole representative of the genus. A rather dwarf, evergreen perennial tufted plant, known only in the Alps and Pyrenees. Leaves are oval-spoon-shaped, often toothed, to 4 cm (1½ in) long, formed into rosettes. The erect stems, up to 15 cm (6 in) long, bear many rose-pink or whitish tubular flowers about 1 cm (½ in) wide with notched-tipped petals, during spring and summer. A sunny position is best, and very porous, enriched soil. Propagate from seed in spring.

Eriogonum ovalifolium
POLYGONACEAE

A more or less hummock-forming species originating from western areas of North America. Leaves oval, densely white-woolly, more or less erect, to 7 cm (2¾ in) long. Flowers in close-set umbels on stems to 20 cm (8 in) high, white or lemon yellow, in summer. Alpine house culture is preferable. Needs full sun and a gritty soil, enriched with leaf mould. Propagate by division or from seed in spring.

Erodium corsicum
GERANIACEAE

A somewhat sprawling or erect, slightly hairy species native to Corsica and Sardinia. Leaves are greyish-green, more or less oval in shape, scarcely heart-shaped at the base, the margins decidedly lobed, to 3 cm (1¼ in) wide. Flowers appear in summer, generally solitary or 2 – 3 together, to nearly 2 cm (¾ in) in diameter, pink or white. An open, bright, sunny position is preferable, and a well-drained soil. Propagate from seed in spring.

Erodium reichardii
GERANIACEAE

A very compact species, similar in many ways to *E. corsicum*, native to the Balearic Islands. The sparsely hairy, greenish leaves vary from 5 – 15 mm (¼ – ⅝ in) in length, somewhat rounded in shape, often with slightly pinnate margins. Flowers appear in summer, varying from white with purple veins to pinkish with red veins, always borne singly. This is a subject for the alpine house, needing a sunny position and a well-drained soil. Propagate by division or from seed in spring.

Eryngium bourgatii
UMBELLIFERAE

An evergreen perennial species originating from the Pyrenees, with stems 30 – 60 cm (12 – 24 in) tall. Leaves spiny, bluish-grey and white-veined, 3-lobed, each lobe bipinnate and somewhat angular, 3 – 7 cm (1¼ – 2¾ in) long. Flowers, in summer, are borne terminally in oval heads about 2 cm (¾ in) long, with slender lanceolate, often spiny, bracts of purplish-blue to 5 cm (2 in) long. Needs sun and a well-drained soil. Propagate from freshly ripened seed.

Eryngium glaciale
UMBELLIFERAE

A fairly dwarf, woody-stemmed plant, 30 – 40 cm (12 – 16 in) high, found in hilly regions of Spain. Leaves are stiff, hard and spiny, obovate, bipinnate, greyish-blue. Almost globose heads, 2 cm (¾ in) across, of soft blue to almost whitish flowers in summer, subtended by bright, silvery grey thorns. Needs the protection of the alpine house in an open, enriched soil and in full sun. Propagate from newly harvested seed.

Erysimum myriophyllum
CRUCIFERAE

A tufted perennial plant native to the mountains of southern Spain, especially in the regions of Valencia and Andalusia. A species that tends to branch from the base, with numerous green-greyish narrow leaves to 2 cm (¾ in) wide. The glossy yellow flowers appear in early summer, the petals about 1.5 cm (⅝ in) long and the sepals 1 cm (½ in) long. A compact, erect, rather elegant plant that has, to a great extent, escaped cultivation. A normal garden soil with fine grit added, in a fairly sunny position meet requirements. Propagate from seed in spring.

Erythrina zeyheri
LEGUMINOSAE

A low-growing, shrubby species with a large, fleshy, tuberous rootstock, found wild from Transvaal to Natal in South Africa. Leaves are large and prickly on both surfaces, bright green, divided into 3 oval leaflets, about 15 cm (6 in) long. Flowers are bright scarlet, borne on stems about 45 cm (18 in) long, appearing in succession during summer. Best suited to the alpine house, grown in a deep pot filled with humus-rich, porous soil. Propagate from seed, sown in spring.

Erythronium dens-canis
LILIACEAE

Commonly known as the dog's tooth violet. A rather dwarf bulbous perennial plant, widely distributed throughout much of Europe to Japan. It has just 2 slender, lance-shaped leaves, basal and set opposite, bluish-green marbled with reddish-brown blotches. Flowers appear in spring, solitary, on slender stalks, pink to deep pinkish-mauve, reflexed and marked purple or orange in the throat, about 5 cm (2 in) wide. Needs sun and an enriched soil. Propagate from seed, freshly harvested.

Erythronium grandiflorum
LILIACEAE

The choice glacier lily, native to western North America. The bulb produces totally plain green, lance-shaped leaves to 15 cm (6 in) long. Flowers, in spring, are bright yellow, solitary or up to 5 together on stems to 3 cm (1¼ in) long, each about 5 cm (2 in) across. There is also a white form from the same region. A bright position in partial shade is beneficial to flowering and a moist, open soil. Propagate from seed, freshly harvested.

Erythronium oregonum
LILIACEAE

This perennial bulbous species is found principally in the region of Oregon, USA. Attractively marbled leaves to 20 cm (8 in) long, with varying light and dark mottling. Flowers about 6 cm (2½ in) in diameter, white or cream, appearing during spring, each with a yellow throat edged with dark brownish-orange, mostly solitary, but sometimes 2 – 3 to a stem. A very slightly shaded position is preferable and a rich, permeable soil. Propagate from seed, freshly harvested.

Eschscholzia californica
PAPAVERACEAE

A perennial, low-growing plant, found wide-spread at various altitudes in the USA in California and neighbouring States. Leaves slender, glaucous green or often somewhat greyish, cut into many segments. Stems to 30 – 40 cm (12 – 16 in) tall, with terminal orange-yellow flowers, 4 – 6 cm (1½ – 2½ in) across, in late summer and autumn. Suited to rock garden culture; often treated as an annual. Propagate from seed in spring.

Euphorbia cyparissias
EUPHORBIACEAE

This dwarf, spreading plant, commonly known as the cypress spurge, is native to Europe, including the Alps. Leaves are stalkless, linear, arranged alternate along the stems, 1 – 3 cm (½ – 1¼ in) long. Flower stems carry terminal heads of up to 18 rays, with rounded, kidney-shaped, yellowish-green bracts, which become reddish, blooming early summer. Grow in ordinary garden soil in slight shade. Propagate by division or from seed after flowering.

Euphorbia griffithii
EUPHORBIACEAE

A hardy, rhizomatous-rooted perennial species found wild in the Himalayas. Leaves lanceolate with reddish ribs, basal, and embracing the stems. Flowers appear in summer, bright red in terminal clusters, each about 1.2 cm (9/16 in) across. Can be used to advantage in the rock garden. Needs a bright sunny position and a well-drained, humus enriched soil. Propagate by careful division of the rootstock, or by cuttings of basal shoots or from seed in spring.

Euphorbia helenae
EUPHORBIACEAE

An attractive, bushy, semi-succulent species, found at altitudes of about 800 m (2,600 ft) in Oriente, Cuba; a localized plant in the Sierre de Nipe. Plants can be male or female. Leaves firm, lance-shaped, about 20 cm (8 in) long. Flowers appear in early summer, borne on a solitary inflorescence – the very deep red bracts are each 1.5 – 5 cm (5/8 – 2 in) long. Needs a rich, mineral-based compost and is best kept in an alpine house. Propagate by stem cuttings in late summer or from seed, freshly harvested.

Euphorbia heterophylla
EUPHORBIACEAE

Known as painted spurge. Generally a low-growing plant, 30 – 45 cm (12 – 18 in) high, found in many parts of the eastern USA and the West Indies. It has fiddle-shaped, dark green leaves about 12 cm (5 in) long, the upper bract-like leaves surrounding the terminal umbel, bright red. Flowers, in summer, are clustered together terminally, yellowish. Needs alpine house protection, a sunny position and rich, open soil. Propagate from freshly harvested seed.

Euphorbia lathyris
EUPHORBIACEAE

The caper spurge. This tall-growing plant is found wild on hilly slopes in southern Europe. Stems, to 1 m (3 ft) or more high, bear stalkless, green, slender leaves. Flowers are borne in summer in more or less terminal umbels, the bracts bright green and the glands having blunt 'horns'. Suited to the rock garden in normal garden soil. Propagate from seed, freshly harvested.

Euphorbia myrsinites
EUPHORBIACEAE

A low, spreading species found in rocky terrain in southern Europe through to western Turkey. Leaves very thick and succulent, grey or bluish-green, oval or rounded, borne along the whole length of the stems. Flowers in terminal umbels, bright yellowish-green, to 10 cm (4 in) wide, appear in early summer. A hardy plant, ideally suited to rock garden culture; needs a porous, slightly calcareous soil with a little added humus, in bright sun or partial shade. Propagate by division in spring.

Euphorbia peplis
EUPHORBIACEAE

A dwarf, low, prostrate species, with purplish stems, found in mountainous rocky areas in southern Europe, sometimes near the coast. It has short-stalked, deep bluish-green, oblong, fleshy leaves, about 1.5 cm (⅝ in) long, borne opposite along the 10 – 15 cm (4 – 6 in) long branches. Flowers borne in summer, greenish, solitary, terminal or lateral, rarely clustered. An unusual plant for the alpine house; needs a rich, gritty soil. Propagate from fresh seed.

Euphorbia regis-jubae
EUPHORBIACEAE

A bushy species, found wild in most of the Canary Islands, invariably on mountain slopes to 1,000 m (3,300 ft) or higher. It has narrowly oblong leaves, particularly slender, 3 – 7 cm (1¼ – 2¾ in) long, dull greyish-green. Flowers borne in summer. Bracts greenish-yellow, mostly in terminal umbels; these tend to fall before the fruits ripen. Needs alpine house culture and a fairly rich, mineral-based soil in full sun. Propagate from seed, freshly harvested.

Euphorbia rossii
EUPHORBIACEAE

A medium sized, freely branching species, with succulent stems 50 cm (20 in) or more tall, native to mountainous areas of Madagascar. Branches rather olive green in colour, 2 – 3 cm (¾ – 1¼ in) thick, with many prominent thorns, and twisting, slender green leaves, to 4 cm (1½ in) long. Flowers, in summer, borne in umbel-like cluster, olive green to reddish. Needs alpine house culture in a rich, open soil. Propagate by cuttings or from seed.

Euphorbia rubella
EUPHORBIACEAE

A dwarf, fleshy species with a cylindrical base, caudex-like, subterranean, only the tips showing above ground. Native to hilly country in Somalia and neighbouring regions. Leaves deep green, dark red underside, 2 cm (¾ in) long, 1 cm (½ in) wide, lying at soil level. Inflorescence with whitish flowers suffused with pale pink. A rare plant; suited to the alpine house and needing a rich, open soil, minimum temperature 15℃ (59℉). Propagate from seed, newly ripened.

Euryops acraeus
COMPOSITAE

Syn. *E. evansii*. A short, bushy species with woody stems, native to the Drakensberg Mountains in South Africa. Rarely exceeds 15 cm (6 in) tall. The erect stems are closely arranged, bearing silvery green linear leaves with blunted tips, to 2 cm (¾ in), more or less in whorls, hairy. The daisy-like flowers appear in late spring and summer, bright yellow, to 3 cm (1¼ in) across, always solitary. A sunny location is advisable, and a good, porous soil. Propagate from cuttings in spring.

Eustephia darwinii
LILIACEAE

A rare bulbous species, native to South America. The oval bulb has a blackish sheath. Leaves are strap-like, 30 – 45 cm (12 – 18 in) long. Flowers, in summer, are borne on a reddish stem to 60 cm (24 in) long in a few-flowered umbel of pendent, orange-red, tubular flowers with dark green tips. A humus-rich, loamy, permeable soil is essential, preferably in an alpine house. Keep dry in winter. Propagate from seed, freshly harvested.

Genista delphinensis

F-G

Felicia amelloides
COMPOSITAE

A dense, small, bushy plant, 30 – 45 cm (12 – 18 in) high, native to South Africa. Leaves broadly ovate, about 3 mm (³⁄₁₆ in) wide, often set opposite along the branches. Flowers in summer, daisy-like, very pale blue with yellow centres, borne from the tips of the stems, standing well above the foliage, 2.5 – 4 cm (1 – 1½ in) in diameter. A half-hardy plant, which is best cultivated in the alpine house; can be grown in the rock garden in a bright, sunny, sheltered site, but may require winter protection. Needs a rich, porous soil. Propagate by cuttings in summer.

Ferraria crispa
IRIDACEAE

A cormous plant originating from South Africa, where it is widespread throughout much of Cape Province. It has a stoutish stem to 30 cm (12 in) or more long, covered with leaf sheaths, the lower leaves arranged distichously. Flowers in late summer in cultivation, dark brownish-red with whitish markings on the inner segments; there is also a pale yellow variety with brownish margins. A plant for alpine house culture, requiring sun and a slightly acid, open soil. Propagate from seed in spring.

Ferula communis
UMBELLIFERAE

The giant fennel. This tall-growing plant is found growing from low to quite high ground in much of the Mediterranean region. Stems, 1 – 3 m (about 3 – 7 ft) tall, are thick and hollow. Leaves, 3 – 4 in number, are bright green, pinnate, longer towards the base. Flowers borne in early summer in terminal umbels, the numerous rays being bright yellowish-green. Requires full sun and a sandy, slightly enriched soil. Propagate from seed, freshly harvested.

Freesia andersoniae
IRIDACEAE

A cormous species to about 15 cm (6 in) tall, originating from South Africa (Griquatown and Barkly West areas). Leaves very erect, linear. Flowers richly scented, 4 – 5 cm (1½ – 2 in) long, waxy-white within, with a deeper yellow-shaded throat, at their best in late spring. This is rarely encountered in cultivation, but, when available, keep in the alpine house in a bright position, and in a humus-enriched, permeable soil. Propagate from freshly harvested seed, in summer or autumn.

Freesia sparrmannii var. alba
IRIDACEAE

A cormous species from Cape Province, South Africa. A variable plant from 20 – 45 cm (8 – 18 in) tall, with slender leaves 7 – 17 cm (2¾ – 7 in) long. Stems overtop the leaves and are usually branched. Flowers appear in spring, pure white, shaded pale yellow at the lower part of the perianth tube, star-shaped and sweetly scented. Best suited to alpine house culture, given a fairly sunny position; allow to dry once leaves and flowers have withered. Needs an open, humus-enriched soil. Propagate from seed, sown in autumn, temperature 15 ℃ (59 °F).

Fritillaria aurea
LILIACEAE

A bulbous plant found wild in mountainous country in central Turkey, generally among lime-stone rocks. Leaves arranged alternate, greyish-green, lanceolate, of varying lengths. Flowers in early summer, borne solitary on fleshy stems 5 – 15 cm (2 – 6 in) long, bell-shaped, yellow with reddish-brown veining, to about 3 cm (1¼ in) in diameter. Requires a bright, sunny, sheltered position, preferably in an alpine house, and an open, slightly calcareous, gritty soil. Propagate from newly ripened seed or offsets.

Fritillaria bucharica
LILIACEAE

A bulbous plant originating from Afghanistan and central Asia on rocky slopes to altitudes over 2,000 m (6,600 ft). Leaves greyish-green, lanceolate, borne along the fleshy stems, which are 10 – 30 cm (4 – 12 in) or more in length. Flowers white, greenish-tinged, to 2 cm (¾ in) long, carried in racemes of up to 10 flowers in spring. Frost-hardy, but needs careful attention; complete dryness is necessary in summer. Needs a well-drained, humus-enriched soil, and a sheltered, sunny site. Propagate from seed when ripe.

Fritillaria carica
LILIACEAE

A bulbous plant from hilly limestone country in southern Greece, western Turkey and the Aegean islands. Leaves greyish-green, usually set alternate along the stems, which vary in length from 5 cm (2 in) to over 12 cm (5 in). Flowers, in late spring and early summer, are bell-shaped, pendent and terminal, yellow or greenish-yellow, up to 2 cm (¾ in) in diameter. Of easy growth, best in an alpine house, in a sheltered, sunny position and a slightly calcareous, gritty soil, which needs to be porous. Propagate from fresh seed or offsets.

Fritillaria chitralensis
LILIACEAE

Syn. *F. imperialis* var. *chitralensis*. A most elegant bulbous species found wild in the Himalayas, particularly the western regions, on rocky slopes 2,000 m (6,600 ft) or more high. This is basically one of the colour forms of the type species. Leaves lanceolate, glossy green, arranged in whorls. Flowers lemon yellow, bell-shaped, about 5 cm (2 in) long, borne terminally in a head of up to 5, appearing in spring. Well suited to rock garden culture, needing a well-drained soil, which dries slightly in summer. Propagate from offsets or seed.

Fritillaria crassifolia ssp. kurdica
LILIACEAE

A rather low-growing species native to mountainous regions of northwest Iran, Iraq and southern Russia. Leaves narrowly lanceolate, set alternate along the short stems. Flowers, in late spring and early summer, are bell-shaped, variable in colour, usually greenish with brownish tessellate marking, 2 – 3 cm (¾ – 1¼ in) in diameter. Best kept in an alpine house; needs a fairly sunny position and a gritty, loamy, peaty soil, enriched with humus. Propagate from offsets or newly harvested seed.

Fritillaria lanceolata
LILIACEAE

Commonly known as the chequer lily. A rather tall, bulbous species found wild in western parts of North America. Leaves oval-lanceolate, arranged in whorls around the stems. Flowers, in summer, carried on fleshy stems 30 – 65 cm (12 – 26 in) or more tall, usually 1 – 4 to a stem, bell-shaped and nodding, brownish-purple with yellow mottling, or yellow with purplish-brown mottling, each about 3 cm (1¼ in) long. Needs sun and a well-drained soil. Propagate from seed.

Fritillaria lusitanica
LILIACEAE

A bulbous species found at low and high altitudes in east, central and southern Spain. Leaves linear, long-pointed, arranged alternate, about 1 cm (½ in) wide. Flowers, in summer, are pendent and variable in colour – usually reddish-brown or greenish, flushed and chequered externally, also with a pale greenish or whitish band running lengthwise, about 4 cm (1½ in) long. Best suited to alpine house culture, needing sun and good ventilation when in bloom. A well-drained soil is essential. Propagate from freshly harvested seed, temperature 13 ℃ (55 ℉).

Fritillaria meleagris
LILIACEAE

Commonly known as the snake's head fritillary.
A variable species, it is native to many parts of
Europe, including the south of England. The
slender stem grows to about 30 cm (12 in), bearing
very narrow, greyish leaves and, in late spring, a
single, pendent, bell-shaped flower about 4 cm
(1½ in) long, usually in shades of pinkish-purple,
although white flowers are known. Slight shade
and moist conditions are advisable, and bulbs
quickly naturalize if set in grassy areas. Propagate
from seed, freshly harvested, or from bulbils.

Fritillaria minuta
LILIACEAE

Syn. *F. carduchorum*. A more dwarf-growing
bulbous plant found wild in northwest Iran and
eastern Turkey on wooded hill sides at altitudes
of 1,000 – 3,500 m (3,300 – 11,500 ft). Leaves bright
shiny green, arranged alternate on the upper part
of the 6 – 8 cm (2½ – 3 in) long stem. Flowers
appear in late spring and early summer, solitary,
reddish-brown or orange-brown, to 1.5 cm (⅝ in)
in diameter. Suitable for a bulb frame or alpine
house. A peaty, gritty soil, enriched with leaf
mould, is recommended, in partial shade.
Propagate from offsets in autumn.

Fritillaria nobilis
LILIACEAE

Probably a dwarf form of *F. latifolia*. A small
bulbous plant found wild in mountainous regions
of eastern Turkey. Short stems carry a few glossy,
grey-green, lance-shaped leaves arranged
alternate, and bell-shaped, purplish-brown flowers
about 4 cm (1½ in) in diameter, both stems and
flowers tending to rest on the ground. This early
summer-flowering plant, rarely exceeding 15 cm
(6 in) high, needs a sunny, sheltered position in the
rock garden, and an enriched peaty soil. Propagate
from seed, newly ripened.

Fritillaria olivieri
LILIACEAE

A rare species, native to Iran, where it grows in
moist meadows at altitudes to 4,000 m (13,000 ft).
This bulbous plant produces a stem to about 50 cm
(20 in) tall, with bell-shaped flowers appearing in
late spring to early summer – the shiny leaves
enhance the attractive colouring of the green and
brown blooms, each about 4 cm (1½ in) long.
Bulbs should be planted in partial shade in an
enriched, moist, well-drained soil in early autumn.
Propagate from seed, freshly harvested.

Fritillaria orientalis
LILIACEAE

Syn. *F. montana*, *F. tenella*. A medium sized
bulbous plant, native to eastern Europe and the
Balkans, mostly to about 40 cm (16 in) high. The
rather greyish-green leaves are mainly set
opposite or whorled, having recurving, tendril-
like tips, excepting the terminal whorled 3.
Flowers are borne terminally in late spring or
early summer, somewhat brownish colour and
chequered with even deeper brown. Needs a
sheltered, sunny position in an open, enriched
soil. Propagate from seed, freshly harvested.

Fritillaria pallidiflora
LILIACEAE

A bulbous species, found in mountainous regions
of northern Siberia. The broadly lanceolate,
greyish-green leaves, 20 cm (8 in) or more long, are
either opposite or alternate. Flowers, in late
spring, are in terminal heads on stems generally
longer than the leaves, up to 4 to a head, pale
yellow, about 4 cm (1½ in) long and 3 cm (1¼ in)
across, bell-shaped, from the upper leaf axils. A
hardy plant, needing a bright, sheltered site and
porous, rich soil. Propagate from seed or bulblets.

Fritillaria ruthenica
LILIACEAE

Syn. *F. minor*. A plant very similar to *F. orientalis*, found principally in more southerly regions of eastern Europe. Leaves grey-green, set opposite or in whorls, including the upper 3, which are always whorled and recurved, tendril-like. Flowers, in early summer, are bell-shaped, generally coloured and chequered blackish-brown, 2 – 3 cm (¾ – 1¼ in) wide, terminal, solitary or few together. Partial shade advised, and a humus-rich, permeable soil. Propagate from seed, freshly harvested.

Fritillaria sewerzowii
LILIACEAE

Also recorded as *F. severtozovii*. A bulbous species, found wild in central Asia in the Tien Shan and Pamir Alai Mountains to altitudes of about 2,000 m (6,600 ft). Leaves more or less lanceolate, arranged alternate along the stems. Flowers, in late spring and early summer, bell-shaped, 2 – 3 cm (¾ – 1¼ in) long, green or greyish-green with brownish markings, from the upper leaf axils on stems to 45 cm (18 in) long. Of fairly easy culture but best kept in an alpine house or a bulb frame. Needs a rich, open soil and sun. Propagate from offsets or seed.

Fuchsia procumbens
ONAGRACEAE

A prostrate, trailing plant from New Zealand, best suited to alpine house culture as it is probably deciduous if left in the open. Rather fleshy, rounded leaves, to 2 cm (¾ in) long. Flowers, in summer, erect, tubular, to 2 cm (¾ in) long, the tube pale orange, the sepals green, reddish tipped – petals are absent. Large red-purple fruits about 2 cm (¾ in) long. Grow in ordinary garden soil; sun or partial shade preferred. Propagate from seed, sown in spring.

Gagea arvensis
LILIACEAE

A low to medium sized bulbous species found in southern Europe and north Africa, mainly on fairly low ground in fields or verges. Plants rarely more than 15 cm (6 in) tall, with minutely hairy stems, and a few slender leaves below the flower head. There are 2 flat, linear, basal leaves about 3 mm (³⁄₁₆ in) wide. Flowers appear throughout the spring, often severaltogether, yellow with greenish outer surface, about 2 cm (¾ in) across. Suited to indoor or outdoor cultivation; needs slightly calcareous, moisture-retentive soil. Propagate from seed, freshly harvested.

Gagea fibrosa
LILIACEAE

A very low-growing, bulbous plant, native to Greece and the Aegean islands. Plants rarely exceed 8 cm (3 in) high when in flower. It has a solitary, rather flat basal leaf to 3 mm (³⁄₁₆ in) wide, always prostrate on the ground. Flowers, in late spring and early summer, to 3 cm (1¼ in) in diameter, yellowish, green externally, borne on minutely hairy stalks. A subject for the alpine house. Needs a sunny position and a very porous, enriched compost. Propagate from seed, freshly harvested.

Galactites tomentosa
COMPOSITAE

A delicate, thistle-like species found in many parts of southern Europe and north Africa. Leaves are arranged alternate, oblong and finely divided with spiny lobes, dark green, often white veined on the upper surface. It has branches 30 cm (12 in) or more tall, each carrying a terminal head of soft purplish to lilac, sometimes whitish, flowers, 2 cm (¾ in) across, in early summer. Needs a very stony but humus-rich soil (as shown), and full sun. Propagate from seed when ripe.

Galanthus nivalis
AMARYLLIDACEAE

This popular species of the snowdrop family is found in many parts of Europe, from Spain to Britain and Russia, invariably in woodland and similar shady places. Plants are usually tuft-forming, rarely exceeding 12 cm (5 in) in height. Leaves in greenish shades, strap-like, appearing at flowering time. Flowers are white, generally with drooping heads, to 2 cm (¾ in) or more long, appearing in late winter and early to late spring. Grow in normal garden soil in slight shade. Division, soon after flowering, is the best method of propagation.

Galaxia barnardii
IRIDACEAE

A fairly low-growing, cormous species, found on hilly country near to Caledon, Cape Province, South Africa. It has a few channelled leaves, 6 cm (2½ in) long, with ciliate margins, formed into a rosette. Flowers, in late spring and early summer, are pinkish-purple with a darker centre, the perianth tube 3 cm (1¼ in) long and deeper purple – opening briefly at midday. Suited to alpine house culture; needs rich, sandy soil. Propagate from seed or cormlets.

Galaxia citrina
IRIDACEAE

A dwarf cormous species, widespread in mountainous regions of Cape Province (Worcester, Calvinia and Wuppertal), South Africa. Leaves, about 7 cm (2¾ in) long, have minutely ciliate edges. Flowers, opening after midday in early summer, are bright yellow, the segments to 3 cm (1¼ in) long and 1 cm (½ in) wide. A choice subject for the alpine house; needs an enriched, sandy soil. Propagate from seeds or offsets.

Galaxia variabilis
IRIDACEAE

A dwarf, deciduous, cormous plant, originating from low mountains near Bokkeveld, Cape Province, South Africa. It has bi-facial, channelled leaves, 3 – 6 cm (1¼ – 2½ in) or more long, with ciliate margins. Flowers, appearing in early summer in cultivation, are variable, pink, yellow or white with yellow throat, the perianth tube 3 cm (1¼ in) long, segments to 3.5 cm (1⅜ in) in length, about 1 cm (½ in) wide. Needs to be kept in an alpine house, in a porous, rich soil. Propagate from freshly harvested seed.

Galtonia candicans
LILIACEAE

A bulbous species originating from South Africa, from Natal to eastern Cape Province, in moist, grassy areas to altitudes of 2,500 m (8,200 ft). Leaves erect or arching, 45 – 60 cm (18 – 24 in) long, formed into basal rosettes. In cultivation flowers in summer, the stems overtopping the leaves, these bearing racemes of pendent, bell-shaped, white flowers, each about 4 cm (1½ in) long, often fragrant. Needs a humus-enriched, but well-drained soil, the bulbs set 12 – 15 cm (5 – 6 in) deep. A sunny but sheltered position is advisable. Propagate from seed or offsets in spring.

Gazania uniflora
COMPOSITAE

One of several species suited for the alpine house. It originates from South Africa, and in Britain is treated as a half-hardy rhizomatous perennial. A prostrate, trailing plant, to about 30 cm (12 in) wide, with slender, lanceolate leaves, bearing many bright golden-yellow, daisy-like flowers, 3 – 4 cm (1¼ – 1½ in) across, during the summer. A sun-loving plant, needing free watering during the growing season but very little in winter. A compost of loam, peat and sand is recommended. Propagate from seed, sown in spring, or cuttings in late summer.

Gelasine azureus
IRIDACEAE

An interesting cormous species, native to southern Brazil and Uruguay, where it is found in grassland at altitudes to about 200 m (650 ft). It has 1 – 2 basal, bluish-green leaves to 30 cm (12 in) long, and 1 longer cauline leaf. The branching, flowering stem has small, leaf-like bracts and terminally produced flowers, bright blue or violet, 2.5 – 5 cm (1 – 2 in) in diameter when fully open, in the morning only. Suited to the rock garden, but corms should be lifted in winter. Propagate from seed, sown fresh in acid soil.

Genista delphinensis
LEGUMINOSAE

Possibly now recognized as *Genistella delphinensis*. A very dwarf, shrubby species, rarely exceeding 20 cm (8 in) high, originating from the rocky slopes of the Pyrenees. A more or less prostrate plant with only few, very small, leaves borne on rather crooked stems. Flowers, in summer, bright yellow, borne on short stems, usually in clusters of 2 – 3. Very suitable for the rock garden. Best grown in full sun and an enriched, open soil. Propagate from heeled cuttings in summer or from seed in spring.

Genista sagittalis var. delphinensis
LEGUMINOSAE

Syn. *G. sagittalis* var. *minor*. A prostrate, spreading species found wild in southern France. Leaves are very small, few in number, more or less oval in shape, rather challenging the small winged branches, which are somewhat leaf-like. Flowers, in summer, bright yellow, in small clusters, in erect spikes. An attractive dwarf plant, rarely more than 6 – 8 cm (2½ – 3 in) high, suitable for rock garden culture, preferably on sloping ground, set in an open, enriched soil. Propagate by division or from seed.

Genista tinctoria
LEGUMINOSAE

A variable shrubby plant found in the Mediterranean area, also in the Caucasus and western Turkey. Leaves simple, oblong-lanceolate, to 3 cm (1¼ in) long, sometimes hairy. Flowers, in late spring and summer, bright yellow, about 1.5 cm (⅝ in) long, borne in terminal racemes; may sometimes be seen in bloom in autumn. Adaptable to either sun or partial shade; best planted in a rock garden in rich, porous soil. Propagate from seed, freshly harvested.

Gentiana acaulis
GENTIANACEAE

Syn. *G. kochiana*. An almost stemless species, which comes from high altitudes in grassy regions of northeastern Spain, the Pyrenees and the Carpathians. Leaves more or less lanceolate or elliptical, 5 – 15 cm (2 – 6 in) long, clear green, forming a basal rosette; 1 – 2 pairs of leaves on the stems, the latter being more oval in shape. Flowers appear in summer, deep blue, the lobes tapering to a stiff point, the throat green-spotted. A plant of particular charm, requiring slight shade and an acid soil. Propagate from seed in spring.

Gentiana asclepiadea
GENTIANACEAE

Commonly known as the willow gentian. This species originates from woodlands in parts of central Europe and eastwards to the Caucasus. It has slender, willow-like leaves set opposite along the stems, 30 – 60 cm (12 – 24 in) long, and from the leaf axils clusters of blue flowers appear in mid- to late summer, the inner surface of the petals having purplish spots and lines. A fairly well-shaded position is recommended, and a humus-rich soil. Propagate from seed, sown in early spring.

Gentiana clusii
GENTIANACEAE

A low, tufted, perennial species, found in the wild in grasslands of the Alps and Apennines at altitudes to 2,500 m (8,200 ft). Greyish-green leaves are more or less lance-shaped. Flowers, deep blue, trumpet-shaped, 4 – 6 cm (1½ – 2½ in) long, are borne solitary in summer. A suitable plant for the rock garden; needs a slightly calcareous soil and sun or partial shade. Propagate from seed, freshly harvested.

Gentiana saxosa
GENTIANACEAE

A dense, mat-forming species, originating from New Zealand. It has rosettes composed of slender, recurving, small glossy green leaves. Arising from each rosette, stems appear, 5 – 10 cm (2 – 4 in) long, bearing, in late summer and early autumn, cup-shaped white flowers, singly or 2 – 3 together, having a brownish-purple veining on each petal. Requires full sun and permeable soil on sloping ground or in an alpine house. Propagate from seed, sown in spring.

Gentiana septemfida
GENTIANACEAE

A variable plant, with botanically recognized forms and widespread distribution in many parts of the Balkan region, Armenia, Iran and the Caucasus. About 30 cm (12 in) high, perennial, tufted, branching freely at the base, with many erect stems. Leaves dark green, mainly lanceolate to linear, up to 4 cm (1½ in), arranged alternate. Flowers bell-shaped, blue or purplish, terminally borne in summer, each 3 – 4 cm (1¼ – 1½ in) long. Of easy culture, requiring a bright position and a peaty, loamy soil mix, enriched with humus. Propagate from seed in early spring.

Gentiana sino-ornata
GENTIANACEAE

A rosette-forming species with more or less prostate stems, native to western parts of China and Tibet, in totally lime-free soil. Leaves are dark green, narrowly linear, set opposite along the stems, each stem bearing a terminal deep blue, trumpet-like flower about 5 cm (2 in) long in autumn. Of easy culture, but demanding an enriched soil, totally lime-free, in partial shade. Propagate by division of the rosettes in late spring or from seed sown in spring.

Gentiana sino-ornata var. alba
GENTIANACEAE

This is but one of a number of varieties of the popular, easy-flowered species. It originates from more or less the same localities as the species, particularly the eastern section of the Himalayas at altitudes over 4,000 m (13,000 ft). In terms of foliage there is little difference from the species. The trumpet-like flower, almost pure white, is the principal feature. General cultivation requirements are as for the species. It is also wise to plan division and replanting every 3 – 4 years.

Gentiana utriculosa
GENTIANACEAE

Commonly known as the bladder gentian. A very low-growing, annual species native to open grass-lands (as shown) in mountainous regions of Europe, generally at high altitudes. The small, lanceolate leaves, 2 – 3 cm (¾ – 1¼ in) long, form a basal rosette, from which arise bright blue flowers, about 1.5 cm (⅝ in) across, on short stalks, in summer. After flowering, the calyx becomes swollen and oval with 5 wings, giving rise to its common name. A rock garden plant; needs enriched, lime-free soil in full sun. Propagate from seed.

Geranium canariense
GERANIACEAE

A perennial species with a woody stem, native to the Canary Islands. Leaves broadly ovate, deeply lobed and dissected, forming a very substantial rosette. The inflorescence is much branched, bearing pink flowers with 5 spreading petals, 2 – 3 cm (¾ – 1¼ in) in diameter, in summer. Only half-hardy, so best grown in an alpine house, in bright light or partial shade. Needs porous soil, enriched with leaf mould. Propagates easily from fresh seed, temperature 15 °C (59 °F).

Geranium cinereum 'Ballerina'
GERANIACEAE

The species is native to the Pyrenees and forms mounds or tufts to 15 cm (6 in) high. Leaves greyish-green, 5 – 7 lobes, carried on thin stalks. This particular form has white or lilac-pink flowers veined purple in late spring, and is most desirable for rock garden culture. A sun-loving plant, requiring a slightly enriched garden soil. Best planted from autumn to spring. Propagate by division in spring.

Geranium columbinum
GERANIACEAE

A dwarf, spreading, slightly hairy plant, native to moist grasslands in southern Europe. Leaves are deep green, divided into 5 or more lobes. Flowers, in late spring, are borne on short stems, 2 – 4 cm (¾ – 1½ in) long, purplish-pink to 1.5 cm (⅝ in) or more across. Suitable for the rock garden; needs partial shade and moisture-retentive, enriched soil. Propagate from seed, freshly harvested.

Geranium malviflorum
GERANIACEAE

An erect, attractive leafy perennial, frequently encountered on rocky hill sides in central and southern Spain. Leaves 7 – 10 cm (2¾ – 4 in) wide, with very deeply cut lobes divided again into slender segments. Bright rose-purple flowers appear in early summer, each 3 – 4 cm (1¼ – 1½ in) in diameter, generally in terminal loose clusters and certainly reminiscent of the flowers of certain *Malva*. Needs a position in sun or partial shade and a very porous soil, benefitting considerably if humus is added. Propagate from seed, sown in spring.

Geranium sessiliflorum var. nigricans
GERANIACEAE

This is a somewhat tufted plant, which forms low, dense clumps and is native to Australia and New Zealand. The bright green leaves, 3 – 4 cm (1¼ – 1½ in) wide, have 5 – 7 lobes and are attractively suffused purplish-brown. Flowers, in summer, almost hidden by the prolific leaves, are white, each to 1.5 cm (⅝ in) across when fully open. Best suited to alpine house culture, in a sunny position and an enriched, permeable soil. Propagate from fresh seed in spring.

Geranium tuberosum
GERANIACEAE

A tuberous-rooted perennial plant, 15 – 30 cm (6 – 12 in) high, native to southern Europe, primarily throughout the Mediterranean region. The stem branches from well above the base, bearing greyish-green, prominently lobed leaves on long stalks. Flowers, 1 – 1.5 cm (½ – ⅝ in) across, appear in early spring, purplish-pink or violet, in clusters, the petals notched. After flowering, plants tend to die down and remain dormant until the following season. Needs good light and a rich, porous soil. Propagate from seed in spring.

Gethyllis ciliaris
AMARYLLIDACEAE

A small, bulbous species found wild on open, sandy areas of Piketberg to Cape Peninsular, South Africa. Leaves are very short and slender, invariably spirally twisted, 10 – 20 cm (4 – 8 in) long. Flowers appear in late spring to late summer, carried terminally on stems about the same length as the leaves, white on the inner surface, reddish outside, 2 – 3 cm (¾ – 1¼ in) in diameter. An attractive miniature specimen for the alpine house. Needs a moisture-retentive, humus-enriched soil; allow to dry off once the flowers and leaves have withered. Propagate from seed in spring.

Geum chiloense
ROSACEAE

Syn. *G. coccineum* of gardens, *G. quellyon*. A variable, clump-forming species with long stems of varying lengths, native to Chile. The large, pinnate green leaves, 20 cm (8 in) or more long, have an obvious terminal heart-shaped leaflet. Flowers appear in early summer, scarlet, each about 3 cm (1¼ in) in diameter. Many hybrids in different colours have been developed. Needs a moisture-retentive soil and a position in sun or slight shade. Propagate from seed in spring.

Gladiolus alatus
IRIDACEAE

A colourful cormous plant originating from Cape Province, South Africa, where it is widespread. Leaves dark green, basal, varying in length to about 30 cm (12 in). Flowers appear in summer, basically reddish, although other colourings are also registered, pinkish shades or orange-red, 1 – 10 to a spike, on stems 8 – 35 cm (3 – 14 in) long. Well suited to alpine house culture; a sunny site and open, humus-enriched soil are essential. Keep dry during the dormancy period, after the foliage has withered. Propagate from seed in spring, temperature 15 ˚C (59 ˚F).

Gladiolus callianthus
IRIDACEAE

Syn. *Acidanthera murieliae*, under which name it is probably better known and sold. A cormous plant, found wild in many parts of eastern Africa at altitudes to 2,500 m (8,200 ft). Leaves basal, erect, linear, glabrous, 15 – 30 cm (6 – 12 in) long. Flowers, in midsummer, borne terminally on stems 30 – 45 cm (12 – 18 in) long, creamy white, with a dark purplish, star-like blotch at the base of the petals, 2 – 10 to a stem. Can be planted annually in a rock garden, in enriched, lime-free soil, and lifted after flowering. Propagate from seed.

Gladiolus carinatus
IRIDACEAE

A rare, cormous species, native to high ground in the Malmesbury area of Cape Province, South Africa. Basal leaves are very slender, 20 cm (8 in) or more long. Flowers are borne in late summer, terminally, on stems 20 cm (8 in) long, pale greyish-blue, sometimes a deeper colour, 4 – 6 cm (1½ – 2½ in) long, and usually scented. A suitable rock garden subject, but needs to be lifted before frosts develop. Propagate from seed, freshly harvested.

Gladiolus communis ssp. communis
IRIDACEAE

A cormous plant found wild in woodland on low mountain slopes in many parts of the Mediterranean area (Spain to Greece and Corsica) and north Africa. Leaves basal, sword-like. Flowers appear in early summer, several together on slender stems to 50 cm (20 in) or more long, purplish-red to rose-pink, lower segments lined white, 3 – 4.5 cm (1¼ – 1¾ in) long. Half-hardy; plant 15 cm (6 in) deep in well-drained, fertile soil in a sheltered rock garden. Propagate by cormlets or from seed, freshly harvested.

Gladiolus floribundus
ssp. floribundus
IRIDACEAE

A cormous plant, to about 45 cm (18 in) tall, found wild in Cape Province (Knysna to Clanwilliam), South Africa, mostly on low mountain sides. Slender leaves are strap-like, 40 cm (16 in) or more long. Flowers, in summer, are white, cream, pale pink or mauve with a prominent purple stripe longitudinally down the centre of each segment. If grown in the rock garden, lift corms after flowering; otherwise best kept in the alpine house. Propagate from seed.

Gladiolus gazensis
IRIDACEAE

A rare cormous species, native to mountainous areas of central Africa, particularly on Mount Pene at altitudes of 3,000 m (10,000 ft) and over. Plants are about 40 cm (16 in) tall when in flower, with long, linear, very slender, green leaves. A flower spike, about 25 cm (10 in) long bears several rose or purple flowers in summer, each flower about 2.5 cm (1 in) long and 3 – 5 cm (1¼ – 2 in) wide, in late spring and early summer. Alpine house culture necessary; needs an enriched, sandy soil. Propagate from seed.

Gladiolus illyricus
IRIDACEAE

A cormous species with stems 30 – 45 cm (12 – 18 in) tall, found wild in the Mediterranean region and western Europe, also in Turkey and Israel; also known in southern England. Stems are sheathed, green or red veined. Leaves slender, about 30 cm (12 in) long. Small flowers, in early summer, purplish-pink, reddish-purple or purple, 3 – 4 cm (1¼ – 1½ in) long, with prominent white lines on the lower segments. Half-hardy in many areas, otherwise hardy – ideal for rock garden culture. Keep almost dry after flowering. Propagate by offset corms or from seed.

Gladiolus italicus
IRIDACEAE

A cormous species found in southern Europe and into western, central areas of France. Stems 40 cm (16 in) or more long, with basal sheaths reddish, often spotted white or pale green. Leaves slender, about 30 cm (12 in) long. Flowers appear in early summer, 6 – 16 to a spike, each pale pink or purplish-red bloom 4 – 5 cm (1½ – 2 in) long, the segments unequal, the upper being larger and broader. A half-hardy plant for either rock garden (where it will need winter protection) or alpine house, in rich, porous soil. Propagate by cormlets or from seed.

Gladiolus liliaceus
IRIDACEAE

An elegant, cormous species, found wild in sandy areas in Cape Province, South Africa, at altitudes to 1,800 m (6,000 ft). Stems slender and flexuose, 25 – 60 cm (10 – 24 in) or more long, carrying a few-flowered spike. Leaves, shorter and narrow, are borne in basal tufts. Flowers, night-scented, are in a variety of colours – yellowish, orange-red – heavily speckled and with a prominent median line on segments. A subject for alpine house culture; needs an open soil. Propagate from seed.

Gladiolus melleri
IRIDACEAE

A tall-growing, almost leafless, cormous species, to about 60 cm (24 in) high, native to upland, rocky regions of Zimbabwe to north Nigeria. Leaves appear briefly, but have gone by the time flowers are borne in late summer. Flowers salmon pink or vermilion, 3 – 6 cm (1¼ – 2½ in) long, with sub-equal segments. Requires alpine house culture, in rich, porous soil; keep totally dry during dormancy. Propagate from newly ripened seed.

Glaucium flavum
PAPAVERACEAE

A medium sized perennial plant, widespread in Europe, including Britain. A colourful plant arising from a fleshy taproot, the glaucous green leaves almost forming a rosette, from which emerges a greyish-green, branching stem with bluish-grey leaves and terminal, bright yellow flowers, 6 – 7.5 cm (2½ – 2⅞ in) across, appearing in early summer and continuing in succession over many weeks. Suitable for rock garden culture in an enriched, sandy soil. Propagate from seed, newly harvested.

Globularia cordifolia
GLOBULARIACEAE

A cushion-forming species, native to many parts of southern Europe and western Asia. The glossy green leaves are slightly notched and arranged in rosettes. Greyish-blue flowers appear in summer, each about 1 cm (½ in) across, borne singly on short stalks. An open, fairly sunny position is advisable, preferably in a very porous, but enriched soil – take care to avoid excessive moisture, especially during dormancy. Plant in late autumn or early spring. Propagates easily from seed.

Globularia meridionalis
GLOBULARIACEAE

Syn. *G. bellidifolia*. A low-growing, creeping, shrub-like plant with many twisted, entangled stems, a native of the southern Alps and the Balkans. Leaves rather lanceolate, dark green, 3 – 9 cm (1¼ – 3½ in) long. In summer the stems bear heads of bright blue flowers to about 2.5 cm (1 in) across. Needs a sunny position in normal garden soil, which must be well-drained. Propagate from seed in spring.

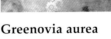

Glottiphyllum oligocarpum
AIZOACEAE

A creeping, prostrate, succulent plant from the Willowmore district of Cape Province, South Africa. The branches carry distichous fleshy leaves of unequal size, about 4 cm (1½ in) long, 2 cm (¾ in) across and 1 cm (½ in) thick at the side, bright whitish-olive green with many dots on all surfaces. Flowers, in autumn and early winter, solitary, 4 – 6 cm (1½ – 2½ in) long, glossy yellow. For alpine house culture in a porous, enriched soil, growing in spring, then resting until flowering time. Propagate from seed sown freshly gathered, temperature 15°C (59°F).

Greenovia aizoon
CRASSULACEAE

A low-growing, freely branching succulent species found wild in Tenerife, Canary Islands. Leaves are broadly roundish-spathulate, bluish-green, forming a rosette 5 – 6 cm (2 – 2½ in) in diameter, densely glandular-pubescent. From the rosette arises a leafy inflorescence with golden-yellow flowers, each 1 – 2 cm (½ – ¾ in) across, in dense clusters, in summer. Requires the security of the alpine house – a bright sunny position, set in a well-draining, humus-enriched soil. Propagate from seed sown in spring, temperature 15°C (59°F).

Greenovia aurea
CRASSULACEAE

A semi-prostrate succulent species, of dwarf habit, native to several of the Canary Islands, where it is found on hill sides. The leaves are somewhat oval to rounded, bluish-green pruinose, formed into rosettes to 4 cm (1½ in) in diameter. Flowers, in early summer, are yellow, borne terminally in a series of slender panicles on short stems. Only half-hardy, so best kept in an alpine house in enriched, open soil. Propagate by division.

Greenovia dodrantalis
CRASSULACEAE

A low-growing, more or less prostrate, succulent plant, which forms cushions. Native to Tenerife, Canary Islands, where it is found at altitudes to 1,200 m (4,000 ft). The wide, saucer-like, bluish-green leaves, with a rather waxy surface, are formed into many small, compact rosettes. The flowers, which appear in summer, are bright yellow, borne on a short, many flowered spike. If grown in the rock garden, requires winter protection; otherwise grow in the alpine house. Needs an enriched, open soil. Propagate from seed.

Gynandriris pritzeliana
IRIDACEAE

A low-growing, cormous species native to the Caledon area of Cape Province, South Africa. Generally only 2 leaves to a plant, spiral and almost prostrate, to over 30 cm (12 in) long, the inner surface having a central white band. Stems branch near the base, bearing flower spikes closely appressed to the stem. Flowers in early summer, segments purplish-blue, 3 cm (1¼ in) long, 1.5 cm (⅝ in) wide, with, towards the base, white blotch, edged with crimson-purple. For alpine house culture, needing a permeable, fertile soil and slight shade. Propagate from fresh seed.

Gynandriris sisyrinchium
IRIDACEAE

A choice miniature species with a cormous root-stock, found in many parts of southern Europe, growing on open or leafy hill sides (as shown) at altitudes to 1,000 m (3,300 ft). The few slender, channelled leaves are somewhat rush-like, rounded on the outside, to about 8 mm (⁷⁄₁₆ in) wide, the 2 lowest often longer than the flower stem. Flowering in late spring, these appear in groups of 2 – 4 from the axils of the papery bracts, blue with white or yellow markings. Needs an open, rich soil in sun or shade. Propagate from seed.

Gypsophila cerastioides
CARYOPHYLLACEAE

A tufted species found in the Himalayan region. It has soft, stalked, basal, greyish-green leaves, more or less spathulate, 2 – 5 cm (¾ – 2 in) long. Borne from early summer to autumn, the white flowers, pinkish-purple veined, each about 1 cm (½ in) across, appear on branched stems to 10 cm (4 in) long. A very sunny location is essential, together with a well-drained, enriched soil. Propagate from seed, sown in spring.

Gypsophila repens
CARYOPHYLLACEAE

Syn. *G. prostrata* var. *fratensis*. A mound-forming, somewhat prostrate species from mountainous areas of central and southern Europe, the branching stems to 20 cm (8 in) or more long, spreading in all directions. Leaves greyish-green, linear, 1 – 3 cm (½ – 1¼ in) long, often paired, covering the branches. Flowers appear in summer, white to lilac, about 1 cm (½ in) across, many in clusters. A fine rock garden plant, needing sun and porous soil. Propagate from seed in spring.

Helianthemum croeceum

H

Haberlea rhodopensis
GESNERIACEAE

A rosette-forming species found in mountainous regions of Greece and Bulgaria. An evergreen perennial, with stems to 12 cm (5 in) or a little more in length. The oval-shaped, softly hairy, dark green leaves have toothed margins, to about 8 cm (3 in) long. The 1 – 5 flowers, tubular in shape with spreading lobes, about 2.5 cm (1 in) across, pale lilac, are borne on slender stems in spring. Needs an enriched soil and partial shade. Propagate from seed in spring.

Haberlea rhodopensis var. ferdinandi-coburgii
GESNERIACEAE

A very similar plant to the type, the rosette being formed of narrow, spathulate, rather thick, toothed leaves. Found principally in the Balkans. Flowers appear in spring in terminal umbels on slender stems, usually 3 – 4, tubular, lilac, nearly 3 cm (1¼ in) across when the unequal petals have spread fully. Needs slight shade and a very open soil. Propagate by leaf cuttings in summer.

Haberlea rhodopensis var. virginalis
GESNERIACEAE

In almost every respect this variety has similar growth habits to the type, and, in the wild, it is to be found in the same habitat. The leafy rosettes combine to form large clusters to about 14 cm (5¾ in) high. Flowers, which appear in spring, are an albino form of the type, these being pure white. Cultural conditions are similar, likewise propagation. Probably best kept in the alpine house.

Habranthus brachyandrus
AMARYLLIDACEAE

A bulbous plant, found wild in Paraguay, south Brazil and north Argentina. Leaves appear before the flowers in spring, very slender, 15 – 20 cm (6 – 8 in) long. Flowers, in summer, borne on stems about 30 cm (12 in) long, more or less trumpet-shaped, petals rose-pink with a bright purplish-pink centre. Alpine house culture is advised, in a humus-rich, porous soil; if grown in the rock garden winter protection is essential. Propagate by division of bulbs or from seed, freshly harvested.

Habranthus martinezii
AMARYLLIDACEAE

A rather dwarf, bulbous species, native to southern Mexico and central America. It has short, flat, linear leaves about 15 cm (6 in) long, all basal. Flowers appear in late summer and autumn, on stems about 20 cm (8 in) long, pinkish-lilac, funnel-shaped, about 3 cm (1¼ in) long and across when fully open. Best suited to alpine house culture, using a well-drained soil with rotted leaf mould and gritty sand added. Propagate by offsets or from newly ripened seed, temperature 15 ℃ (59 ℉).

Haemanthus katherinae
AMARYLLIDACEAE

A particularly attractive, bulbous plant found wild in Natal, Transvaal and Zimbabwe, southern Africa, on low hilly slopes. Leaves thick and fleshy, to about 30 cm (12 in) long, glossy, deep green, 12 – 15 cm (5 – 6 in) wide at the base. Heads of scarlet flowers, to 14 cm (5¾ in) or more across are produced in spring on stems 30 cm (12 in) or more long. For alpine house culture; needs full sun and a soil of equal parts sand, loam, peat and leaf mould. Propagate by offsets at potting time or from freshly ripened seed.

Halimium commutatum
CISTACEAE

A member of the rock-rose family, native to low ground in Portugal and Spain. A low-growing, branching shrub to about 50 cm (20 in) high. Leaves very slender, shiny above, white downy undersurface, 1 – 3 cm (½ – 1¼ in) long, the margins revolute. The pale yellow flowers appear in late spring, each about 1 cm (½ in) across, borne solitary or in terminal clusters of 2 – 3. A very open, sandy soil is required, but, even so, water must not be too restricted. Plant in a sunny position in autumn. Propagate from seed or by cuttings.

Haplocarpha ruepellii
COMPOSITAE

A flat, rosette-forming species, to 15 cm (6 in) high, originating from southeast Africa. The prominently toothed leaves are bright green on the upper side, silvery below, and the rosettes formed tend to spread quite freely. Flowers, each about 2 cm (¾ in) across, appear throughout much of the summer, with bright yellow rays and blackish anthers. It adapts to ordinary garden soil, in either sun or partial shade. Propagates best from seed.

Helianthemum alpestre
CISTACEAE

Syn. *H. oelandicum* ssp. *alpestre*. A low-growing, prostrate plant of spreading habit, originating from mountainous areas of central and southern Europe. Plants tend not to exceed 20 cm (8 in) in height, the hairy stems bearing elliptic to linear-lanceolate leaves about 1.5 cm (⅝ in) in length. Flowers are freely borne in summer, golden-yellow, to about 2 cm (¾ in) in diameter. Needs a sunny site and ordinary, well-drained soil. Propagate by cuttings in summer.

Helianthemum canum
CISTACEAE

A low, bushy plant, hairy in almost all its parts, a native of southern Europe to Turkey, frequently encountered in the Mediterranean region. The slender, very narrow leaves often form rosette-like clusters at the tips of the shoots and are more or less greyish in colour. Flowering in early summer, the small yellow flowers, about 1.5 cm (⅝ in) across, appear in racemes of 3 – 5 blooms. Needs bright light and a slightly alkaline, porous soil. Propagate from seed, freshly harvested.

Helianthemum croeceum
CISTACEAE

A rather variable, often prostrate, low, shrubby plant found in southern Europe from Portugal to Italy and Sicily on rocky mountain sides. Leaves oblong to lanceolate, sometimes more rounded, fleshy, the upper surface coated with fine hair. Flowers appear in early summer, shades of yellow or white, to 2 cm (¾ in) long. An ideal plant for either rock garden or alpine house, needing bright light and an enriched, open soil. Propagate from seed, sown in spring.

Helichrysum arwae
COMPOSITAE

A much-branched, dwarf, somewhat bushy species, introduced from Yemen. Leaves are carried on very short branches, slender-spathulate, 2 – 4 cm (¾ – 1½ in) long, silvery grey, formed into an open rosette. Flowers appear in summer, borne on very thin stems, white, the petals tending to incurve and be rather papery. Probably best kept in an alpine house, in a very open, slightly calcareous soil but with a little added humus. Propagate by division or from seed.

Helichrysum conglobatum
COMPOSITAE

A low shrublet found wild in sandy, rocky areas from north Africa and southern Italy to Cyprus and eastwards. Leaves are broadly linear or spathulate, to about 3 cm (1¼ in) long, greyish-green. Flowers appear in late spring and early summer, bright yellow, borne in rounded heads to 5 cm (2 in) or more across, on stems 45 cm (18 in) long. There is also a more dwarf form with shorter stems and smaller flower heads. Half-hardy, suited to the rock garden; needs open, sandy soil. Propagate from freshly gathered seed.

Helichrysum coralloides
COMPOSITAE

A low-growing, shrubby species originating from New Zealand, rarely exceeding 30 cm (12 in) in height. Leaves are borne on erect, branching stems, almost scale-like and white-woolly and overlapping. Tiny yellow flowers, 5 – 6 mm (¼ – ⁵⁄₁₆ in) wide, appear in summer, in small, solitary heads. Best kept in the alpine house as it requires warmth as well as sun throughout the growing season; needs an open soil. Propagate by cuttings in summer.

Helichrysum frigidum
COMPOSITAE

A small, tuft-forming species of branching habit and generally prostrate growth, found in high mountainous areas of Corsica. Both leaves and stems are densely coated with fine silvery hairs, the leaves being sessile and fairly prominently pointed. The silvery white flower heads, 1 cm (½ in) or more across, appear in summer, solitary and terminally, lasting for several weeks. Suited to alpine house culture. Needs sun and a slightly alkaline soil. Propagate from seed in spring.

Helichrysum meyeri-johannis
COMPOSITAE

A low-growing species with rhizomatous, stoloniferous rootstock, found wild in moist alpine meadows in Kenya. Leaves, formed into loose rosettes, are greyish-green, white-woolly, especially on the underside. Flowers appear in summer on erect, leafy stems to 30 – 35 cm (12 – 14 in) high, in a dense terminal corymb of red, pink or white heads. For alpine house culture, requiring a moisture-retentive, humus-enriched, porous soil. Propagate from seed or by division in spring.

Helichrysum plumeum
COMPOSITAE

A branched, variable shrub, to about 30 cm (12 in) or little more tall, found only in South Island, New Zealand. The crowded branches, 2 – 3 mm (⅛ – ³⁄₁₆ in) across, are densely covered with minute, thick, triangular, scale-like leaves, 4 – 8 mm (³⁄₁₆ – ⁷⁄₁₆ in) long, coated with loose, pale yellow or whitish hairs, which persist, so creating a rather downy effect. Flowers are born terminally in summer, yellowish or reddish-pink, about 5 mm (¼ in) wide, contrasting with the very pale greenish leaf colouring. Needs sun and a porous, enriched soil. Propagate from seed in spring.

Helichrysum rupestre
COMPOSITAE

An erect, shrubby plant, found wild in high rocky altitudes in Spain and other areas in southern Europe. Stems to about 50 cm (20 in) long, clothed with slender, green, slightly white-felted leaves, to 8 cm (3 in) long, but not aromatic when crushed. Flowers, in early summer, are borne in quite dense, terminal clusters, to 7 cm (2¾ in) across, flower bracts bright yellow. Only half-hardy, so alpine house culture is advised; needs open soil. Propagate from seed.

Helichrysum selago var. minor
COMPOSITAE

A dense, small, bushy species with erect stems, native to New Zealand. The plant varies somewhat in height; the more dwarf form, 18 – 20 cm (7½ – 8 in) high, has earned its title *minor*. The small, pointed, scale-like, overlapping leaves, about 3 mm (³⁄₁₆ in) long, are dark green above, white-felted below. The flowers appear in summer in solitary heads to 6 mm (⁵⁄₁₆ in) wide, yellowish-white. For alpine house culture, in a sunny site and gritty, enriched soil. Propagate from seed in spring.

Helichrysum sibthorpii
COMPOSITAE

Syn. *H. virgineum*. A woody-based, tufted species originating from northeastern Greece and the Balkans. Leaves greyish-green, white-woolly, more or less oblong or linear-spathulate, to 6 cm (2½ in) long. Flowers small, papery, white, enclosed within bright pink bracts, in clusters about 1.5 cm (⅝ in) in diameter, in late spring or early summer. Best suited to alpine house culture, needing a porous, fairly rich soil. Propagate by division or from seed.

Helichrysum stoechas
COMPOSITAE

Known as the curry plant. An erect, dwarf shrub, native to varying altitudes in southern Europe and north Africa, mostly in rocky areas. Stems to 50 cm (20 in) long, with strongly aromatic, white-felted leaves, 3 cm (1¼ in) long, with revolute edges. Flowers, in late spring and early summer, with yellow flower heads borne terminally in clusters to 3 cm (1¼ in) wide. Alpine house culture is advised; needs sun and enriched, gritty soil. Propagate from fresh seed.

Helleborus cyclophyllus
RANUNCULACEAE

A somewhat tufted, stemless species, found in wooded areas on hill sides in the Balkan region. Usually all basal leaves, toothed, undersurface hairy, divided into 5 – 9 leaflets. Flowers, yellowish-green or whitish, about 6 cm (2½ in) long, borne in early summer. Useful for rock garden culture; needs rich, well-drained soil and partial shade. Propagate by division or from newly ripened seed.

Helleborus foetidus
RANUNCULACEAE

A fairly widespread plant, occurring in many parts of Europe, including Britain, but principally encountered in the Mediterranean islands in comparatively shady areas. The greyish-green leaves are divided into 7 – 10 narrow leaflets. Flowers appear in branched clusters during the winter months, and are pale greenish with a purplish-brown rim, invariably drooping and bell-like, to 2 cm (¾ in) long. The one disadvantage is their unfortunate smell. Plant in autumn in enriched garden soil, in a shady position. Propagate from seed, freshly harvested.

Hepatica americana
RANUNCULACEAE

A colourful woodland species from North America and parts of Europe. A somewhat tufted plant with dark green leaves, the 3 lobes of which are rather rounded. The flowers, which are similar to those of the anemone, appear in early spring, a delicate blue, carried on stalks to 30 cm (12 in) long. Best in slightly shaded areas, set in a well-drained, enriched soil where it often multiplies freely. Propagate from seed or by division of the rootstock in autumn.

Hepatica nobilis
RANUNCULACEAE

Syn. *H. triloba*. A mainly tuft- or clump-forming species, found in the wild throughout much of Europe, America and Asia. The 3-lobed leaves are a particular feature. Flowers occur in late spring and early summer, generally blue, but sometimes pink or white, to 2.5 cm (1 in) wide, borne on stems about 10 cm (4 in) long, with 3 oval bracts subtending each flower. Very well suited to rock garden culture, preferring slight shade and a partially alkaline soil. Propagate from seed in early spring.

Herbertia hauthalii
IRIDACEAE

Syn. *Cypella hauthalii*. A short-stemmed, bulbous plant from mountainous regions of Paraguay. Leaves are almost grass-like, very slender, 20 – 30 cm (8 – 12 in) long. Flowers, borne in early summer, are lilac-blue with spathulate segments to 9 cm (3½ in) long; the var. *opalina* (shown here) has whitish flowers. Best kept in the alpine house; needs a minimum temperature of 10°C (50°F) and to be kept dry during dormancy. Propagate from seed in spring.

Herbertia lahue ssp. caerulea
IRIDACEAE

A fairly short, bulbous species, found in coastal prairies from Texas, USA, to Argentina, Uruguay and central Chile. It has 1 – 6 basal leaves as long as or longer than the inflorescence and sheathing the base. Inflorescence with several flowers, about 5 cm (2 in) across, bluish-purple, the outer segments slightly darker, opening in early summer. A superb item for the alpine house, requiring a slightly porous soil enriched with decomposed leaf mould. Propagate from seed, newly harvested.

Hereroa hesperantha
AIZOACEAE

An erect, branching, succulent plant to about 30 cm (12 in) high, found in hilly country in Namibia and southwest Africa. Stems about 20 cm (8 in) long, with leafy branches about 1 cm (½ in) long. Leaves bright green, trigonous, widening at the tips and altogether swollen, 2 – 6 cm (¾ – 2½ in) long. Flowers bright golden-yellow, to 2 cm (¾ in) in diameter, in bloom in summer. Best kept in an alpine house in humus-rich, open soil. Propagate by cuttings or from seed.

Hermodactylus tuberosus
IRIDACEAE

Syn. *Iris tuberosa*. Commonly known as the widow iris. A fascinating tuberous-rooted species, found wild in many parts of southern Europe. Leaves linear, deciduous. Flowers appear in late spring to midsummer, depending on location and temperature – yellowish-green, velvety, with outer segments speckled purplish-brown, fragrant, about 5 cm (2 in) long. Can be grown successfully in a sheltered rock garden, preferably in a raised bed, set in porous soil enriched with humus, and kept dry during dormancy. Propagate from seed in autumn.

Hesperoxiphion peruvianum
IRIDACEAE

A fairly large bulbous plant, found wild at altitudes of 2,500 m (8,200 ft) or more from Bolivia to Peru. The stem, simple or branched, is 10 – 50 cm (4 – 20 in) or more long, with bract-like cauline leaves. Basal leaves, 2 – 3 in number, are 60 cm (24 in) long, lance-shaped. Flowers are borne in late summer, about 6 cm (2½ in) across, yellow, faintly lined with reddish-brown. Can be grown in a sheltered rock garden given rich, permeable soil, but bulbs should be lifted when dormant. Propagate from newly ripened seed.

Hieracium lanatum
COMPOSITAE

Commonly known as the woolly hawkweed. A tufted, perennial, almost stemless species, originating from the Maritime Alps. The whole plant is coated with white, wavy, feather-like hairs. It has one or more simple or branched stems to 30 – 35 cm (12 – 14 in) tall, with white, tomentose, basal and stem leaves, more or less spathulate, each leaf 5 – 12 cm (2 – 5 in) long. Each stem with few or several heads having numerous linear bracts and yellow flowers, florets toothed at the tips, in summer. Needs a calcareous soil and sun. Propagate from seed when harvested.

Hippeastrum vittatum
LILIACEAE

A rather large bulbous plant, found wild in the Peruvian Andes. The wide, strap-shaped, bright green leaves are 30 – 40 cm (12 – 16 in) long. Flowers, borne on stems 45 – 60 cm (18 – 24 in) tall in late spring, are trumpet-shaped, to 15 cm (6 in) in diameter, 2 – 3 to a stem, white with numerous scarlet longitudinal lines on the petals. Needs alpine house culture in an open, loamy, peaty soil. Propagate from seed, freshly harvested.

Hippocrepis balearica
LEGUMINOSAE

A woody-based, perennial, bushy species, found wild in the Balearic Islands. Leaves pinnate, the leaflets in 5 – 10 pairs, linear to oblong. Numerous individual flowers, about 1.5 cm (⅝ in) long, yellow, sweetly scented, in loose globular, terminal clusters, in summer. Will accept rock garden culture if sheltered from excessive rain and cold, otherwise best in an alpine house, in a porous, calcareous soil with decomposed leaf mould added. Propagate from seed in spring.

Hippocrepis glauca
LEGUMINOSAE

A spreading, clustering plant found on dry hill sides, often limestone (as shown) from Spain to Greece. It has a woody base and glaucous foliage, the pinnate leaves being divided into 4 – 7 paired leaflets, white-downy on the undersurface. The bright yellow flowers, about 1 cm (½ in) long, are carried in early summer in terminal clusters of up to 8 separate flowers on long stalks. Needs sun and a calcareous soil. Propagate from seed, in spring.

Homeria breyniana var. aurantiaca
IRIDACEAE

Syn. *H. collina*. A popular cormous plant, which, in flower, may reach 45 cm (18 in) in height. Native to southern and southwestern parts of South Africa. Stem slender, usually 2-branched, with long, linear leaves attached singly along its length. Flowers orange-red, more yellowish throat, 3 – 4 cm (1¼ – 1½ in) across when fully open, in late summer and early autumn. Proves to be hardy in many southern parts of Britain but nevertheless needs protection during severe weather. Needs good light and a porous, enriched soil. Propagate from seed, freshly harvested.

Houstonia caerulea
RUBIACEAE

A densely clump-forming plant, native to North America, where it is called bluetts. The loose clumps are composed of 8 cm (3 in) long stems bearing small, spoon-shaped, pale green leaves, which are quite glossy. Flowers appear in summer, soft blue, 4-petalled, with a yellow eye, about 1 cm (½ in) long, borne on very slender stalks. A plant for the alpine house, where it needs partial shade and a moisture-retentive soil. Propagate by division in spring.

Huernia hystrix
ASCLEPIADACEAE

A dwarf, succulent species, native to Transvaal, South Africa, where it grows on rocky terrain in open woodlands at medium altitudes. It has 5-angled, bluish-green, leafless stems to about 10 cm (4 in) high. Flowers, in late summer and autumn, are wide, bell-shaped and 5-lobed, about 4 cm (1½ in) across, green externally, yellow inside, densely covered with reddish-brown lines and dots. Requires alpine house culture in slight shade and a normal cactus compost. Propagate from cuttings or seed in spring.

Huernia kirkii
ASCLEPIADACEAE

A low-growing, succulent species, found at medium to quite high altitudes in Transvaal and Mozambique. Stems, to about 4 cm (1½ in) long and 1.5 cm (⅝ in) wide, 4-angled, with prominent pointed 'teeth'. Flowers, borne in early summer, are 4 – 5 cm (1½ – 2 in) in diameter with pointed lobes, the tube 2.5 cm (1 in) wide, with dark purplish lines; lobes pale yellow, irregularly marked with numerous red dots. Needs alpine house culture in rich, open soil. Propagate from cuttings or seed.

Huernia verekeri var. verekeri
ASCLEPIADACEAE

A dwarf, clump-forming, succulent plant, found on high ground in many parts of semi-tropical Africa (Malawi, Zimbabwe, Zambia, Mozambique and Angola). Stems, about 10 cm (4 in) long, are 5-angled and toothed. Flowers, borne in summer on short pedicels, are about 3.5 cm (1⅜ in) in diameter, with yellowish lobes and a prominent reddish corona. Requires alpine house culture in an enriched, porous soil. Propagate from cuttings or seed.

Hyacinthella atchleyi
LILIACEAE

A fairly short, bulbous plant to about 15 cm (6 in) tall, found principally in Greece. There are 2 – 3 basal leaves, prominently veined, to 1 cm (½ in) wide. The flower stem is leafless and carries a raceme of deep blue flowers, each about 5 mm (¼ in) long, on short pedicels 4 mm (³⁄₁₆ in) in length, in late winter and early spring. Needs a fairly sunny position and well-drained, enriched soil. Propagate from freshly harvested seed.

Hyacinthella glabrescens
LILIACEAE

Syn. *H. hispida* var. *glabrescens*. A bulbous species, found wild in a restricted area of southern Turkey. It has glabrous leaves, all basal, with smooth margins, narrowing to a pointed tip, about 2 cm (¾ in) wide at the base. Flowers, in summer, semi-tubular, 5 – 6 mm (¼ – ⁵⁄₁₆ in) long, deep violet-blue, borne in loose racemes on rather fleshy stems. A bright, sunny position is advisable, and a permeable, enriched, slightly gritty soil. Propagate from seed sown soon after ripening, temperature 15 °C (59 °F).

Hylotelephium spectabile
CRASSULACEAE

More commonly known under its earlier generic title of *Sedum*, this is one of the more popular alpine species. It is native to China and Korea. It has a thick, fleshy rootstock, bearing very erect, stout shoots to 25 cm (10 in) tall and to 8 mm (⁷⁄₁₆ in) thick, and 9 – 15 nodes, each with 2 – 4 thick, fleshy, ovate to circular leaves, the lowest 3 – 9 cm (1¼ – 3½ in) long. Flowers pinkish, to 1 cm (½ in) across, borne in a corymb, in summer. Will grow in ordinary garden soil in partial shade. Propagate by division or from seed in spring.

Hymenocallis amancaes
AMARYLLIDACEAE

A large bulbous plant, found wild in Peru in rocky areas at altitudes to 3,000 m (10,000 ft). Leaves bright green, strap-like, 30 – 40 cm (12 – 16 in) long. The flowers, at their best in summer, are bright yellow, funnel-shaped, with fringed margins, to 7 cm (2¾ in) long, borne on a stem 40 cm (16 in) or more long. Needs to be kept in an alpine house, in a fairly rich, permeable soil. Bulbs should be allowed to remain dry throughout the winter, but kept warm. Propagate from freshly harvested seed.

Hypericum aegyptiacum
GUTTIFERAE

A low, spreading, shrubby species, found in, the eastern Mediterranean region and parts of north Africa. Leaves are small, tough, narrowly oblong, bluish-green and quite densely arranged. Bright yellow flowers are borne solitary and terminally in late winter and early spring, each up to 1.5 cm (⅝ in) wide, somewhat flax-like. Needs sun and a well-drained soil. Propagate by cuttings in late summer or from seed in spring.

Hypericum cerastoides
GUTTIFERAE

A choice, easily flowered species, originating from Turkey and the Balkans. It quickly develops numerous, more or less prostrate, hairy stems with pale greenish leaves, to 3 cm (1¼ in) long, set opposite along their lengths. Flowers are freely borne from the terminal end of the stems, usually in late spring; the bright yellow flowers, 2 – 4 cm (¾ – 1½ in) across, last several days. A sunny position is advantageous, preferably protected from cold winds. Any well-drained garden soil is suitable. Propagate by division or from cuttings in spring.

Hypericum polyphyllum
GUTTIFERAE

A tufted, woody-based perennial species with semi-erect stems, found wild in western Turkey. Leaves are lanceolate or narrowly oblong, glaucous green in colour, to 3 cm (1¼ in) long, carried on semi-erect stems. Flowers yellowish-white, to 6 cm (2½ in) across, often dotted with black, very small spots, in early summer. A hardy species for the rock garden, needing a well-drained garden soil. Propagate by division in late summer or from cuttings or seed in spring.

Hypoxis setosa
HYPOXIDACEAE

A rhizomatous species with several basal leaves arranged rosulate, native to South Africa, principally the eastern Cape Province. Leaves linear, dull green, 15 – 20 cm (6 – 8 in) or more long. Flowers appear in summer, bright yellow, with 6 narrowly ovate petals, borne on a much shorter, slender stem, generally solitary and terminal, subtended by bracts. Best kept in the alpine house, in a warm, sunny position. Needs an enriched soil, with fine, gritty sand added. Propagate from seed in spring, temperature 15°C (59°F).

Hypsela reniformis
CAMPANULACEAE

A mat-forming species with very slender stems, found wild in Chile. It has round or kidney-shaped leaves, rather glossy green, about 1 cm (½ in) long, alternate. Small white or pink flowers in summer, with reddish veining and yellow-spotted throat, tubular, with spreading lobes, about 1 cm (½ in) long. Needs partial shade and a moisture-retentive soil. Propagate by division or from seed or cuttings in spring.

Iris vicaria

I-K

Iberis pruitii
CRUCIFERAE

A variable, tufted species found wild in southern Europe on hills and mountains, from Spain to Greece. Plants have ascending or spreading stems, forming a bushy plant to about 15 cm (6 in) tall. Leaves spathulate, rather fleshy, with smooth edges, though sometimes with toothed tips. White flowers dominate the plant in early summer, borne in dense flat-topped terminal clusters. Perhaps better suited to alpine house culture; needs a well-drained soil and a sunny position. Propagate from cuttings or seed in spring.

Iberis sempervirens
CRUCIFERAE

A semi-procumbent, evergreen, shrubby plant native to much of the Mediterranean mainland in southern Europe, about 20 cm (8 in) high with somewhat spathulate leaves 2 – 4 cm (¾ – 1½ in) long. Flowers in early summer, in flat-topped clusters or racemes 10 cm (4 in) long, pure white. A position in full sun and a rich, permeable soil are essential. Totally hardy, so useful for the rock garden. Propagate from cuttings in spring or from freshly ripened seed.

Impatiens niamniamensis
BALSAMINACEAE

Syn. *I. congolensis*. An unusual species found in many parts of central and eastern Africa. It has long-petiolate leaves, 10 – 15 cm (4 – 6 in) in length, 3 – 5 cm (1¼ – 2 in) broad, pubescent with crenate margins. Flowers appear in early to late summer, red and yellow, about 4.5 cm (1¾ in) long, borne on pedicels from the leaf axils, sometimes 2 together. A desirable plant for the alpine house, requiring a rather acid, well-drained soil. Propagate from seed, which is freely produced.

Incarvillea mairei
BIGNONIACEAE

A clump-forming, perennial species, native to Tibet and Nepal to China. The greyish-green leaves, about 15 cm (6 in) long, are basal, divided into 5 – 9 leaflets, to 4 cm (1½ in) long, oblong in shape, the terminal one longest. Flowers appear in early summer, reddish-purple, with white or yellow centre, each up to 10 cm (4 in) wide, in racemes to 30 cm (12 in) tall. Will accept sun or shade; needs an enriched, porous soil. Propagate by division.

Ipheion uniflorum 'Album'
LILIACEAE

This is an albino form of the species, having all the characteristics of the type, but varies in bearing rather attractive, almost pure white flowers. Seed does not necessarily produce this unusual form, so to propagate it is advisable to separate offsets from the parent bulbs during dormancy. If grown in the open, provide a bright, sunny or partially shaded position.

Ipheion uniflorum 'Wisley Blue'
LILIACEAE

A South American bulbous plant, primarily from Argentina and Uruguay, and an improved form developed at the Royal Horticultural Society Gardens at Wisley. It has linear, grass-like leaves of pale to greyish-green, all basal and forming tufts to 20 cm (8 in) long. Flowers of deep purplish-blue, borne on stems to 15 cm (6 in) long, appear in spring, each about 4 cm (1½ in) wide. A hardy plant; needs permeable, enriched soil and partial shade. Propagate by dividing the bulblets during dormancy or from seed in spring.

Iris attica
IRIDACEAE

Syn. *I. pumila* ssp. *attica*. A dwarf species, almost stemless, native to Greece, Turkey and Macedonia. Plants rarely exceed 10 cm (4 in) high when in flower. The leaves are generally about 8 cm (3 in) long, 9 mm (⁷⁄₁₆ in) wide, strongly falcate, greyish-green. Flowers, in early summer, solitary, wholly bluish-purple, or yellow, white or bi-coloured, the falls reflexed. A most desirable species for rock garden culture; needs a sunny position in a fairly acid soil. Propagate by division or from seed.

Iris bucharica
IRIDACEAE

Syn. *I. orchioides*. A bulbous plant with rather thin roots, found in the wild in parts of Russia and Afghanistan. A popular species, 20 – 40 cm (8 – 16 in) tall, with shiny olive green leaves to 20 cm (8 in) long. The flower stem has 5 – 7 flowers from the leaf axils in mid- to late spring – golden-yellow, the falls 4.5 cm (1¾ in) long, the blade 1.2 cm (⁹⁄₁₆ in) or more wide, the golden-yellow crest marked with blackish-green lines and dots, standards white or cream. An open, alkaline soil is best; needs some protection from the elements. Propagate from seed, freshly harvested.

Iris collettii
IRIDACEAE

A fairly erect species, somewhat similar to *I. decora*, found in northern Burma and south-western China, and still considered a rarity. Leaves vary in length, often elongating after flowering. Flowers appear in early summer, borne on very short, slender stems, each to 3 cm (1¼ in) across, slightly scented, pale blue with golden-yellow crest, standards narrower than falls, pale bluish-violet with deeper veins. It appears to prefer partial shade and a rather acid soil, and is relatively hardy. Propagate from seed, freshly harvested.

Iris decora
IRIDACEAE

Syn. *I. nepalensis*. A species native to many parts of the Himalayas (Nepal, Sikkim) and China (Yunnan), on hill sides to over 4,000 m (13,000 ft). Leaves, about 30 cm (12 in) long, have very prominent ribs. The slender stem produces a terminal head of 2 – 3 lavender blue to reddish-purple flowers 4 – 5 cm (1½ – 2 in) in diameter, and 1 – 2 reduced leaves, in summer, the falls having white or purplish veins and a yellowish-orange crest becoming white at the apex. Needs bright light, porous soil and careful watering at all times. Propagate from seed, freshly harvested.

Iris graminea
IRIDACEAE

A rhizomatous-rooted plant, originating from many parts of central Europe, including quite high altitudes in the Pyrenees. Leaves, 20 – 40 cm (8 – 16 in) long, 2 cm (¾ in) wide, are clump-forming. In early summer stems, shorter than the leaves, bear 1 – 2 flowers, blue and purple, 7 – 8 cm (2¾ – 3 in) in diameter, from rather leaf-like bracts. A useful plant for the rock garden; needs rich, open soil. Propagate by division or from seed.

Iris innominata
IRIDACEAE

A rhizomatous species found wild in northern California and southwestern Oregon, USA. The dark green, slender leaves, about 30 cm (12 in) or little more long, 4 mm (³⁄₁₆ in) wide, are densely arranged. Slender stems about 25 cm (10 in) long have spathes of 1 – 2 flowers, extremely variable, white, yellow, lilac or bluish, the falls 4.5 cm (1¾ in) long, 1.8 cm (¹¹⁄₁₆ in) wide, the standards 4 cm (1½ in) long, 7 mm (⅜ in) wide, in early summer. Needs a very permeable, lime-free soil and a position in sun or partial shade. Propagate by division or from seed in spring.

Iris japonica
IRIDACEAE

Syn. *I. fimbriata*. A very choice species, originating from China and Japan, flowering in late spring and early summer. Dark green leaves, about 50 cm (20 in) long, usually glaucous on the underside. Flowers somewhat flattish, 4 – 5 cm (1½ – 2 in) in diameter, pale lavender blue, the segments with crisped edges. Falls have a large orange area with yellowish-brownish markings, standards wide-spread, about 2.5 cm (1 in) long, 1 cm (½ in) wide. Prefers a lime-free soil, and needs sun or partial shade and careful watering at all times. Propagate by division or from seed.

Iris kerneriana
IRIDACEAE

A rather slender species, native to Turkey, ideally suited for the alpine garden. Plants rarely exceed 30 cm (12 in) in height. Leaves slender, green, spirally with pointed tips, deciduous. Stem simple, with 3 clasping leaves at the apex. Flowers, in early summer, straw yellow, 7 – 10 cm (2¾ – 4 in) in diameter, falls pale primrose yellow, deeper shade in centre, the margins crisped and recurved, standards creamy yellow, erect, slightly twisted, about 4 cm (1½ in) long. Best in full sun and a slightly acid soil. Propagate from seed, freshly harvested.

Iris korolkowii
IRIDACEAE

A horizontal-rhizomatous species, found on open rock faces at altitudes of 1,600 – 3,000 m (5,300 – 10,000 ft) or more in Afghanistan and Iran. Leaves are pale grey, glaucous green, 30 cm (12 in) or more long. Flowers, borne in late spring on stems over 30 cm (12 in) tall, are greenish-white, brownish veined – the colourings can be variable. Well suited to rock garden culture given a rich, gritty soil. Propagate by division or from seed.

Iris kuschakewiczii
IRIDACEAE

A bulbous plant to about 15 cm (6 in) tall, originating from the Tien Shan Mountains in Turkestan. Stem densely covered with 4 – 5 slightly curving leaves to 1.5 cm (⅝ in) wide, the margins hard and minutely bristly. Flowers, appearing in early summer, are pale violet, to 8 cm (3 in) in diameter, the falls elongated, with a white crest, mottled and lined with deep violet on either side, standards about 1.5 cm (⅝ in) long, usually 1 – 4 flowers to a stem. Needs good drainage and dry dormancy; best grown in a raised bed. Propagate from seed.

Iris lacustris
IRIDACEAE

A dwarf-growing species found in the Great Lakes area of North America. Leaves slender, erect, to about 15 cm (6 in) long. The stem has cauline leaves and attractive sky blue flowers, in late spring to early summer, the falls, to 2 cm (¾ in) long, with prominent yellow crest flecked brown and a whitish patch, the margins bluish-purple; standards violet or white near base, rounded or notched at the apex, and pale violet style branches, 1.2 cm (⁹⁄₁₆ in) long. Needs slight shade and a well-drained soil. Propagate by division of rootstock or from fresh seed.

Iris lutescens
IRIDACEAE

Syn. *I. chamaeiris*. This species, found in northeast Spain, southern France and Italy, is extremely variable, particularly as regards the flower colour, which can be yellow, bluish-violet, sometimes almost white (as shown). Leaves greyish-green, 15 – 30 cm (6 – 12 in) or more long, to 1.5 cm (⅝ in) wide. Stems 5 – 18 cm (2 – 7½ in) long, with 1 – 2 flowers in late spring, 6 – 7 cm (2½ – 2¾ in) in diameter, beard yellow or whitish, standards erect. An alkaline soil and good drainage are essential; needs a position in sun or partial shade. Propagate by division or from seed.

Iris magnifica
IRIDACEAE

A bulbous species originating from the mountains of Pamir-Alai in central Asia. Plants in flower to about 50 cm (20 in) tall, bright green leaves, 3 – 5 cm (1¼ – 2 in) wide, carried at intervals along the stem, and 5 – 7 flowers borne at the leaf axils. Flowers appear in late spring, about 7.5 cm (2⅞ in) in diameter. Falls white, tinged pale bluish-lilac, crest whitish, edged orange-yellow; standards have a deep mauve ridge in the centre. A dry dormancy is advisable. Best grown in a raised bed in enriched, open, well-drained soil. Propagate from seed, freshly harvested.

Iris maracandica
IRIDACEAE

A low-growing plant, scarcely more than 15 cm (6 in) high, occurring in the wild on the Pamir-Alai Mountains of central Asia. Leaves are well developed at flowering time, to 2 cm (¾ in) wide, almost covering the stem. The stem is very short, bearing 1 – 4 yellow flowers with widely winged haft to the falls, in late spring. A most useful plant for the alpine house, needing a bright, sunny position and a porous, slightly alkaline soil. Propagate by division, as bulbs often multiply freely.

Iris microglossa
IRIDACEAE

A perennial-rooted, bulbous plant, native to dry mountain slopes at altitudes of 1,700 – 2,700 m (5,600 – 9,000 ft) in northeast Afghanistan. Leaves are greyish, ciliate, 25 cm (10 in) long and 2.5 cm (1 in) wide. Stems, 10 – 30 cm (4 – 12 in) long, bear 1 – 4 flowers. Flowers, pale mauvish-blue to almost white, to about 5 cm (2 in) in diameter, appear in late spring. A species for the rock garden, where it needs enriched, permeable soil and to be in the sun. Propagate from seed, freshly harvested.

Iris milesii
IRIDACEAE

A green-rhizomatous species, of variable height, native to altitudes of 2,000 m (6,600 ft) or more in the western Himalayas (Punjab, Assam). Pale green leaves are broadly ensiform, 45 – 60 cm (18 – 24 in) long. Stems, usually overtopping the foliage, usually branched with bract-like leaves subtending each branch. Spathes are many flowered, the flowers, borne in early summer, being purplish with an orange crest, 6 – 10 cm (2½ – 4 in) wide. An ideal subject for the rock garden. Propagate by division or from seed.

Iris missouriensis
IRIDACEAE

A most variable species, found in the USA from the Rocky Mountains to Arizona and also known in Canada and Mexico. The slender, deciduous leaves are 30 – 40 cm (12 – 16 in) or more long, to 7 mm (⅜ in) wide, glaucous green, overtopping the flowers. The stems carry 2 – 4 flowered spathes. Flowers appear in early summer, pale lilac to bluish-violet, often white, the falls prominently veined, often with a brownish-yellow signal patch, standards barely shorter than the falls. Needs sun and rich soil. Propagate by division or from seed in early spring.

Iris orchidioides
IRIDACEAE

Syn. *Juno orchidioides*. A bulbous species from central Asia, found on stony mountain slopes at altitudes up to 2,000 m (6,600 ft). Leaves 15 – 30 cm (6 – 12 in) long, 1 – 3 cm (½ – 1¼ in) wide, partially covering the stem. Stems about 30 cm (12 in) long, with 3 – 4 flowers from the leaf axils. Flowers, in late spring, about 5 cm (2 in) in diameter, falls widely winged, with a deep yellow area and a toothed keel, brownish lines on either side. Needs slight shade and an enriched, open soil; best grown in a raised bed. Propagate from seed, freshly gathered.

Iris planifolia
IRIDACEAE

A bulbous species to about 15 cm (6 in) tall, found wild in southern Europe and north Africa, usually on high ground in rocky limestone areas. Leaves glossy green, arching, to 3 cm (1¼ in) wide, almost concealing the stem. Flowers 1 – 3, bluish-violet with darker veins surrounding the bright yellow crest, 6 – 7 cm (2½ – 2¾ in) in diameter, from early spring to early summer. A plant best suited to alpine house culture, in a slightly calcareous soil. Propagates best from newly ripened seed, sown in temperature 12 – 15°C (54 – 59°F).

Iris prismatica var. alba
IRIDACEAE

A tall species, found wild in swampy ground in Carolina, USA, through to Nova Scotia, Canada. Leaves, very slender, almost grass-like, are to 50 cm (20 in) or more long, 2 – 5 mm (⅛ – ¼ in) wide. Flowers, borne in early summer, have pale yellowish-white falls, to 3 cm (1¼ in) long, standard white, sub-erect to 2.6 cm (about 1 in) long. Suited to rock garden culture; needs a very moisture-retentive, enriched soil and to be planted in a truly moist position in slight shade. Propagates freely from seed, newly harvested.

Iris pseudocaucasica
IRIDACEAE

An intriguing, low-growing plant, 6 – 20 cm (2½ – 8 in) high, arising from fleshy roots, found in the wild in Transcaucasia, Turkey, Iran and Iraq. The 3 – 4 leaves are generally produced at flowering time, to 18 cm (7½ in) long, 3 cm (1¼ in) wide, falcate and veined white. Stem 10 cm (4 in) long, almost totally enclosed by leaves, with 1 – 4 flowers in late spring and early summer, yellowish-blue or pale blue, the blade of the falls having a yellow crest, the standards about half as long as the falls. Needs sun and an enriched compost. Propagate by division or from seed.

Iris pumila
IRIDACEAE

A rather dwarf species found wild in dryish places in many parts of eastern and southeastern Europe. Plants about 15 cm (6 in) tall, with greyish-green leaves 10 – 15 cm (4 – 6 in) long, to 1.5 cm (⅝ in) wide. Stem about 1 cm (½ in) long, the perianth tube to 10 cm (4 in) long, usually 1 flower. Flowers, in late spring, scented, yellow, blue or purplish, to 6 cm (2½ in) in diameter, falls bearded, yellow or bluish, blade 4 cm (1½ in) long, 1.2 cm (⁹⁄₁₆ in) wide, crest brownish-purple. Needs a sunny position and a slightly alkaline, well-drained soil. Propagate by division or from seed.

Iris reticulata
IRIDACEAE

A bulbous, variable and very popular species, indigenous to the Caucasus, Turkey, Iran and Iraq at high altitudes. Stem often only 10 cm (4 in) long, having 2 – 4 somewhat quadrangular leaves, rarely more than 30 cm (12 in) long. Flowers in early spring, blue, purple to reddish-purple, often with a yellowish crest; falls have a greenish section marked with purplish dots and lines on the under-surface; standards larger than falls, erect, but paler in colour. Grow in open ground in normal garden soil. Propagate by division.

Iris rosenbachiana
IRIDACEAE

A low-growing, bulbous species found wild in Afghanistan and the adjoining Pamir-Alai Mountains of central Asia. It has 3 – 6 leaves in a tuft, eventually about 25 cm (10 in) long, tapering towards the tips. Flowers, in summer, are borne on a short stem in the leaf axils, variable, purple or mauve, 5 – 6 cm (2 – 2½ in) in diameter; falls elongated, the haft often wider than the blade, the blade having an orange crest. Best grown in a bulb frame or an alpine house, in a rich, open soil. Propagate from seed, freshly harvested.

Iris sintenisii
IRIDACEAE

A rhizomatous species of rather small growth, which occurs wild in southeastern Europe and Turkey, usually in low mountain pastures or wood clearing at altitudes to 1,500 m (5,000 ft). Generally to 30 cm (12 in) tall; the leaves, rather fan-like, form tufts and are about 2 – 5 mm (⅛ – ¼ in) wide. Flowers appear in early summer, deep purple or prominently veined on pale ground; falls constricted, 4 cm (1½ in) long, about 1 cm (½ in) wide, standards shorter. Very well suited to the rock garden, given a sunny position and a rich soil. Propagate by division or from seed.

Iris suaveolens
IRIDACEAE

Syn. *I. rubromarginata*. A low-growing, dwarf plant to 15 cm (6 in) high, found in many parts of eastern Europe, Turkey and the Black Sea region. Plants have a rhizomatous rootstock bearing fan-shaped leaves 12 cm (5 in) long, 1 cm (½ in) wide. Stems have 1 – 2 flowers, in spring, yellow, brown and purple (or a combination of all), about 5 cm (2 in) wide, scented, with falls shorter and narrower than the standard; the beards usually yellow, standards usually deeper coloured. Needs a slightly alkaline soil and bright sun. Propagate by division or from seed.

Iris tectorum
IRIDACEAE

Syn. *Evansia tectorum*. A species found in central and southwestern areas of China, possibly also in Japan. The pale green leaves, to 30 cm (12 in) or more long and to 5 cm (2 in) wide, are arranged fan-like. Flowers, which appear in early summer, are borne on wiry stems, which are simple or slightly branched, and are bright lilac and bluish-purple, to 10 cm (4 in) across. Falls have broad, rounded blade, veined lilac and mottled lilac-blue and a white crest with dark spots. Best in lime-free soil, in sun or partial shade. Suited to the rock garden.

Iris unguicularis
IRIDACEAE

A tufted species found wild in north Africa, invariably on low hill sides among scrub. A horizontal, rhizomatous rootstock produces sword-shaped leaves, usually about 6 to a tuft, 45 cm (18 in) or more long, about 1 cm (½ in) wide. Stems short, almost absent, but with a perianth tube to 10 cm (4 in) long. Flowers, in autumn to spring, lavender blue, fall with yellow keel on white ground near base, standards with lilac blade and reddish veined yellow haft. Propagate by division or from seed in spring.

Iris vicaria
IRIDACEAE

A bulbous plant 30 – 37 cm (12 – 15 in) tall in flower, originating from rocky slopes in mountainous regions of central Asia. Leaves falcate, to 15 cm (6 in) long, 3 cm (1¼ in) wide, well developed at flowering time in late spring, and set at intervals along the stem. Flowers bluish-violet, 4 – 5 cm (1½ – 2 in) in diameter, 2 – 6 to a stem. Falls pale bluish-violet, the haft with violet lines and a yellow crest, standards 2.5 cm (1 cm) long, pale violet with deeper veins. Likes a bright position and a slightly alkaline, porous soil. Propagate from seed, freshly harvested.

Isophysis tasmanica
IRIDACEAE

An exceptionally rare sub-alpine species, native to high altitudes on mountains in Tasmania. Leaves, to 20 cm (8 in) long, form a dense, tufted plant. Inflorescence, always overtopping the foliage, to 35 cm (14 in), with somewhat triangular spathes to 3.5 cm (1⅜ in) long. Flowers, borne in summer, terminal and solitary, dark brown, reddish, more rarely yellow, are 8 – 9 cm (3 – 3½ in) across. Needs alpine house culture in a rich, permeable soil. Propagate from seed, freshly harvested.

Ixia flexuosa
IRIDACEAE

A cormous-rooted species from hills and mountains in more northerly parts of Cape Province, South Africa. It has slender, erect, rather sturdy green leaves. Flowers, small, scented, pale pink, mauve or white, appear in early summer, borne terminally on long, often branching stems about 45 cm (18 in) long – 3-15 to each spike. If regularly lifted after the leaves and flowers have withered, they can be grown outside; otherwise best kept in an alpine house. Needs a permeable, humus-enriched soil. Propagate from seed.

Ixiolirion ledebourii
AMARYLLIDACEAE

Possibly synonymous with *I. montanum*. A bulbous plant, native to central and western areas of Asia. Stems to about 45 cm (18 in) tall, with grass-like leaves forming tufts. Flowers, in early summer, borne in terminal umbels, each trumpet-like flower about 4 cm (1½ in) long, deep to pale blue. Can be planted and grown successfully in the rock garden or alpine house in well-drained soil, but needs protection from frost. Propagate from fresh seed.

Jeffersonia diphylla
BERBERIDACEAE

A comparatively rare plant, which originates from woodland areas of North America. The low-growing, somewhat bushy plant tends to form tufts. The leaves are rounded and lobed, glaucous, often tinted violet, on wiry, brownish stems. Flowers appear in spring, borne solitary on long stalks, a rich creamy white, about 2 cm (¾ in) in diameter, cup-shaped. Certainly a rather difficult plant to locate, but definitely a special item for the alpine house, requiring slight shade and moist, rather peaty soil. Propagate from seed.

Jovibarba hirta
CRASSULACEAE

Syn. *Sempervivum hirtum*. A very variable, low-growing, spreading succulent plant from the eastern Alps. Differing habitats appear to produce dissimilar plants. Generally the rosettes remain slightly open, to 2 – 5 cm (¾ – 2 in) wide, these made up of many sharp pointed, yellowish-green leaves, which are invariably reddish-brown on the outer surface. Flowers, which appear in early summer, carried on very stout stems to 20 cm (8 in) long, are bright yellow, borne terminally. Suited to the rock garden; needs a position in shade in porous soil. Propagate by division in late summer.

Kalanchoe jongsmansii
CRASSULACEAE

A trailing, mat-forming succulent species, found on high ground in Madagascar. The small, fleshy to woody branches are to 20 cm (8 in) long. Leaves, more or less oblong, to 4 cm (1½ in) long, 1 cm (½ in) wide, are fleshy and bright green. Flowers, borne terminally in summer on short, slightly hairy stems, are bright golden-yellow, somewhat cup-shaped to about 3 cm (1¼ in) long. Alpine house culture is essential; needs porous, enriched soil and indirect light. Propagate from seed, newly ripened.

Kalanchoe manginii
CRASSULACEAE

A somewhat pendent species with many branches, found wild in fairly high, hilly country in southern Madagascar. Branches, 10 – 30 cm (4 – 12 in) long, carry many succulent, dark glossy green, more or less oval leaves, to 3 cm (1¼ in) long, 8 mm (⁷⁄₁₆ in) thick and over 1 cm (½ in) wide. Flowers, borne in early summer mainly from the tips of the branches, are tubular-bell-shaped, about 2.4 cm (1 in) long, red. A subject for the alpine house. Propagate from cuttings or from seed.

Kalanchoe pumila
CRASSULACEAE

A densely clustering, succulent species, native to mountainous regions of central Madagascar. Many branches bear numerous ovate, greyish-green leaves, 2 cm (¾ in) or a little more long, minutely pruinose, the upper margins crenate. Flowers, borne in early summer in terminal panicles on stems to 20 cm (8 in) long, are pinkish, about 1 cm (½ in) across. Best kept in the alpine house in an enriched, open soil. Propagate from stem cuttings.

Kalanchoe schumacheri
CRASSULACEAE

A clustering, low-growing, often pendent species of uncertain origin, but believed to originate from Madagascar. It has semi-erect or horizontally spreading branches, clothed with dull greenish, more or less rounded leaves, about 1.5 cm (⅝ in) long. Flowers, in early summer, whitish with pinkish tips to the petals, are borne in terminal clusters, each 6 – 9 mm (³⁄₁₆ – ⁷⁄₁₆ in) across. Needs alpine house culture, in open, moisture-retentive soil. Propagate by division.

Kelissa brasiliensis
IRIDACEAE

Syn. *Herbertia brasiliensis*. A particularly choice bulbous plant, to 15 cm (6 in) tall, found only in Rio Grande de Sol, Brazil. Leaves are basal, 2 – 11 cm (¾ – 4½ in) long, 6 mm (⁵⁄₁₆ in) wide. Stems carry a few bracts and a solitary leaf and are 2-flowered. Flowers, in late autumn, are violet, about 4 cm (1½ in) across, the segments unguiculate and claws yellow with reddish-brown spots; blade of outer segments pale violet with deep purplish markings. Still very rare; needs sun and an acid, open soil. Propagate from seed, sown in spring.

Knautia arvensis
DIPSACACEAE

An erect, slender species widespread throughout much of central and southern Europe, growing in scrub and dry, grassy places (as shown), which, when cultivated, provides a pleasing result and is useful in the rock garden. Stems about 30 cm (12 in) tall, almost leafless except for a few basal leaves and on lower part of stems. Blue flowers in summer, terminal, in a rounded head about 3 cm (1¼ in) across. Prefers partial shade. Propagate from seed in a sandy, humus-enriched, porous soil in spring.

Lewisia cotyledon

L

Lachenalia aloides
LILIACEAE

Syn. *L. tricolor*. Commonly known as the leopard lily. A bulbous species, with stems to about 30 cm (12 in) long, found wild in southern parts of South Africa. Leaves fleshy, lanceolate, bright green flecked with purplish-blue. Flowers, slightly pendent, tubular, about 2 cm (¾ in) long, red and yellow, tipped green, 7 – 10 to a stem, appear in late spring and early summer, borne terminally in a loose raceme. Needs rich, open soil and a bright, sunny site; best in an alpine house. Propagate from freshly harvested seed, temperature 15°C (59°F).

Lachenalia contaminata
LILIACEAE

A bulbous plant found wild in low, sandy areas of southern parts of Cape Province, South Africa. It has long, strap-shaped, pointed, dark green, somewhat freckled leaves which are wide spreading. Flowers in late spring or early summer on fleshy stems to 20 cm (8 in) long, white, in many flowered racemes. More suited to alpine house conditions, needing a sunny position and an enriched gritty soil. Dry off after flowering. Propagate from seed, gathered immediately it is ripened.

Lampranthus conspicuus
AIZOACEAE

A very colourful succulent plant, native to hilly country in Cape Province, South Africa. Plants can achieve heights of about 45 cm (18 in), with semi-prostrate stems and branches to 2 cm (¾ in) thick. Leaves, semi-cylindrical and about 6 cm (2½ in) long, are green with reddish mucro – stems and leaves forming large masses. Flowers, in summer, are about 5 cm (2 in) across, purplish-red with yellow centres. For alpine house culture. Propagate from cuttings or from seed.

Lampranthus haworthii
AIZOACEAE

A freely branching, spreading, succulent plant, found wild on hill sides in Cape Province, South Africa. The semi-cylindrical, fleshy, green leaves are densely pale grey pruinose, to 4 cm (1½ in) long, 5 mm (¼ in) wide. Flowers, densely produced in late summer and autumn, are pinkish-purple, to about 7 cm (2¾ in) across. Needs a sunny position in the alpine house; may be half-hardy in a sheltered position in the rock garden. Needs a rich, open soil; keep dry in the coldest weather. Propagate from cuttings or from seed in spring.

Lapeirousia silenoides
IRIDACEAE

A short, cormous plant, to about 18 cm (7½ in) tall, found in the wild in hilly country in Namaqualand, southern Africa. Each corm bears a single basal leaf, to 10 cm (4 in) in length, and a few cauline leaves. Flowers borne in early summer, zygomorphic, with a curved tube to 5 cm (2½ in) long; upper segments magenta to cerise, central one hooded; the lower segments similarly coloured with yellow base and deep red spot. Needs rich, porous soil and full sun; keep dry during dormancy. Propagate from seed or cormlets.

Lapidaria margaretae
AIZOACEAE

A short, mat-forming succulent species, native to rocky, hilly regions of southwestern Africa (Greater Namaqualand). Leaves, about 1.5 cm (⅝ in) long and 1 cm (½ in) wide and thick, grey-ish-green, emerge from the spreading stems. Flowers, in late summer, are golden-yellow, to 5 cm (2 in) across, and borne on pedicels about 6 cm (2½ in) long. Requires alpine house culture in an open, humus-enriched compost in sun. Propagate by division or from seed.

Larentia roseii
IRIDACEAE

A bulbous species, found wild in Mexico (Sinaloa, Michoacan), in moist, grassy areas at altitudes of about 700 m (2,300 ft). Leaves basal, to 30 cm (12 in) long, linear or ensiform, glabrous, the cauline leaves 4 cm (1½ in) long (upper), the lower leaves 16 cm (6½ in) long. Spathes terminal, with 2 flowers in spring and early summer, the flowers dark purple or violet, the segments about 2.5 cm (1 in) long, 1.3 cm (9⁄16 in) wide. Needs to be kept in an alpine house, in a humus-enriched, open soil. Propagate from freshly harvested seed.

Launaea spinosa
COMPOSITAE

A much-branched, shrubby plant to about 30 cm (12 in) high, the branches becoming spiny with age, native to dry hills in southern Spain. Leaves linear and coarsely toothed or shallowly lobed, dark green. Flowers appear in summer on the newly produced branches, pale yellow, about 2 cm (¾ in) wide, borne terminally. A sun-loving plant, requiring an enriched, porous soil, suited to a sheltered rock garden. Propagate from freshly harvested seed sown in sandy soil, temperature about 12°C (54°F).

Lavandula stoechas
LABIATAE

A dwarfer species of lavender, generally around 30 cm (12 in) high, found on hill sides and open wooded areas in much of the Mediterranean region of southern Europe. The soft, greyish-green, narrow leaves are densely coated with white, velvety hairs. Flowers appear in spring and early summer, the 4-angled spikes composed of hairy bracts and dark, rich purple, 2-lipped flowers, 6 – 8 mm (5⁄16 – 7⁄16 in) long. This fragrant small shrub is ideal for the rock garden, given a place in full sun and well-drained garden soil. Propagate by cuttings in late summer or from seed in spring.

Ledebouria cooperi
LILIACEAE

This has also been known as *Scilla adlamii*. A bulbous, low-growing plant originating from southern areas of South Africa. The dark green, wide, lanceolate leaves are basal and semi-prostrate, often marked with brownish-purple lines, deciduous. Flowers purple or greenish-purple, borne in summer in a terminal cluster on short stems 10 cm (4 in) in length. Best cultivated in an alpine house, in a rich, peaty, sandy soil in bright light. Propagate from offsets in spring.

Leopoldia comosa
LILIACEAE

Syn. *Muscari comosum*. A fairly tall or medium sized bulbous species, to 60 cm (24 in) in height, found in southern Europe and north Africa. Very slender leaves to 45 cm (18 in) long, 2 cm (¾ in) wide at the base, gradually tapering towards the tips, generally 3 – 6 in number. Flower spikes appear in early summer – the upper flowers erect, bluish-violet, the lower larger, 8 mm (7⁄16 in) long, bluish-brown with pale teeth, more urn-shaped and short-stalked. Ideal for the rock garden in humus-enriched, gritty soil and in sun or slight shade. Propagate from seed in spring.

Leopoldia comosa var. plumosum
LILIACEAE

Syn. *Hyacinthus comosus* var. *plumosum*; has also been included within *Muscari*. As far as is known, this originates from western Asia – a bulbous plant, leaves and stems to 15 – 25 cm (6 – 10 in) tall, with several erect, slender leaves, all basal. Flowers, densely tufted, feather-like, mauvish-blue, in a lax raceme, appear from early to late spring, often into summer. A hardy plant for the rock garden, needing a permeable, humus-enriched, gritty soil, in sun or partial shade. Propagate by division or from ripened seed.

Leptospermum scoparium var. nanum
MYRTACEAE

A small, shrubby plant, to about 30 cm (12 in) tall, found wild in New Zealand. It has dark, slightly twisted stems, with dark green, more or less oblong leaves, about 1 cm (½ in) long, with slightly pointed tips. in summer the pale pink flowers, opening to about 1.5 cm (⅝ in) wide, are borne in profusion. Best suited to alpine house culture, needing sun and well-drained soil. Propagate by heeled cuttings in summer.

Leptospermum scoparium var. nichollsii
MYRTACEAE

A prostrate, bushy plant rarely exceeding 24 cm (9½ in) high, found mainly on South Island, New Zealand. The small, dark green, linear leaves are mainly suffused bronze-purple, hardly more than 1 cm (½ in) long. Flowers appear in early summer, densely arranged across the plant, generally carmine with a darker eye, although paler colours are known. Best suited to alpine house culture; needs an enriched soil and bright sun. Propagate from heeled cuttings in late summer or from seed in spring.

Leucocoryne ixioides
AMARYLLIDACEAE/ALLIACEAE

A rather charming, half-hardy, bulbous species, found wild in Chile. Leaves are basal, rather slender, usually 2 – 3, to about 30 cm (12 in) in length. Flowers appear in spring, 5 – 9 to an umbel, pale blue with a white centre, fragrant, 3 – 4 cm (1¼ – 1½ in) across. An excellent plant for alpine house culture, needing bright sun and a rich, loam-based soil. Allow the soil to dry completely after the flowers and leaves have withered. Propagate from offsets or seed in spring.

Leucojum aestivum
AMARYLLIDACEAE

A small bulbous plant, very similar in many ways to *L. autumnale*, found wild in central and southern Europe to the Caucasus. Leaves strap-shaped, about 30 – 45 cm (12 – 18 in) long, to 1.5 cm (⅝ in) wide, bright green. Flowers, in summer, solitary or in small clusters, white, to 1.5 cm (⅝ in) long, on stems to 30 cm (12 in) or more tall. A hardy plant, useful for the rock garden, but needs shelter from excessively cold weather. Can also prove decorative for alpine house culture. Grow in pots in a John Innes No. 2 compost; outside in ordinary garden soil. Propagate from offsets or newly ripened seed.

Leucojum autumnale
AMARYLLIDACEAE

A short, tuft-forming, bulbous species native to the Mediterranean region. The linear, green leaves are usually seen after the flowers, which appear in late summer and early autumn, borne on stems to about 15 cm (6 in) long, either solitary or 2 – 3 together, white slightly tinted pink at the base, bell-shaped, about 1 cm (½ in) long, in a solitary spathe. Suited to a warm, sunny rock garden or to alpine house culture. Grow in pots in a John innes No. 2 compost; in the rock garden in ordinary garden soil. Propagate from newly ripened seed in spring.

Leuzia conifera
COMPOSITAE

Syn. *Centaurea conifera*. A low-growing, tufted perennial plant, 15 – 20 cm (6 – 8 in) tall, found in Mediterranean regions of southern Europe and northwestern Africa. Leaves oval to lanceolate, the upper divided into slender segments, the lower usually undivided, bright green, white-felted on the undersurface. Cone-like heads of glossy, papery bracts produce small, insignificant, pinkish-purple to whitish flowers in summer. Suitable for alpine house culture, in an open, enriched soil. Propagate from seed when ripe.

Lewisia Ashwood strain
PORTULACACEAE

This attractive hybrid was raised in the USA by the Ashwood Nursery. It has rather bluish-green, spathulate leaves, similar to those of *L. cotyledon*, about 10 cm (4 in) long, formed into a basal rosette. Flowers are borne terminally on slender stalks in early summer, deep rose-pink petals, edged completely in white, about 3 cm (1¼ in) in diameter. Although relatively hardy, it is possibly best kept in an alpine house, in partial shade and an open, rich soil. Propagate by division.

Lewisia Birch hybrid
PORTULACACEAE

A compact, low-growing hybrid, raised in Britain at the ingwersen Nursery. It has more or less oval, slightly succulent green leaves formed into a very leafy rosette. Flowers appear in late spring, in pinkish shades, borne in terminal clusters on stems 15 cm (6 in) or more long. It prefers alpine house culture, needing a gritty, fairly rich, porous soil. Propagate by division in early spring or autumn, using a sandy, peaty mix until thoroughly established.

Lewisia columbiana
PORTULACACEAE

A species widely distributed throughout much of North America. It has a thick, fleshy rootstock, producing slender, almost succulent flat leaves in tufts. Flowers, in spring and summer, vary from pale pinkish-white to far deeper shades of bright pink, 3 cm (1¼ in) or more wide, borne on stems about 30 cm (12 in) long, in panicles, the petals prominently toothed. Needs a lime-free, porous soil, and a bright position; best in a sloping bed. Propagate by division or from seed in spring.

Lewisia cotyledon
PORTULACACEAE

An evergreen, perennial, rosette-forming species, found wild in northern California and southern Oregon, USA. There are a number of forms and varieties, some of which are natural and can be located in the wild. Leaves are spathulate, 4 – 10 cm (1½ – 4 in) long. Flowers in late spring and summer, white, often prominently tinged with shades of pink in panicles to 30 cm (12 in) or more long. Needs a gritty, lime-free soil and slight shade; best in a sloping bed. Propagate by division in spring, or from seed, which is best stored in a refrigerator for 3 – 4 weeks before sowing.

Lewisia cotyledon 'Howellii'
PORTULACACEAE

In most respects this is very similar to the species; possibly only a variant. The leaves are somewhat more slender, often partially incurved, with decidedly crinkled, strongly wavy margins, formed into attractive rosettes, each rosette 15 cm (6 in) wide. Flowers are larger than the species, rose-pink to orange-pinkish shades, borne terminally on long stems in many flowered clusters in late spring and early summer. Cultivation is the same as for the species.

Lewisia leana
PORTULACACEAE

(Sometimes spelt *leeana*.) A thick-rooted plant with a wide habitat in more northern parts of California and Oregon, USA. Leaves, grey-green, are fleshy and form a neat rosette. Flowers vary in colour from rich deep red to magenta to almost white, borne on rather thin stems, 20 cm (8 in) or more long, in many flowered panicles in early summer. Needs a slightly acid, permeable soil and a sunny position. Propagate from seed.

Lewisia nevadensis
PORTULACACEAE

Syn. *L. bernardina*. A species with a fleshy root-stock, producing many basal leaves, native to moist areas in mountains from Washington to Oregon to Nevada and the San Bernardino Mountains in California, USA. Leaves deciduous, linear to lanceolate, to 7 cm (2¾ in) long. Flowers white, 2 – 3 cm (¾ – 1¼ in) across, borne solitary, rarely 2, on short stems, which are partly sub-terranean, appearing in summer. Needs a rich, moisture-retentive soil, in full sun. Propagate from newly harvested seed in spring, temperature 15°C (59°F).

Lewisia pygmaea ssp. longipetala
PORTULACACEAE

A deciduous plant arising from a thick taproot, originating from the Sierra Nevada in California, USA. Stem erect, invariably longer than the slender leaves, which are 6 – 7 cm (2½ – 2¾ in) long and about 8 mm (⁷⁄₁₆ in) wide. Flowers, in spring, are said to be rose-red, although a whitish form with reddish markings (as shown) is known, with a few dark, glandular teeth on the margins. Needs a fairly bright, sunny position and an open, peaty, loamy soil. Best suited to alpine house culture. Propagate from seed, freshly harvested.

Lewisia rediviva
PORTULACACEAE

Commonly known as bitter root. A deciduous species with a thick, edible rootstock, native to northwestern areas of North America. Leaves fleshy, reddish-green and rather narrow, scarcely 5 cm (2 in) long, forming a low rosette, which withers as flowering begins in spring. Flowers white or rose-pink, about 5 cm (2 in) across, carried on very short stems to 3 cm (1¼ in) long. Best suited to an alpine house, where plants can be kept almost dry in winter; needs lime-free compost. Propagate from seed, freshly harvested.

Lewisia rediviva var. minor
PORTULACACEAE

A deciduous mountain plant, found invariably at very high altitudes in California and Nevada, USA. Leaves more or less club-shaped to narrowly oblanceolate, forming a basal rosette. Flowers appear on rather short stems in early summer, white or pink, to about 2.5 cm (1 in) long. Needs sun and slight warmth and a neutral or lime-soil with added grit. Probably best suited to alpine house culture. Propagate from newly harvested seed or by division.

Lewisia tweedyii
PORTULACACEAE

An unusual species from Washington State, USA, and British Columbia, Canada. It has a stout root-stock, evergreen foliage, the obovate, fleshy leaves to 15 cm (6 in) long often suffused with red and formed into a loose rosette. Stems, about 15 cm (6 in) long, carry large, wide-petalled flowers, about 4 cm (1½ in) wide, salmon pink, sometimes paler shades, even yellow and white, 1 – 3 to a stem, in late spring and early summer. Needs a dry dormancy period and lime-free, gritty, peaty soil. Best suited to alpine house culture. Propagate from seed in spring.

Lewisia tweedyii var. rosea
PORTULACACEAE

An evergreen perennial plant found wild in British Columbia, Canada, and Washington State, USA. It has a fleshy, branching rootstock, producing a basal rosette of glabrous, obovate leaves to 15 cm (6 in) long. Flowers appear terminally on short stems in late spring to summer, rose-pink with paler shades in the lower parts of the petals, 3 – 4 cm (1¼ – 1½ in) across, in racemes of 1 – 3. Probably best suited to alpine house culture, needing an enriched soil, in slight shade. Propagate by division or from seed in spring.

Libertia caerulescens
IRIDACEAE

A tufted species found wild in the Chilean Andes in totally alpine conditions. Leaves are rigid, narrowly lanceolate, to 30 cm (12 in) long. Flowers, whitish-blue, on short pedicels, the inner segments bluish-white, the outer brownish-green and smaller, appear during summer on stems 45 cm (18 in) or more long. This has proved totally hardy, and is well suited to the rock garden; needs a slightly shaded position, sheltered from extreme weather, and moisture-retentive soil. Propagate by division or from seed in spring.

Libertia grandiflora
IRIDACEAE

An evergreen, tufted species with grass-like foliage, found wild at altitudes of 1,000 m (3,300 ft) in North Island, New Zealand. All leaves are basal, 40 – 60 cm (16 – 24 in) long. In late spring and early summer the stout inflorescence, overtopping the foliage, bears numerous flowers, 2 cm (¾ in) in diameter, in clusters, pure white with brownish-green keel. An ideal subject for the rock garden in ordinary garden soil. Propagate by division or from seed.

Libertia ixioides
IRIDACEAE

A rhizomatous plant found wild in New Zealand, usually near streams among rocks. It has basal leaves, 30 – 45 cm (12 – 18 in) or more long, slender and pointed. Flowers, white, about 2 cm (¾ in) in diameter, appear throughout summer and early autumn on a fine inflorescence, 45 – 60 cm (18 – 24 in) long. A hardy, perennial plant for the rock garden; needs a moisture-retentive, humus-enriched soil and a bright, but slightly shaded position. Propagate by division or from seed in spring.

Lilium candidum
LILIACEAE

The Madonna lily. A popular, bulbous species, native to rocky slopes and calcareous hill sides to altitudes of 600 m (2,000 ft) in the Balkans and Near East. Leaves are bright green, alternate and lance-shaped, the basal leaves to 30 cm (12 in) long, stem leaves shorter. Inflorescence, borne on stem 1.2 m (4ft) tall, appears in summer. Flowers, pure white, wide bell-shaped, about 8 cm (3 in) long, are in terminal clusters. Totally hardy in the rock garden. Propagate by separating bulblets.

Lilium pyreniacum
LILIACEAE

A well-known bulbous species, originating from the Pyrenees. Leaves narrowly lanceolate, to about 15 cm (6 in) long and 2 cm (¾ in) wide. Flowers appear in early summer, sulphur yellow, 3.5 cm (1⅜ in) wide, black lines and dots in the centre, unpleasantly scented. It has proved completely hardy, and is, therefore, suited to rock garden culture in a well-drained, slightly enriched soil, in sun or partial shade. Propagate by division or from seed, freshly harvested.

Linaria aeruginea
SCROPHULARIACEAE

This spreading, perennial, low-growing plant is found wild on dry rocky hills and mountains in southern and eastern Spain, including the Balearic Islands. Leaves linear to narrowly lanceolate, with revolute margins, the upper leaves set alternate, the lower in whorls. Flowers appear in early summer, varying in colour, violet, purplish-brown, more rarely whitish or yellowish, about 2.5 cm (1 in) long with a 1 cm (½ in) long spur. Best grown in a sunny position, in a freely draining soil in the rock garden. Propagate by root cuttings or from seed in spring.

Linaria alpina
SCROPHULARIACEAE

A rather choice, tufted, perennial plant, encountered frequently in the European Alps, primarily in rocky limestone areas. It has rather trailing, semi-prostrate stems to 25 cm (10 in) long, bedecked with linear to oblong-lanceolate, blue-grey leaves to 1 cm (½ in) or more long. Flowers appear during much of the summer, to 2 cm (¾ in) long, orange and violet, in racemes. Needs full sun and ordinary garden soil. Propagate from cuttings or from seed in spring.

Linaria amoi
SCROPHULARIACEAE

A medium sized subshrub, 30 – 45 cm (12 – 18 in) tall, found on steep, south-facing, limestone slopes at altitudes of 1,000 m (3,300 ft) and over in southwest Spain. Leaves are greyish-green, linear-lanceolate, set alternate, forming quite a dense but loose mass. Flowers, during mid-summer, are rich red-purple carried in long racemes on fairly tall, greenish stems; each flower 1.5 – 2 cm (⅝ – ¾ in) long. Needs bright light and an open, gritty soil enriched with limestone chippings. Propagate from freshly harvested seed.

Linaria hirta
SCROPHULARIACEAE

An erect, rather hairy species 15 cm (6 in) or more tall, even to 60 cm (24 in), found wild in fields and low, rocky areas in much of Spain and Portugal. Leaves oblong-lanceolate, inclined to clasp the spike. Flowers borne terminally in clusters, pale yellow, to 3 cm (1¼ in) long with a reddish-orange spur about 1.5 cm (⅝ in) long, in late spring and early summer. An annual but easily grown and propagated; very suitable for the rock garden, needing ordinary garden soil with added sand and leaf mould. Propagates readily from fresh seed.

Linum arboreum
LINACEAE

A shrubby species, only half-hardy, found wild in the Aegean region (Greece, Crete). Plants may reach 60 cm (24 in) or more in height, clothed with rather leathery, spathulate leaves to 2 cm (¾ in) long. The few-flowered inflorescence bears bright yellow blooms, each to 4 cm (1½ in) wide, in summer. Can be grown successfully in a sheltered rock garden, in well-drained, humus-enriched soil, in sun, preferably protected from cold winds. Propagate from seed in spring.

Linum capitatum
LINACEAE

A low-growing species, found growing wild in mountainous areas on rocky slopes in central and southern Italy and in the Balkan region. It has a woody base, producing basal, leafy rosettes of narrowly lanceolate leaves. Flowers yellow, about 2 cm (¾ in) long, appear in a terminal cluster in early summer, on annual flowering stems to 40 cm (16 in) long and set with slightly fleshy, alternate leaves. Suitable for alpine house culture, needing a fairly rich, open soil. Propagate from seed in spring, temperature 15℃ (59℉).

Linum narbonense
LINACEAE

A medium sized, hairless species with ascending stems, found in rather dry areas in the Mediterranean region of Europe and Africa. The slender, lanceolate leaves of greyish-green are about 5 mm (¼ in) wide. The azure blue flowers, 2 cm (¾ in) or more across, are borne terminally in early summer on slender, branching stems. A useful alpine, requiring a sunny site and well-drained soil; the flower colour varies slightly according to position. Propagate from seed in spring.

Linum perenne
LINACEAE

An attractive but variable plant, widespread throughout much of central and southern Spain, and especially the Pyrenees, in dry grassy places, at altitudes of about 1,600 m (5,300 ft). Leaves stiff, linear to narrowly lanceolate, about 2.5 cm (1 in) long and 1 – 3 mm ($\frac{1}{16}$ – $\frac{3}{16}$ in) wide, 1-veined, set alternate along the stems. Flowers to 2.5 cm (1 in) across, pale to bright blue, carried on straight stalks, borne terminally in branched panicles in summer. Suitable for the rock garden; needs a rich, sandy soil. Propagate from seed in spring.

Linum suffruticosum
ssp. salsoloides
LINACEAE

A tufted, perennial, often deciduous species, found wild in central Spain to northwestern Italy. Leaves linear, somewhat bristly, 1 mm ($\frac{1}{16}$ in) wide. Flowers appear in early summer, pure white, to about 2 cm ($\frac{3}{4}$ in) long, often with pink, yellow or violet centres, borne terminally on slender stems, which are very frequently branched. Grow in the rock garden in well-drained, slightly enriched soil, but, if grown as an annual, gather seed for the next year (although they tend to drop seed wherever planted, so propagate themselves).

Linum tenuifolium
LINACEAE

An attractive perennial species found wild on dry hill sides in many parts of Spain and France. Leaves flat, narrow, slightly hairy, about 1 mm ($\frac{1}{16}$ in) wide. Flowers appear in summer, pure white or pinkish, the petals about 1 cm ($\frac{1}{2}$ in) long, the smaller sepals all pointed. Can be grown successfully in a sheltered, sunny position outdoors or in an alpine house. Needs a very open, humus-enriched soil. Propagate from seed sown in spring, temperature about 12°C (54°F).

Liriope muscari
LILIACEAE

A dense, clump-forming species, found wild in Japan and China. It has slender, strap-shaped, dark green leaves, 30 – 50 cm (12 – 20 in) or more long, erect or arching. Flowers appear in late summer and autumn, lavender coloured, to 1 cm ($\frac{1}{2}$ in) wide, in dense terminal racemes, which are 30 cm (12 in) or even longer. Well suited to rock garden culture; needs a bright position in a well-drained, humus-enriched soil. Propagate by division in spring or from seed, freshly harvested, temperature 12°C (54°F).

Lithodora diffusa 'Heavenly Blue'
BORAGINACEAE

An evergreen, prostrate, shrubby plant, originating from Portugal and Spain, to about 10 cm (4 in) tall, with widely spreading stems and foliage. It has linear-oblong, hairy leaves of deep green, about 2 cm ($\frac{3}{4}$ in) long, and flowers, variously coloured, in early summer. This attractive cultivar has bright gentian blue flowers, somewhat funnel-shaped, to 1.5 cm ($\frac{5}{8}$ in) long, borne in profusion on leafy stems. Needs sun or partial shade, and is best planted in acid soil. Propagate from cuttings in summer.

Lithodora fruticosa
BORAGINACEAE

Syn. *Lithospermum fruticosum*. A densely branched, shrubby plant, about 45 cm (18 in) high, found in the wild in dry, rocky areas on low mountain sides in Spain and southern France. Leaves dark green, more or less slender-oblong and slightly hairy. Flowers are borne in early summer, deep blue, rarely white, to 1.8 cm ($\frac{11}{16}$ in) wide. Can be grown in the rock garden but must have a sheltered position; needs rich, gritty soil. Propagate from cuttings or from seed.

Lithodora zahnii
BORAGINACEAE

A semi-prostrate, shrubby species, to 30 cm (12 in) high, originating in rocky areas of Greece. The leaves are very tough and leathery, greyish-green, narrowly lanceolate, arranged alternate. Flowers, about 1.5 cm (⅝ in) across, are borne in terminal cymes on leafy stems in summer, pale blue, tubular, with 5 spreading lobes. Best kept in an alpine house. Needs a very porous, humus-enriched soil, in full sun or slight shade. Propagate by cuttings in summer or from seed in spring.

Lithospermum oleifolium
BORAGINACEAE

A low-growing, shrubby species, rarely exceeding 15 cm (6 in) in height, native to the Pyrenees. Leaves elliptic to obovate, to 4 cm (1½ in) long, undersurface covered in silky, white hairs. Flowers appear in summer, pinkish at first, becoming pale blue, each about 1.5 cm (⅝ in) long, in few-flowered terminal clusters. Probably best suited to alpine house culture. Needs a sunny site and a well-drained, enriched soil, with a preference for lime. Propagate by cuttings in summer or from seed in spring.

Lobularia maritima
CRUCIFERAE

Syn. *Alyssum maritima*. Commonly known as sweet alyssum. A widely spreading, low-growing species found wild in southern Europe but naturalized in much of the continent. Leaves linear to oblanceolate, to 6 cm (2½ in) long, usually hoary. Flowers appear from early summer to late autumn, white, to 6 mm (⁵⁄₁₆ in) wide, in terminal racemes. A totally hardy plant, which proves useful for ground-cover in a rock garden; needs an open, rich soil, which must be well-drained. Propagate by division or from seed.

Lomatophyllum occidentale
ALOACEAE

A short-stemmed, somewhat succulent, rosette-forming plant, native to hilly country in western areas of Madagascar. The stiff, greyish-green, lance-shaped leaves, 80 cm (32 in) or more long, have toothed margins and are mostly recurving. Flowers, from late winter to late spring, are borne in a many flowered raceme, each flower tubular in shape, dull yellow with pale bluish tips. Suited to alpine house culture; needs a gritty, open soil. Propagate from seed.

Lunaria annua
CRUCIFERAE

A rather robust species, found widespread in most areas of northern to southern Spain, Portugal and France. To about 45 cm (18 in) tall, with erect stems set with somewhat heart-shaped, coarsely toothed leaves, about 15 cm (6 in) long. Flowers, about 2 cm (¾ in) across, rose-pink or reddish-purple, rarely white, in terminal clusters, in early to midsummer. Can be used in the rock garden, planted in ordinary garden soil with gritty sand added. Propagate by division or from seed.

Lychnis coronaria
CARYOPHYLLACEAE

Often known as dusty miller. A slender-stemmed biennial plant, native to hilly country in parts of southeastern Europe. Both stems, to 60 cm (24 in) high, and leaves, more or less lance-shaped to 10 cm (4 in) long, are white-woolly. Flowers, in late summer, are about 3.5 cm (1⅜ in) wide, deep rose-pink or purple-cerise, rarely white. Suited to the rock garden given permeable, fertile soil and a position in the sun. Propagate from seed in spring.

Lycoris aurea
AMARYLLIDACEAE

Thought by some to be synonymous with
L. africana. Commonly known as the golden spider
lily. A bulbous species, found in the wild in hilly
country in Korea. Basal leaves wither as leafless
flower stem, to about 30 cm (12 in) long, appears.
Flowers, in late summer, are terminal, bright
yellow with narrow wavy segments, about 7.5 cm
(2⅞ in) long. A subject for the alpine house; needs
open, rich, moisture-retentive soil. Propagate from
fresh seed.

Lycoris incarnata
AMARYLLIDACEAE

A bulbous species, found widespread in central
China. Stems vary from 30 – 45 cm (12 – 18 in) in
height. Leaves strap-like, all basal, appearing and
withering before the flowers appear. Flowers
borne terminally in late summer, 7 – 10 cm
(2¾ – 4 in) across, sweetly scented, pale pink, 2 – 3
or more. Can be grown successfully in the rock
garden in a sunny, sheltered position and a
humus-enriched, porous soil. Propagate by
division or from seed in spring.

Lycoris squamigera
AMARYLLIDACEAE

Syn. *Amaryllis hallii*. Commonly known in the USA
as the resurrection lily. A bulbous species, found
wild in Japan. Leaves are strap-shaped, to about
2.5 cm (1 in) wide, withered before flowering time.
Flowers in summer, fragrant, pink or pinkish-
purple, funnel-shaped, about 10 cm (4 in) long,
sometimes tinged yellow in the throat. A fairly
hardy plant, suitable for outdoor culture in the
rock garden in a sunny position, sheltered from
cold winds. Needs an open, rich soil. Propagate
by division or from fresh seed.

Lysimachia punctata
PRIMULACEAE

An erect species, native to Europe, including
Britain. Stems 30 – 50 cm (12 – 20 in) or more long,
with more or less ovate leaves with ciliate margins
arranged opposite along the whole length of the
stems. Flowers appear in summer, bright yellow,
about 1.5 cm (⅝ in) across, borne in clusters from
the leaf axils, particularly towards the tips of the
stems. Benefits from a sunny site and an enriched,
peaty, moisture-retentive soil. Propagate from seed
or by division in spring.

Meconopsis grandis x sheldonii

M-N

Maireana sedifolia
CHENOPODIACEAE

A small, bushy plant, 30 – 60 cm (12 – 24 in) high and wide, found in the wild in open areas on fairly high ground in Victoria, Australia. Branches and leaves are densely arranged and tomentose. Somewhat succulent leaves, ovoid, to 1 cm (½ in) long. Flowers are very small – often only a reddish stigma is visible. Orange fruits, turning red, are about 1 cm (½ in) in diameter. Needs alpine house culture and a very porous but moisture-retentive soil. Propagate by cuttings, after summer flowering, or from freshly ripened seed.

Malva sylvestris
MALVACEAE

A semi-erect, perennial species, originating in southern Europe, now widespread in many parts of the continent. It has hairy stems and branches, the leaves more or less rounded, with 5 – 7 distinct lobes, which are toothed. The flowers are 3 – 4 cm (1¼ – 1½ in) across, purple striped with a deeper shade, usually 2 flowers together, in summer. It has proved reasonably hardy and can be considered an excellent plant for the rock garden; needs well-drained, humus-enriched soil. Propagate by cuttings or from seed in spring.

Mammillaria boolii
CACTACEAE

A small, globular cactus, native to a restricted area on mountain slopes at altitudes over 500 m (1,600 ft) near San Carlos Bay, Mexico. The plant is about 3 cm (1¼ in) high and wide, the areoles slightly woolly with small spines. Flowers, in summer, are 1 cm (½ in) or a little more in diameter, pinkish, solitary. Best given alpine house conditions, in a rich, porous soil and a sunny position. Keep dry in winter. Propagate from seed, sown in spring.

Massonia longipes
LILIACEAE

A fascinating bulbous plant, found growing wild in very dry areas of Cape Province, South Africa. Plants have 2 opposite leaves, invariably on the ground, broad, smooth, ovate, 12 cm (5 in) or more long. Flowers can be expected in early summer, white, dense clusters between the leaves, with protruding stamens. An eye-catching plant for the alpine house; needs a sunny site and a very well-drained, humus-enriched soil. Propagates best from seed, sown immediately after harvesting.

Matthiola incana
CRUCIFERAE

A perennial, woody species, 30 – 80 cm (12 – 32 in) tall, found in dry, rocky areas of Turkey, Cyprus and other parts of the eastern Mediterranean region. Leaves oblong-lanceolate, 5 – 10 cm (2 – 4 in) long, rarely and only slightly toothed. Flowers appear in spring and early summer, purple, pinkish and white, sometimes multi-coloured, 2 – 3 cm (¾ – 1¼ in) wide. A totally hardy plant, it is parent of the stocks that are so popular with gardeners. Needs a sunny position and enriched, slightly moisture-retentive soil. Propagates best from seed, sown in spring.

Mazus reptans
SCROPHULARIACEAE

Syn. *M. rugosus*. A prostrate, tuft-forming species, originating from the Himalayas. Tufts, to about 15 cm (6 in) high, are formed of narrow, spathulate, toothed leaves of fresh green. Flowers, in summer, about 2 cm (¾ in) long, purplish-blue, flecked with bright yellow and white. Best suited to alpine house culture; needs a sunny site and well-drained, enriched soil. Propagate by division or cuttings or from seed in spring.

Meconopsis grandis x sheldonii
PAPAVERACEAE

This is a species that originates from the Himalayas, a perennial with basal leaves more than 15 cm (6 in) long on long stalks, oblong-ovate. Flowers blue or purple in summer. Of the several cultivars developed, *sheldonii* has proved exceptional – a cross between *M. grandis* and *M. betonicifolia*, resulting in a display of truly vivid blue flowers. Useful for outdoor culture in the rock garden in a rich, gritty soil. Propagate from seed, carefully pollinated, possibly by hand.

Medicago marina
LEGUMINOSAE

A prostrate species, originating from sandy regions, even seashore, in southern Europe, mainly in the Mediterranean area. It has slender stems to about 15 cm (6 in) long, trailing to form large clusters. Leaves pinnate, divided into 5 – 7 ovate leaflets, coated entirely with minute white-woolly hairs, the margins incurved. Flowers, bright yellow, 6 – 8 mm ($^5/_{16}$ – $^7/_{16}$ in) long, borne on short stalks in summer. An alpine house subject; needs sun and a sandy soil, enriched with humus. Propagate by division or from seed in autumn.

Merendera filifolia
LILIACEAE

A charming miniature cormous species, found wild in the Balearic Islands, southern France and north Africa at low altitudes in sparse grassy areas or scrub. The leaves, which are almost thread-like and only a few centimetres long, follow the flowers, which appear in late summer or spring, 4 – 5 cm (1½ – 2 in) in diameter, bright rose-pink, seemingly arising direct from the corm at ground level. Can be grown successfully in an alpine house or bulb frame, needing a rich, permeable soil. Propagate from freshly ripened seed.

Merendera kurdica
LILIACEAE

A low-growing, cormous plant, originating from Kurdistan, at altitudes to 3,000 m (10,000 ft). Leaves appear together with the flowers and are broad, glossy green, to 4 cm (1½ in) long. Flowers are bright lilac-pink, appearing in early summer, these enabling the plant to reach 6 – 8 cm (2½ – 3 in) or more in height. A fascinating little plant, best grown in an alpine house or heated bulb frame, in well-drained soil enriched with decomposed leaf mould. Propagate from seed in spring.

Merendera pyrenaica
LILIACEAE

Perhaps better known as *M. montana*, this small cormous species is found in mountain pastures in Spain and Portugal, also the Pyrenees. Leaves narrowly strap-shaped, basal, 4 – 6 mm ($^3/_{16}$ – $^5/_{16}$ in) wide, appear after flowering. Flowers in autumn, rose or purplish-lilac, with spreading petals, at almost ground level. Totally hardy and well suited to rock garden culture, needing an enriched, loamy soil with sharp, gritty sand added. Propagate from freshly ripened seed or by division of the corms after flowering.

Merendera sobolifera
LILIACEAE

This fairly small, low-growing species arises from its slender, creeping corm. A hardy plant, found wild in southeastern Europe to Afghanistan, mostly in moist, sandy areas. Leaves, which appear after flowering and die down in summer, are grey-green. Flowers, in spring, are white or pale pinkish-mauve, with petals scarcely more than 1.5 cm ($^3/_8$ in) long and considered insignificant. Needs sun and an enriched, sandy soil. Propagate from fresh seed or by division.

Merendera trigyna

LILIACEAE

Syn. *M. caucasia* and, possibly, *M. nivalis*. A cormous plant, found wild in Iran, Turkey and the Caucasus, with leaves that start to appear with the flowers. These 2 – 3 linear, lanceolate leaves become erect, to 5 cm (2 in) long. Flowers appear in early spring, varying in colour, white, rose-lilac or bluish- or pinkish-mauve. Reasonably hardy, but best grown in an alpine house in sun; needs a fairly rich, porous, peaty soil. Propagate from newly ripened seed or from offsets.

Mesembryanthemum crystallinum

MESEMBRYANTHEMACEAE/AIZOACEAE

A low-growing, creeping species, found wild in Namibia and subsequently introduced to the USA, Australia, the Canary Islands and the Mediterranean region. A succulent plant with ovate or ovate-spathulate, thick, fleshy leaves, papillose with undulating margins. Flowers appear in summer, usually 3 – 5 together, each 2 – 3 cm (¾ – 1¼ in) across, white. A subject for the alpine house, planted in an open, humus-rich, sandy soil, in full sun or partial shade. Propagate by division or from seed in spring.

Milla biflora

LILIACEAE

A species with a small corm, native to Mexico and Central America, producing a series of basal, linear leaves, 30 – 45 cm (12 – 18 in) long, which remain prostrate. Flowers, borne on a slender stem about 4 mm (³⁄₁₆ in) thick, 50 cm (20 in) or more tall, appear in mid- to late summer, white, star-like, 5 cm (2 in) in diameter, carried on pedicels to 15 cm (6 in) long. Requires bright sunlight and a well-drained, sandy, enriched soil. Best lifted in autumn, and in cooler areas is best kept in an alpine house. Propagate from seed in spring.

Minuartia verna

CARYOPHYLLACEAE

Syn. *Arenaria verna*. A variable, densely mat-forming species, found in many parts of Europe, including Britain. Leaves are bright green, very small, slender, stiff, almost needle-like, forming a dome-shaped mass. Flowers in summer, pure white, with oval petals, are borne on short stems 5 – 7 cm (2 – 2¾ in) long. An excellent rock garden plant; needs bright light and an enriched, sandy soil. Propagates best from seed, sown in spring.

Moltkia x intermedia

BORAGINACEAE

Considered to be a hybrid between *M. petraea* and *M. suffruticosa*, both of which are found in mountainous regions of central Europe (Italy, Greece). A short, shrubby plant to about 25 cm (10 in) tall, with dark green, rather narrow leaves of varying lengths. Flowers appear in summer, deep rich blue, sometimes slightly paler shades, borne in dense cymes, terminally on the stems. Needs a humus-rich soil and sun. Propagate by cuttings in summer.

Monardella odoratissima

LABIATAE

A low-growing, creeping species, native to north-west North America. It has rather woody stems, 12 – 20 cm (5 – 8 in) long, slightly ascending, bearing greyish, narrow, aromatic leaves. Somewhat tubular flowers are carried in terminal heads of blue or pale purple in summer. A very fine plant for the rock garden; needs sun and an open, fertile soil. Propagate by division or from seed in spring.

Moraea carsonii
IRIDACEAE

A cormous species, to about 35 cm (14 in) high, found in the wild in moist areas in scrub at altitudes to 2,250 m (7,400 ft) in, for example, Kenya, Uganda and Zimbabwe. The slender stem has several branches, with an erect, solitary, stiff leaf, 30 cm (12 in) long, from the middle of the stem; other leaves basal. Flowers, purplish-blue with yellow markings, are borne in early summer in terminal clusters, each about 4 cm (1½ in) across. Needs alpine house culture in rich, open soil. Propagate from seed.

Moraea fugax var. filicaulis
IRIDACEAE

A cormous, variable species, found in low to medium, mostly sandy areas of Namaqualand, southern Africa. Leaves, 1 – 2 in number, are very slender and channelled, as long as or longer than the inflorescence. Scented flowers, blue, mauve, yellow or white, are borne terminally in early summer on stems about 40 cm (16 in) long, each flower about 8 cm (3 in) across. Requires alpine house culture in enriched, gritty soil. Propagate from seed, freshly harvested.

Moraea polystachys
IRIDACEAE

A cormous species from a wide habitat, extending from Transvaal and northeast Cape Province in South Africa to Namibia, at fairly high altitudes. Leaves, 3 – 4 in number, are about 50 cm (20 in) long, slender and prominently ribbed. In early summer the stem bears a branching inflorescence of clusters of blue or purplish flowers with yellowish blotches at the base of the segments, 5 – 6 cm (2 – 2½ in) wide when fully open. Best kept in an alpine house in a rich, open soil. Propagate from seed.

Moraea serpentina
IRIDACEAE

A cormous plant rarely more than 20 cm (8 in) tall, found wild in gravelly, sandy regions of Bushmanland and Karoo, South Africa. Plants have one basal leaf, flat, slenderly lanceolate, prominently pubescent on margins and under-surface. Stem branched from base, bearing spathes of a few flowers, white to yellow, flushed mauve or pink, the outer and inner segments about 3 cm (1¼ in) long, in early summer. An ideal plant for an alpine house; needs a rich, porous soil. Propagate from seed, sown soon after harvesting.

Morisia monanthos 'Fred Hemingway'
CRUCIFERAE

A rather improved form of the low-growing, prostrate species of the monotypic genus, native to Corsica and Sardinia. The dark green, narrow, pinnately divided, stemless leaves, to 7 cm (2¾ in) long, form compact rosettes. Flowers are bright yellow, solitary, to 1.5 cm (⅝ in) across, on long stems, appearing in the spring from the centres of the rosettes. Bright sun and a well-drained soil are essential. Propagate by division after flowering or in spring.

Muscari armeniacum
LILIACEAE

A bulbous plant, rarely more than 30 cm (12 in) tall, native to Turkey and Bulgaria. It carries 6 – 8 greyish-green, narrow leaves, about 30 cm (12 in) in length, about 6 mm (5⁄16 in) or more wide, appearing in autumn. Flowers, bright blue, about 8 mm (7⁄16 in) long, in terminal spikes, appear in late spring and early summer. Thrives in sun or shade; needs a well-drained, humus-rich soil. Suited to the rock garden. Propagate from seed, directly after harvesting.

Muscari botryoides var. alba
LILIACEAE

A bulbous species, with stems 10 – 15 cm (4 – 6 in) long, found in many parts of central and southern Europe to the Caucasus. Leaves 2 – 4, to 30 cm (12 in) long, to 1 cm (½ in) wide, widest at the tips, greyish-green. Flowers from late spring to early summer, almost globular, to 5 mm (¼ in) long, pure white, in more or less bell-shaped racemes. A useful plant for the rock garden; thrives in slightly moist areas, preferably in sun. Propagate from seed when ripe or in spring.

Muscari neglectum
LILIACEAE

A bulbous species, to 30 cm (12 in) tall, found wild in southern Europe in the Mediterranean region in woods or grassland at altitudes to 2,000 m (6,600 ft). Leaves, 3 – 6 in number, are slender, 3 – 6 mm (³⁄₁₆ – ⁵⁄₁₆ in) wide and 24 cm (9½ in) or more long. Flowers, borne in a dense, terminal raceme in late spring, are deep indigo blue tipped with white, urn-shaped, 4 – 8 mm (³⁄₁₆ – ⁷⁄₁₆ in) long. An ideal plant for the rock garden, set in normal garden soil. Propagates rapidly from seed.

Muscarimia macrocarpum
LILIACEAE

Syn. *Muscari moschatum* var. *flavum*. A bulbous species with a fleshy, perennial rootstock, found wild in Turkey and the Greek islands. Leaves glaucous, long-tapering, to 1.5 cm (⅝ in) wide at the base. Flowers fragrant, yellow, almost tubular in shape, with brownish perianth lobes, borne in dense spikes on stems about 20 cm (8 in) long, in spring. Suited to alpine house culture. Needs a sunny position and an enriched, open soil. Propagate from seed, newly ripened.

Narcissus assoanus
AMARYLLIDACEAE

Syn. *N. juncifolius*. A fairly short, bulbous species, found growing on rocky hill sides in southern Spain and southern France. Leaves very slender, basal, invariably longer than the flower stem, 1 – 2 mm (¹⁄₁₆ – ⅛ in) wide. Flowers appear in late spring, borne terminally 1 – 3 to a stem, bright golden-yellow, the corona more than half as long as the spreading petals, sweetly scented. Needs sun or slight shade and an open, gritty, alkaline soil. After flowering, plants should be allowed to remain dry. Propagate from seed or offsets.

Narcissus bulbocodium var. conspicuus
AMARYLLIDACEAE

This is one of several forms of the popular hoop-petticoat daffodil, to be discovered in many parts of southern Europe and north Africa, usually at high altitudes, in either full sun or partial shade. The dark green, linear, erect leaves of this bulbous plant are scarcely more than 1.5 mm (¹⁄₁₆ in) wide, generally 2 – 4 to a bulb. The graceful, golden-yellow flowers appear in spring, lasting several days. Plant in late summer in well-drained, enriched soil, at a depth of 8 – 10 cm (3 – 4 in). Propagate by seed in autumn.

Narcissus bulbocodium var. nivalis
AMARYLLIDACEAE

A dwarf, bulbous variety, found wild in hills and mountains in Spain, Portugal and western France. Leaves very narrow, almost cylindrical, often prostrate or semi-erect. Flowers appear in early spring on stems 6 – 8 cm (2½ – 3 in) long, golden-yellow, about 2.5 cm (1 in) long, the perianth segments about as long as the corona, and long, prominent styles. Best grown in containers, using a standard potting compost. Keep dry after flowering. Propagate from seed, sown in a gritty loam mixture in autumn, preferably in a cold frame.

Narcissus bulbocodium 'Tenuifolius'
AMARYLLIDACEAE

Apparently an 'improved' form of the species, native to southern Europe and north Africa. This has very slender, filiform leaves, these and the stems to 8 cm (3 in) long. Flowers appear in early spring, bright, almost golden-yellow, the corona narrowly funnel-shaped. Can be grown success-fully outside, either in containers or in a sloping rock garden in sun or partial shade, in a well-drained soil. Propagate from offsets in autumn.

Narcissus cyclamineus
AMARYLLIDACEAE

A comparatively dwarf bulbous species, found in moist areas of northwestern Spain and Portugal. The strap-shaped leaves are bright green, very slender, 10 cm (4 in) or more long, depending where it is planted. The deep yellow, cyclamen-like flowers, about 4 cm (1½ in) long, are borne solitary, the narrow petals sharply reflexed, exposing the slender corona and covering the ovary, appearing in late winter and early spring. Needs shade and well-drained soil. Propagate from seed, freshly harvested.

Narcissus 'Duke of Windsor'
AMARYLLIDACEAE

A rather choice hybrid of seemingly unknown origin. Both leaves and stems are 30 cm (12 in) or more long. A single flower, with white tepals and a large, orange cup, is borne on each erect stem. Of easy culture and recommended for the rock garden. Needs a well-drained, slightly enriched soil in full sun; water freely in growing season. Propagate by division of bulblets at planting time.

Narcissus poeticus
AMARYLLIDACEAE

Commonly known as the pheasant's eye narcissus. A sweetly scented, bulbous species found in moist meadows near the Mediterranean coastline from Spain to Greece. Leaves narrow, strap-like, to about 20 cm (8 in) long. Flowers appear in late spring or early summer on stems about 30 cm (12 in) long, pure white, about 10 cm (4 in) across, with a yellowish-red-edged cup and pointed petals. Needs sun and a moisture-retentive, rich soil. Propagate from offsets when dormant.

Narcissus rupicola
AMARYLLIDACEAE

A dwarf species, sometimes tufted, found growing in rocky terrain in mostly calcareous soil at altitudes to over 2,000 m (6,600 ft) in north and central parts of Spain and Portugal. A dainty plant, with slender green leaves, no more than 3 mm (³⁄₁₆ in) wide. Flowers borne solitary in late spring, deep yellow, slightly scented, about 3 cm (1¼ in) across, the cup about 4 mm (³⁄₁₆ in) deep. Thrives in full sun, in an open, slightly calcareous soil. Propagate from seed, freshly harvested.

Narcissus serotinus
AMARYLLIDACEAE

A low-growing, sweetly scented species native to many parts of southern Europe, found in rocky places on dry hill sides. The flowers, which usually precede the leaves, have spreading white petals, 2 – 3 cm (¾ – 1¼ in) wide, and a shallow yellow cup, borne singly on slender stems, appearing in late autumn. The very slender leaves, about 1 mm (¹⁄₁₆ in) wide, which follow, are rush-like, only 1 – 2 to a bulb. Plant in a gritty, enriched soil, in sun or slight shade; keep almost totally dry during summer, watering once growth becomes apparent. Propagate from seed, freshly harvested.

Narcissus tazetta ssp. aureus
AMARYLLIDACEAE

Also known as 'Soleil d'Or'. A widely distributed plant, which has become naturalized in many parts of southern Europe and north Africa, also in China and Japan. A sweetly scented, bulbous plant with strap-like leaves to 20 cm (8 in) or more long. Flowers, borne in terminal clusters early in the year, are bright yellow with a deep orange cup, about 4 cm (1½ in) across. Well suited to the rock garden, in rich garden soil. Propagate from fresh seed.

Narcissus willkommii
AMARYLLIDACEAE

A perennial bulbous species, native to moist, grassy areas in hilly country in southwest regions of Spain and Portugal. It has very slender, slightly greyish-green leaves, 2 – 3 mm (⅛ – 3/16 in) wide, often forming tufts. Flowers, borne in spring in terminal clusters of 2 – 3 blooms, are deep yellow, to 2 cm (¾ in) across. Ideally suited to the rock garden; plant in moisture-retentive soil. Propagate from seed as soon as it has ripened.

Nassauvia revoluta
COMPOSITAE

A rare, rosette-forming, dwarf species, found in the mountains of Patagonia, South America. Rosettes 5 – 8 cm (2 – 3 in) wide. Leaves greyish-green, somewhat succulent and congested, forming neat columns to 10 cm (4 in) high. Little is known about the flowers, but they are reported to be very small and white, flowering in spring. It would appear to be best potted in an enriched, very porous soil and kept in an alpine house. Propagate by division once flowering is over, or from seed if available.

Nemastylis geminiiflora
IRIDACEAE

A fascinating bulbous plant, widely distributed in the wild in many southern and central states of the USA. It has 2 – 3 basal leaves, about 40 cm (16 in) long, and 2 – 3 cauline leaves, 15 – 30 cm (6 – 12 in) long. Stems have 1 – 4 heads, about 35 cm (14 in) long, bearing spathes of 1 – 2 flowers. These appear in early summer and are bright blue or purplish-blue, the segments obovate, about 3 cm (1¼ in) long, 1.5 cm (⅝ in) wide, opening by day, closing at night. Needs a sunny position and porous, nutritious soil. Grow in an alpine house. Propagate from seed, freshly harvested.

Neohenricia sibbettii
AIZOACEAE

A mat-forming, low-growing, succulent species, found in the wild on rocky hill sides in Orange Free State, South Africa. The bluish-green or greyish-green, fleshy leaves, about 1 cm (½ in) long, 2 – 5 mm (⅛ – ¼ in) thick, are covered with many minute, white tubercles. Flowers, borne in summer on short pedicels to 1.5 cm (⅝ in) long, are whitish, about 1 cm (½ in) across, open at night. Best given alpine house culture, in open, humus-rich soil in sun. Propagate from cuttings or from seed.

Nepeta x faassenii
LABIATAE

A perennial hybrid of N. mussinii crossed with N. nepetella, both of which originated in the Apennines. A freely branching, erect plant, more closely resembling N. mussinii, usually 30 cm (12 in) or more in height. The more or less lanceolate, greenish-grey, downy leaves are to 3 cm (1¼ in) long. Flowers appear in early summer, violet-bluish, each about 1.5 cm (⅝ in) long and freely borne towards the upper parts of the branches. Prefers a bright position and enriched, open soil. Propagate by cuttings in spring.

Nerine bowdenii var. wellsii
AMARYLLIDACEAE

A rare, exotic, bulbous species, originating from high altitudes in the Drakensberg Mountains, South Africa. Leaves, appearing at the same time as the flowers, are glossy green, about 30 cm (12 in) long. Flowers, in late summer, are dusty pink, slightly wavy, the tepals to 7 cm (2¾ in) long, borne in terminal umbels on stems to about 60 cm (24 in) tall. Almost hardy if planted fairly deep in a protected rock garden in rich, open soil. Propagate from seed, freshly harvested.

Nierembergia repens
SOLANACEAE

Syn. *N. rivularis*. A mat-forming plant with slender, subterranean stems, native to Argentina, Uruguay and Chile. Leaves appear almost at soil level, about 3 cm (1¼ in) long, oblong in shape, dull green and standing very erect. The cup-shaped, white flowers are about 3 cm (1¼ in) wide, borne in summer on very short stalks, just overtopping the foliage. Best kept in an alpine house, in a sunny position and in well-drained soil. Propagate by division in spring.

Nigella damascena
RANUNCULACEAE

Commonly known as love-in-a-mist. A medium sized annual species found in rocky and grassy areas at different altitudes in the Mediterranean region. While not generally considered an alpine plant, it is nevertheless useful for the rock garden. Leaves are divided into very slender leaflets, the upper ones in a whorl subtending the flower. Flowers solitary, terminal, white to blue, 4 cm (1½ in) across, in summer. Needs fertile, well-drained soil. Propagate from seed in spring or autumn.

Oxalis adenophylla

O

Odontospermum maritimum
COMPOSITAE

Syn. *Astericus maritimus*. A short, hairy shrublet found in rocky areas near the coast or on inland hill sides in the Mediterranean region. A clustering, almost mat-forming species, with many stems and branches bearing more or less spathulate to obovate stalked leaves. Flowers appear in summer, deep yellow, 3 – 4 cm (1¼ – 1½ in) across, terminally, on short, hairy stems. Well suited to the rock garden, needing sun and a permeable, alkaline soil. Propagate from seed in spring.

Oenothera acaulis
ONAGRACEAE /OENOTHERACEAE

Syn. *O. taraxacifolia*. A fairly hardy, tufted plant, originating from Chile. The leaves very much resemble those of the common dandelion, being hairy and coarsely toothed, forming a rosette shape, but remaining widely spread and semi-prostrate, each leaf to 20 cm (8 in) long. Flowers appear in late spring and throughout much of summer, are white, sometimes very slightly pinkish, cup-shaped, about 8 cm (3 in) across, mainly opening in the evening. Needs sun or slight shade and a rather gritty, enriched soil. Propagate from seed, freshly harvested.

Omphalodes cappadocica
BORAGINACEAE

A tufted species with rhizomatous rootstock, native to Turkey and the Balkans. Leaves oval-heart-shaped, to 9 cm (3½ in) long, on long stalks, dark green, often with incurving margins. Flowers appear in early summer, in terminal clusters, each flower about 8 mm (7/16 in) wide, dark blue with white eye, on stems about 20 cm (8 in) tall. Best suited to alpine house culture; needs partial shade and a rich, well-drained soil. Propagate from seed in spring.

Onira unguiculata
IRIDACEAE

Probably better known as *Herbertia unguiculata*. A dwarf-growing, bulbous plant with soft, plicate, strap-like leaves, 30 cm (12 in) long, 3 – 7 mm (3/16 – 3/8 in) wide, found wild in Brazil and Uruguay. The stem is mostly subterranean, having 1 – 4 spathes. The flowers, which open in early summer, are about 5.5 cm (2¼ in) across, pale violet, the inner segments about 2.5 cm (1 in) long, whitish, with numerous lilac-purplish spots. Very well suited to alpine house culture; needs a permeable soil, enriched with leaf mould. Propagate from seed in spring.

Ononis fruticosa
LEGUMINOSAE

A handsome, dwarf, shrubby plant found in lime-stone areas of Spain and the Pyrenees. It has hairless, rather leathery, trifoliate leaves with stalkless, oblanceolate, finely toothed leaflets. Flowers, bright pink, appear in summer, terminally on branches to 30 cm (12 in) long, lasting several days. Probably best kept in an alpine house; needs bright light and a permeable, calcareous soil. Propagate from seed, sown in spring, temperature 15°C (59°F).

Ononis natrix
LEGUMINOSAE

A dwarf, bushy plant, 40 – 60 cm (16 – 24 in) tall, much-branched, widespread in rocky areas of southern Europe at altitudes to about 2,000 m (6,600 ft). Leaves trifoliate, somewhat sticky, the leaflets often toothed. Flowers, borne in leafy panicles in early summer, are yellow, to 2 cm (¾ in) long, with reddish veins externally. Suited to the rock garden; needs slightly calcareous soil. Propagate from seed in spring.

Ophiopogon planiscapus 'Nigrescens'
LILIACEAE

An evergreen, perennial plant originating from Japan. A somewhat tufted species with purplish, almost black leaves, 20 cm (8 in) or more in length. Flowers appear in late summer, in racemes about 12 cm (5 in) long, white, suffused deep purple. A reasonably hardy plant in southern Britain, perhaps not so elsewhere. Flourishes in an alpine house, in a humus-rich soil, in partial shade. It tends to seed freely after flowering, the deep bluish seed germinating very quickly, temperature 12°C (54°F).

Ophrys lutea
ORCHIDACEAE

A rather dwarf, terrestrial orchid, found wild in rocky or grassy habitats in low mountainous areas of southern Europe. Basal leaves pale green, oval and pointed; stem leaves are short and slender. Flowers, 1 – 2 or more, borne terminally on stems 15 – 30 cm (6 – 12 in) long in late spring; sepals green, petals green or yellowish; 3-lobed lip about 1.5 cm (⅝ in) long with a brown centre and yellow edge. Best kept in an alpine house in orchid compost. Propagate from fresh seed.

Ophrys scolopax ssp. scolopax
ORCHIDACEAE

A most variable species, some varieties being botanically recognized. It occurs in sparse grassy areas at quite low altitudes in southern Europe. An attractive plant, to 45 cm (18 in) tall, with bright green lanceolate leaves arising from the base and slightly smaller ones, which are more pointed, sheathing the flower stem. Spikes carry 3 or more flowers of pink or purplish-pink sepals and a somewhat rounded lip of reddish-brown, with white or yellowish markings, in late spring. Needs a bright position in humus-rich, open soil. Propagate from fresh seed.

Ophrys sphegodes
ORCHIDACEAE

A variable, short to medium sized species with tuberous rootstock, found wild on hills and low mountain slopes in the Mediterranean region. Leaves green, oval-lanceolate, arranged in a basal rosette. Spikes carry 2 – 10 flowers in early spring – petals greenish-purple or brownish-green, velvet lip brown, lobed or unlobed, about 1.2 cm (⁹⁄₁₆ in) long and often as much wide, with H-shaped speculum in lilac-blue or purple. Thrives in an alpine house, in a calcareous soil. Propagate from seed.

Ophrys tenthredinifera
ORCHIDACEAE

A most attractive ground orchid, found from Spain to western Turkey, mainly in rocky or grassy areas. Tuberous-rooted, it varies in height from 10 – 30 cm (4 – 12 in), basal leaves more or less lanceolate, stem leaves narrower. Flowers appear in spring, 3 – 8 to a stem, sepals brilliant pink with green median line, petals triangular, pink, lip yellow with reddish-brown centre area, bluish-white base. Needs sun and rich, open soil. Best kept in an alpine house. Propagate from seed.

Opuntia pulchella
CACTACEAE

A rather choice, low-growing, spreading species found wild in Arizona and Nevada, USA, usually on low mountain slopes among rocks. Joints are cylindrical and rather slender, to 6 cm (2½ in) long, covered with low warts and small, pale yellowish areoles bearing pale spines. Flowers appear during summer, purplish-rose, about 5 cm (2 in) across when fully open, followed by club-shaped red fruits about 2 cm (¾ in) long. Needs to be kept in an alpine house, in a porous, humus-enriched soil. Propagate by stem-joints in summer.

Opuntia schottii
CACTACEAE

A low-growing, spreading, bushy species, found on fairly high mountain slopes in Texas and New Mexico, USA. Plants rarely exceed 20 cm (8 in) high, with club-shaped, greyish-green joints to 7 cm (2¾ in) long, 2 cm (¾ in) thick, with many warts and areoles having whitish glochids and spines to 2 cm (¾ in) long. Flowers appear in summer, bright yellow, about 3 cm (1¼ in) across. Needs alpine house culture in rich, porous soil. Propagate from cuttings or from seed.

Opuntia verschaffeltii
CACTACEAE

A low-growing, clustering species, found wild on low mountain sides in Bolivia. The dull-green, cylindrical stems, to 15 cm (6 in) long and 1.5 cm (⅝ in) thick, bear cylindrical leaves 1 – 5 cm (½ – 2 in) long, these frequently persisting. Areoles have several hair-like spines, to 6 cm (2½ in) long. Flowers, in late summer, are reddish, about 4 cm (1½ in) in diameter. Needs alpine house culture, in normal cactus soil. Propagate by stem cuttings or from newly ripened seed.

Orbea ciliata
ASCLEPIADACEAE

Syn. *Diplocyatha ciliata*. A mat-forming succulent plant from fairly high ground in Karoo region of Cape Province, South Africa. Stems to about 5 cm (2 in) long, 4-angled with pointed 'teeth'. Flowers, in summer, bell- to funnel-shaped with spreading lobes, whitish and pointed, the margins white, hairy. Best kept in an alpine house; needs an enriched, permeable soil. Propagate by stem cuttings or from newly ripened seed.

Orbeopsis lutea ssp. lutea
ASCLEPIADACEAE

Syn. *Caralluma lutea* ssp. *lutea*. A low, branching succulent species, found in many areas of high ground in Botswana, Zimbabwe and South Africa. The branches, 5 – 10 cm (2 – 4 in) long, to 2 cm (¾ in) thick, are 4 -angled, pale green. Flowers, in summer, usually in umbels, 5 – 7 cm (2 – 2¾ in) across, the corolla lobes lance-shaped and tapering, yellowish and densely spotted with red or dark brownish. A plant for the alpine house; needs rich, open soil. Propagate from cuttings.

Orbeopsis lutea ssp. vaga
ASCLEPIADACEAE

Syn. *Caralluma lutea* ssp. *vaga*. A plant found at low to medium altitudes in southwest Africa (Namibia and Angola) and in hilly areas of Cape Province, South Africa. The 4-angled stems, to 10 cm (4 in) high, 2 cm (¾ in) thick, have prominent pointed 'teeth'. Flowers, borne in mid-summer, are basically yellowish but densely spotted with reddish-brown on the broad, pointed lobes. Requires alpine house culture in a humus-rich soil. Propagate from cuttings.

Orchis collina
ORCHIDACEAE

A short, tuberous-rooted perennial orchid, often encountered in the Mediterranean region in grass-lands and rocky places. Basal leaves 2 – 4, broadly oblong, sometimes dark-spotted, formed into a rosette. Stem almost totally sheathed with leaves tinged pale purplish and bracts similarly coloured and veined. Flowers in spring, on a slender spike to about 15 cm (6 in) long, petals and sepals purple or dark olive green, the upper ones forming a hood, lip about 1 cm (½ in), unlobed, purplish-pink. For alpine house culture, in calcareous, gritty soil. Propagate from fresh seed.

Orchis coriophora ssp. fragrans
ORCHIDACEAE

A fairly low-growing species, found in the Mediterranean region of Spain, to altitudes of about 1,000 m (3,300 ft). Leaves long, narrow and pointed, sheathing the stem towards the top. Flowers in early summer; bracts about 1 cm (½ in) long, assembled in short, dense spikes, the hood pointed, composed of brownish-purple sepals and petals, the lip about 8 mm (⁷⁄₁₆ in) with 3 lobes, the centre larger, deep reddish-green or purplish-green, the spur 1 cm (½ in) in length. For alpine house culture in a slightly calcareous soil. Propagate by division or from seed.

Orchis italica
ORCHIDACEAE

A rather slender, perennial orchid, usually found wild in forested areas at low to medium altitudes in much of southern Europe. It has a few wavy-edged, rather lance-shaped leaves, often spotted, and a few sheathed stem leaves. Flowers, in early summer, are borne terminally on stems to 40 cm (16 in) high in dense clusters; sepals and petals pale pink, purple veined, the lip pinkish and spotted purple, with prominent 'arms' and 'legs'. Best kept in the alpine house in rich, open soil. Propagate from seed.

Orchis militaris
ORCHIDACEAE

A tuberous-rooted orchid, to 15 cm (6 in) high, found wild in many parts of Europe, including Britain, generally in moist, wooded places in calcareous terrain. Leaves dark green, unspotted, 1 – 2 sheathing the base of the stem. Flowers in early summer, 20 – 30 or more carried on a slender stem, pinkish or pale purple with darker veining on petals and sepals, these forming the helmet, lip white-tipped and spotted purple, 4-lobed with up-turned ends. Useful for rock garden culture, planted in calcareous soil. Propagate from fresh seed.

Orchis purpurea
ORCHIDACEAE

A variable, tuberous-rooted perennial species, found wild in many parts of Europe, including Britain, also in Asia and north Africa. An erect plant with shiny green, unspotted leaves forming a basal rosette. Flowers in early summer in a dense terminal spike, fragrant, but varying in terms of colour. The purple or maroon hood, 1 – 1.4 cm (½ – ⅝ in) long, composed of petals and sepals, the lip 3-lobed, pink, violet or white, and spotted, the spur short and downward pointing. Suited to the rock garden, in calcareous soil and shade. Propagate from seed.

Orchis ustulata
ORCHIDACEAE

A dwarf, tuberous-rooted species, found widespread in Europe, including Britain, on calcareous hill sides and in wooded areas. Stem 15 – 30 cm (6 – 12 in) long, leafless in the upper part, arising from a rosette of fresh green, unspotted, erect leaves. Flowers borne in a cylindrical head in early summer, white and maroon, the hood rich deep maroon, the lip 4-lobed, white or pale pink, spotted red or purple, the 2 upper lobes widely spreading, the spur 1 – 3 mm (¹⁄₁₆ – ³⁄₁₆ in) long. Can be grown in the rock garden; calcareous soil is essential. Propagate from seed.

Oreosedum album
CRASSULACEAE

Probably better known under its original generic title, *Sedum*. A low-growing, mat-forming species to be found in many parts of western Europe and through to Turkey and Russia, in rocky territory. A variable plant: this is the type species, but many varieties are botanically recognized. The small, green, cylindrical to ovate leaves are compressed into dense 'cushions', to 20 cm (8 in) in diameter, from which emerge clusters of small white flowers, borne on leafy stalks in early summer. Grow in ordinary garden soil in sun or slight shade; can be invasive. Propagate by division in spring.

Oreosedum album ssp. gypsicolum
CRASSULACEAE

A subspecies, found in southern parts of Spain and in Morocco, principally in low mountainous country. In cultivation may be best set within rocks, where it will nestle readily. The rather top-shaped, ovate leaves tend to overlap to form almost elongated rosettes, each leaf about 6 mm (5/16 in) long. The flower stems are also bedecked with leaves and bear loose clusters of white or whitish-pink flowers in late spring and early summer. A gritty, slightly enriched soil will encourage good growth and flowers. Propagate by division.

Origanum amanum
LABIATAE

A compact, tufted, somewhat mat-forming perennial, which grows wild in Anatolia, Turkey. Plants cluster to about 15 cm (6 in) in diameter, the leaves pale green, obovate-lanceolate. Flowers, lilac-pink, have a long flowering season, from midsummer into autumn, borne on short stems in clusters, to 4 cm (1½ in) long, with dark pink bracts subtending the long-tubed blooms. Best suited to alpine house culture, given a sunny position and a permeable, enriched soil. Propagate from seed in early spring.

Origanum amanum var. album
LABIATAE

In almost every respect identical to the species and from the same habitats. The tiny green leaves are set opposite and help to form a dense mat, 8 – 10 cm (3 – 4 in) in diameter. Slender stems carry white flowers in summer, in shape and size similar to the species, somewhat slender trumpet-like. Essentially a subject for the alpine house, needing a very sunny position and enriched garden soil. Can be propagated, with care, by rooted cuttings; otherwise from seed in spring.

Origanum dictamnus
LABIATAE

A small, shrubby plant, to about 20 cm (8 in) or a little more high, native to Crete. The rather wiry stems are bedecked with ovate, almost circular green leaves, white-felted on both surfaces, to 2.5 cm (1 in) long, borne opposite. Flowers appear during much of the summer, with terminal, drooping heads of pink flowers, about 1 cm (½ in) long, set in rose-pink bracts, similar to miniature hops. Needs sun and warmth, so is best grown in an alpine house in a well-drained soil. Propagate from cuttings or seed in spring.

Ornithogalum lanceolatum
LILIACEAE

A low-growing plant with bulbous rootstock, native to Turkey and Lebanon, where it is found in open, mountainous areas to altitudes of 2,000 m (6,600 ft). An attractive dwarf species, which develops a basal rosette of wide, lanceolate, rich green leaves, which frequently remain mostly prostrate or only semi-erect. Flowers appear in racemes during spring, white, to about 2 cm (¾ in) in diameter, marked with a green line lengthwise on each petal. Hardy, but needs a sunny location and a well-drained soil. Propagate from seed when ripe.

Ornithogalum nanum
LILIACEAE

A very dwarf bulbous species, rarely more than 5 cm (2 in) high when in full bloom, found wild in the Balkan region and Italy, generally at low altitudes in grassy areas. Leaves linear, spreading, greyish-green, forming a basal cluster. Flowers about 1.5 cm (5/8 in) across, white with a green median line, borne in a dense terminal cluster. It seems only half-hardy, so best grown in a bulb frame or an alpine house, in a well-drained, fairly rich soil. Propagate from freshly harvested seed.

Ornithogalum saundersiae

LILIACEAE

A robust, bulbous plant, originating from Swaziland and Transvaal, South Africa, at altitudes of about 1,000 m (3,300 ft). It has broad, greyish-green leaves, 60 cm (24 in) or more long, 1.5 cm (⅝ in) broad, soft and strap-like. White flowers, about 2.5 cm (1 in) wide, with a conspicuous dark green ovary, appear in late summer in a somewhat rounded inflorescence. Can be grown in the rock garden, but after flowering must be lifted and stored in a frost-free place; best kept, therefore, in an alpine house, in rich, open soil. Propagate from seed in spring.

Ornithogalum sintenisii

LILIACEAE

An interesting and rather unusual bulbous species, which is found in the wild in northern Iran and neighbouring areas. It has very slender, linear, green leaves, which tend to recurve, often becoming quite twisted. Flowers appear in spring, white with a wide, green band on the underside of each of the 6 petals, 1.5 – 2 cm (⅝ – ¾ in) in diameter, borne on an inflorescence to about 8 cm (3 in) high. Totally hardy, needing as sunny a position as possible and an enriched, open soil. Propagate from ripe seed.

Ornithogalum umbellatum

LILIACEAE

A bulbous species, usually producing many bulbils or offsets, found in low and high altitudes in Spain and north Africa, usually in rocky territory. Plants are short, 8 – 30 cm (3 – 12 in) tall when in flower. Leaves dark green with a whitish median line, about 2 mm (⅛ in) wide. Flowers appear in early summer, pure white with a green band on the back of each tepal, 3.5 cm (1⅜ in) or more wide, in a somewhat flat-topped raceme. Needs bright light and a well-drained soil. Propagate by bulbils when dormant.

Orostachys iwarenge

CRASSULACEAE

Possibly only a form of *O. malacophyllus*, to which this unusual plant from Japan is similar in most respects. An evergreen succulent with dark green, fleshy, farinose leaves formed into a fairly close rosette. Flowers, which, to 1 cm (½ in) in diameter, are produced on a long, cylindrical inflorescence in summer. A rather rare species, needing a slightly shaded position and a soil rich in humus; water and feed during summer but keep scarcely moist in winter. Propagate from ripe seed, freshly harvested.

Orthrosanthes polystachus

IRIDACEAE

Syn. *Sisyrinchium polystachyum*. A rhizomatous rootstock providing a somewhat tufted plant, which originated from Western Australia (Darling and Warren districts). Leaves glabrous, 25 – 60 cm (10 – 24 in) long. Flowers appear in spring or early summer, borne on a stem 45 cm (18 in) or more long, pale blue, several together – 2 – 2.5 cm (¾ – 1 in) long. Only half-hardy, so best kept in an alpine house in a sandy, humus-enriched soil. Propagate from seed, sown in spring.

Oscularia pedunculata

AIZOACEAE

A low-growing, spreading, succulent species, often producing large mats, found wild in Cape Province (Tulbagh, Worcester and Caledon districts), South Africa. Leaves united at the base, triangular, with 2 – 4 reddish teeth along each angle, pale greyish-green, to 1.5 cm (⅝ in) long, 8 mm (⁷⁄₁₆ in) wide. Flowers in summer, sometimes much earlier, pale pink, to 1.5 cm (⅝ in) wide, usually 3 together on short stems. Needs alpine house conditions and an open, humus-enriched soil. Propagate by division or from newly harvested seed.

Oxalis acetosella
OXALIDACEAE

This is the common wood sorrel, which is native to much of Europe, including Britain, through to Japan. It is rhizomatous, barely 10 cm (4 in) high, the leaflets obcordate, to 2 cm (¾ in) long. Flowers are borne solitary, in spring, white with pale purplish veining, about 1.5 cm (⅝ in) long. More often it is var. *rosea* that is seen in cultivation, the flowers being pink with purple veining, and this is less invasive. Thrives best in partial shade in well-drained soil. Propagate by division or from seed in spring.

Oxalis adenophylla
OXALIDACEAE

A tuberous-rooted plant, often concealed by rotted fibrous leaves, native to Argentina and Chile. Many grey-green, much-divided leaves provide a rather tufted plant. Flowers appear from early spring until well into the summer, about 3 cm (1¼ in) in diameter, lilac-pink in colour with a prominent maroon eye. An excellent rock garden plant, equally suited to the alpine house. Best planted in autumn; needs a well-drained soil and a position in full sun. Propagate by division or from seed.

Oxalis articulata
OXALIDACEAE

A low-spreading species, originating from Brazil but now naturalized in many parts of southern Europe, principally on quite high ground. A perennial plant with a short, swollen rootstock but no bulbils. Leaflets, more or less oblong, slightly hairy, are orange-spotted on the undersurface. Flowers, several borne together in terminal umbels in late spring, are purplish-pink, each about 1.5 cm (⅝ in) long. Suitable for the rock garden in enriched soil. Propagate by division or from seed.

Oxalis eckloniana
OXALIDACEAE

A low-growing, tuberous-rooted plant, found wild in many of the more southern regions of South Africa. Leaves are all basal, stalked, trifoliate, bright green. Flowers appear in mid- to late summer, purplish-pink or yellow, borne on a slightly pubescent scape to 10 cm (4 in) long. Can be grown successfully in the rock garden, on sloping ground, in a sunny, sheltered position. Needs a porous soil, enriched with decomposed leaf mould. Propagate from seed or by division in autumn or spring.

Oxalis x 'Ione Hecker'
OXALIDACEAE

This is one of several hybrids that have been produced and that are becoming available to horticulturists and plant enthusiasts. It has proved to be a very successful cross between *O. laciniata* and *O. enneaphylla*, bearing the flowering qualities of both parents. Dull green leaves on short stems are well dissected. Flowers, which appear in late spring and early summer, are pinkish with prominent lines on the petals in deeper shades, 4–5 cm (1½–2 in) wide. Well suited to the alpine house, in bright light. Propagate by division in spring.

Oxalis laciniata
OXALIDACEAE

A tuft-forming rhizomatous species, found wild in Patagonia, South America. It has slender trefoil leaves, bluish-grey, with many wrinkled, narrowly linear leaflets. Flowers appear in early summer, to 4 cm (1½ in) in diameter, deep purplish-blue, sometimes rose-pink, sweetly scented. This dwarf plant, rarely more than 5 cm (2 in) high when in flower, is best grown in an alpine house in a humus-enriched, open soil, or in the rock garden in a slightly shaded position on sloping ground. Propagate by division or from seed.

Oxalis lobata
OXALIDACEAE

A low-growing, tuberous-rooted species, originating from high altitudes to about 2,000 m (6,600 ft) in South America, particularly Chile. Rarely more than 6 cm (2½ in) high when in bloom. Deep green leaves, to about 1 cm (½ in) in diameter, are divided into obovate leaflets. Flowers, bright yellow, appear in autumn, always solitary, about 1.5 cm (⅝ in) in diameter. Best kept in an alpine house, because it could be easily damaged by frost. Needs a sunny position and a fairly rich, permeable soil. Propagate by division or from seed in spring.

Oxalis obtusa
OXALIDACEAE

A low-growing plant with a small tuberous rootstock, native to Cape Province, South Africa. Leaves form something of a rosette shape, green or greyish-green, divided into 3 notched leaflets. This beautiful species has rich pinkish flowers, 2.5 cm (1 in) across, with deeper veining and a yellowish throat, making an impressive display over several weeks in early summer. It cannot be considered totally hardy, so is best kept in an alpine house, in full sun and an open, humus-enriched soil. Propagate by division or seed.

Oxalis pes-caprae
OXALIDACEAE

Syn. *O. cernua*. Commonly known as the Bermuda buttercup. A small, bulbous, perennial species, originating from South Africa but naturalized around the world. Plants to about 30 cm (12 in) high when in flower. Leaves bright green, mainly trifoliate, the leaflets to 2 cm (¾ in) long. Flowers appear in spring and summer in terminal umbels, bright lemon yellow, about 2.5 cm (1 in) long. Will flower in sun or shade; needs a permeable, humus-enriched soil. Best grown in an alpine house. Propagate by division in autumn.

Oxalis versicolor
OXALIDACEAE

A low-growing, cushion-forming species from Cape Province (Clanwilliam to Peninsular and Caledon districts), South Africa. It has leafy stems about 10 – 20 cm (4 – 8 in) long, with deep green leaves to 2 cm (¾ in) long, divided into 3 slender, lanceolate leaflets. Flowers are produced in summer, white or yellow with deep reddish-purple margins. It is scarcely half-hardy, so is best kept in an alpine house; needs a porous soil enriched with leaf mould. Propagate by division of the rhizomes or from seed in spring.

Oxytropis lambertii
LEGUMINOSAE

A low-growing, stemless species found wild in mountainous areas in southwest and west Texas, USA. It has long leaves, about 20 cm (8 in) in length, divided into leaflets, ovate to linear with pointed tips, coated with silvery silky hairs. Flowers purple or rose-purple, rarely white, 2 – 3 cm (¾ – 1¼ in) long, in racemes just over-topping the foliage, produced in summer. Very useful for the rock garden, grown in a well-drained soil in bright light. Propagate from seed in spring, temperature about 15°C (59°F).

Primula forrestii

P

Pamianthe peruviana
AMARYLLIDACEAE

A choice species from the Andes, in north Peru and southern Ecuador, from both temperate and tropical zones. It develops a clump of very slender leaves, about 18 cm (7½ in) long. Flowers, borne in a terminal umbel in early spring on a stem about 50 cm (20 in) long, are white, each about 20 cm (8 in) across, the segments having a pale yellowish-green median line. For alpine house culture. Propagate from fresh seed.

Paronychia capitata
CARYOPHYLLACEAE

A very low-growing, mat-forming species, widespread throughout most of the Mediterranean region on dry hill sides (as shown). The spreading branches have small, paired, lance-shaped leaves, about 1 – 6 mm (1⁄16 – 5⁄16 in) long, the margins edged with stiff hairs. Flowers appear in rounded heads of silvery bracts, longer than the actual flowers. Best kept in an alpine house, in full sun; needs a slightly calcareous soil. Propagate by division.

Patersonia glabrata
IRIDACEAE

A rhizomatous species, native to hilly country in Victoria and New South Wales, Australia, always near the coast. Grass-like leaves about 30 cm (12 in) long, those at the base wider than the upper ones. In late spring to early autumn a slender inflorescence, 8 – 15 cm (3 – 6 in) long, carries silky bracts and bluish-purple flowers, about 6 cm (2½ in) across when fully open. Best cultivated in the alpine house in a rich, porous soil. Propagate by division or from seed.

Patersonia occidentalis
IRIDACEAE

A creeping, rhizomatous species from coastal plains in Western Australia, central Australia and Victoria. Leaves are formed into tufts, about 40 cm (16 in) long, very tough and rigid. Flowers, in summer, 1 – 3 to a spikelet, each 4 – 5 cm (1½ – 2 in) in diameter, pale blue or lilac-blue, with white throat, outer segments to 3.5 cm (1⅜ in) long, 2 cm (¾ in) wide, inner segments minute. A half-hardy plant, best grown in a pot in an alpine house, in humus-rich, open soil, although if given a sheltered position it may prove hardy. Propagate by division or from seed.

Patersonia sericea
IRIDACEAE

A rhizomatous plant from high ground in eastern regions of Australia and Tasmania, mostly in partially wooded areas. Leaves are stiff, pilose, 20 – 40 cm (8 – 16 in) long. Flower stem is much shorter than the leaves, with bracts coated with deciduous, brownish, silky wool. Flowers borne in early summer, in clusters, rich purple or deep blue; outer segments to 3 cm (1¼ in) long, ovate and somewhat truncate; inner segments minute. Alpine house culture is advised; needs an open, rich soil. Propagate from seed, freshly harvested.

Pelargonium australe
GERANIACEAE

A short, shrubby-stemmed species, found widespread in Tasmania, New Zealand and parts of Australia, to about 30 cm (12 in) high. Leaves cordate, slightly lobed and bluntly crenate, 3 – 8 cm (1¼ – 3 in) wide, softly hairy, dark green. Flowers pink and white, borne in stalked umbels in summer, 4 – 12 flowers to an umbel, petals 6 – 8 mm (5⁄16 – 7⁄16 in) long, marked with deep rose or purplish veining. Essentially a plant for the alpine house, in full sun or partial shade. Needs an open, humus-enriched soil. Propagate by cuttings or from fresh seed.

Pelargonium incrassatum
GERANIACEAE

A tuberous, tufted, perennial species, found in Namaqualand, Cape Province, South Africa, to about 20 cm (8 in) high when in flower. Leaves glabrous, deeply pinnatifid, slightly fleshy, the leaflets lobed. Stem simple or branched, bearing terminal umbels of cerise or magenta flowers with darker streaks, in late spring and summer. A choice plant for the alpine house; needs equal parts of loam, peat and sharp sand. Propagate by cuttings or from freshly harvested seed.

Pelargonium lobatum
GERANIACEAE

A tuberous-rooted plant, which forms tufts – a perennial, only 7 cm (2¾ in) tall, introduced from Cape Province (Picketberg, Peninsular to Humansdorf), South Africa. Leaves cordate at base, then tripartite, the lobes having crenate margins. Flowers black-brown with yellow base and margins, appearing in early summer. Needs to be grown in an alpine house, in a porous soil enriched with leaf mould, with careful watering at all times. Propagate by cuttings or from freshly harvested seed.

Pelargonium violarium
GERANIACEAE

Syn. *P. tricolor*. A tuberous-rooted species, found wild near Ladysmith, Natal, South Africa. It has a short stem, branching, the branches short and spreading. Leaves lanceolate with dentate margins. Flowers appear in early summer in umbels of 2 – 3, the upper petals dark red, veined black, the lower white, sometimes suffused red. Rarely exceeds 15 cm (6 in) in height when in flower. A choice subject for alpine house culture; needs a peaty soil with a little loam and leaf mould added, plus fine, gritty sand. Propagate by division or from seed.

Penstemon davidsonii
SCROPHULARIACEAE

Syn. *P. menziesii*. A variable, mat-forming, low, shrubby species from British Columbia, Canada, and Oregon, USA. To about 15 cm (6 in) tall, with woody stems bearing grey-green entire, elliptic or obovate leaves, somewhat fleshy, about 1 cm (½ in) long, occasionally slightly toothed. Flowers, in summer, violet-purple or deep pink, 3 – 4 cm (1¼ – 1½ in) long. A sunny position is important and a permeable, enriched soil. Propagate by cuttings in spring.

Penstemon fruticosus
SCROPHULARIACEAE

Syn. *P. crassifolius*. An erect subshrub, 20 cm (8 in) or more high, found in Oregon, USA, and British Columbia, Canada. Leaves more or less lanceolate, to about 5 cm (2 in) in length, mostly entire, but sometimes toothed. Flowers appear in summer from towards the upper part of the stems, rather tubular in shape, with outward-spreading tips to the petals, to 4.5 cm (1¾ in) long, pale purplish or lavender coloured. A very bright position and well-drained soil are essential. Propagate from seed in spring.

Penstemon glaber
SCROPHULARIACEAE

Syn. *P. gordonii*. A perennial species, which has become confused because several hybrids have developed, originating from North Dakota to Nebraska, USA. Plants attain 30 cm (12 in) or more in height, the stems bearing lanceolate to oblanceolate green leaves, 10 cm (4 in) or more long. Flowers, in summer, bluish-purple, about 3 cm (1¼ in). Other colours – shades of red and blue – are most likely to be of hybrid origin. A bright, sunny position and well-drained soil are essential. Propagate from seed in spring.

Penstemon hirsutus 'Pygmaeus'
SCROPHULARIACEAE

An evergreen, shrubby species, originating from the USA, rarely exceeding 10 cm (4 in) in height. Leaves dark green, more or less oval in shape, with pointed tips. Flowers are at their best in summer – tubular in shape, lipped, hairy, white, flushed blue or purplish on the outer surface. Reasonably hardy, ideally suited for rock garden culture, on slightly sloping ground in a well-draining, humus-enriched soil. Propagate by division or from seed, temperature 15 °C (59 °F).

Penstemon pinifolius
SCROPHULARIACEAE

A fairly low-growing species, native to North America. Generally 20 – 30 cm (8 – 12 in) high when in full bloom, with very slender leaves, which develop into quite dense clusters. Flowers appear throughout much of the summer, scarlet, about 2 cm (¾ in) long, tubular in shape, widely opening at the tips, borne in racemes on elongating greenish stems. Needs a sheltered position in as sunny a place as possible, and a very porous soil. Best suited to an alpine house. Propagate from seed, freshly harvested.

Penstemon virens
SCROPHULARIACEAE

A shrubby species, to about 45 cm (18 in) high, native to North America. In general, leaves are arranged opposite along the rather short flower stems, invariably subtending several clusters of blue flowers, which are set at intervals along their length, appearing in summer. Late spring is the best planting season; needs a sunny position with good drainage, and a soil enriched with decayed manure or leaf mould. Propagate by division in spring.

Petrophytum caespitosum
ROSACEAE

A densely tufted species, cushion-forming, found in mountainous regions of northwest America. Tufts are composed of small greenish leaves coated with fine silky hairs. Small white flowers, carried on short stems, appear in summer in dense racemes to 15 cm (6 in) long. A hardy plant for the rock garden, needing partial shade and a slightly acid, well-drained soil. Propagate by cuttings after flowering or from freshly ripened seed.

Petrophytum hendersonii
ROSACEAE

Syn. *Spiraea hendersonii*. An evergreen, shrubby, mat-forming plant, found in the Olympic Mountains of Washington State, USA. The dark bluish-green, oblanceolate leaves, about 2 cm (¾ in) long, become bronzed in winter. Flowers, creamy white and very small, appear in early summer in fluffy racemes, to about 7.5 cm (2⅞ in) long. Needs slight shade and a porous, acid soil. Propagate from freshly harvested seed.

Petrosedum anopetalum
ssp. montanum
CRASSULACEAE

A low-growing, clustering, succulent plant to about 9 cm (3½ in) high or more, with decumbent stems rooting at the nodes, found on low mountain slopes in central and southern Spain. Branches develop from near the top of short stems, densely covered with fleshy, greyish-green leaves to 1.2 cm (⁹⁄₁₆ in) long, directed upwards and set opposite. Flattened heads of many yellow flowers appear in midsummer, on stems to 24 cm (9½ in) long, sparsely leafed. Fairly hardy, but perhaps better accommodated in an alpine house, in porous soil. Propagate from seed or by division.

Petrosedum sediforme
CRASSULACEAE

Syn. *Sedum sediforme*. An evergreen, succulent plant with sturdy, fleshy stems and branches, widespread in southern Spain on hill sides and mountain slopes. Stems may be to 30 cm (12 in) long, the non-flowering branches covered with pale green, semi-elliptic, fleshy and pointed leaves 1.3 cm (⁹⁄₁₆ in) long, arranged in 'ranks'. Flowers, pale greenish-yellow, each about 1 cm (½ in) across, borne on fairly erect stems in terminal heads in summer. Reasonably hardy; a useful plant for the rock garden in a bright position, in porous soil. Propagate by division.

Petunia axillaris
SOLANACEAE

A large-flowering species, often tuft-forming, native to hills in south Brazil and Argentina. Stems 40 – 50 cm (16 – 20 in) or more long. Leaves more or less lance-shaped, to 1 cm (½ in) long, arranged alternate along the stems. Flowers, in summer months, are funnel-shaped, pure white, to about 5 cm (2 in) across, sweetly scented at night. For the garden or alpine house in well-drained, fertile soil and in a sunny position. Propagate from seed.

Phaiophleps nigricans
IRIDACEAE

Better known as *Sisyrinchium striatum*. A fibrous-rooted species, 30 – 60 cm (12 – 24 in) tall, native to Argentina and Chile. Stem erect, narrowly winged, arising from a basal cluster of lanceolate leaves. Flowers in late summer and early autumn, pale greenish-yellow, finely veined with purple and brown, in a lengthy raceme along the stem, tending to multiply freely. Suited to the rock garden in ordinary garden soil with added humus. Propagate by division or from seed.

Phlomis lychnitis
LABIATAE

A small, white-felted, shrubby plant, found on stony hill sides throughout much of the Iberian Peninsula and southern France. Stems eventually reach 60 cm (24 in) or more high. Leaves slender or spatula-shaped, often with small apical teeth, grey upper surface, white-felted beneath. Flowers, yellow, to 3 cm (1¼ in) long, appear in early to midsummer, borne in a series of whorls subtended by oval bracts. Suited to the rock garden in permeable soil and in a sunny position. Propagate by division or from seed.

Phlox bifida 'Starbright'
POLEMONIACEAE

A tufted, rhizomatous species, originating in southern and western regions of the Great Lakes in North America. Plants to about 20 cm (8 in) tall, with linear to lanceolate leaves to 5 cm (2 in) long. Flowers appear in early summer; those of this cultivar are particularly attractive, lavender blue, opening to about 2 cm (¾ in) across, the petals slightly cleft. A plant for the rock garden, in well-drained, humus-enriched soil in a bright, sunny position. Propagate by stem cuttings or from seed in spring.

Phlox borealis
POLEMONIACEAE

A prostrate, mat-forming, evergreen species of uncertain origin, possibly from America. The slender, linear leaves, to 2 cm (¾ in) long, are fairly compacted together. Flowers appear in late spring, pink, lilac or occasionally white, about 2 cm (¾ in) across, on short stems in terminal clusters. An ideal rock garden plant; needs partial shade and a moist, enriched soil. Propagate by division or from seed in spring.

Phlox mesoleuca
POLEMONIACEAE

A low-growing, perennial species, originating from Texas and Arizona, USA. A clump-forming plant with very long, thread-like, linear, dark green leaves up to 12 cm (5 in) in length. Flowers appear in summer, reddish-purple, pink, white or yellow, with a small whitish centre. A very attractive garden plant, particularly for the rock garden, set in a moisture-retentive soil, enriched with thoroughly decomposed leaf mould. Propagate by root cuttings or from seed in spring.

Phlox subulata
POLEMONIACEAE

A mat-forming species, to 1 m (3ft) in diameter, with prostrate stems, found growing wild in the mountains of northeast USA. Evergreen leaves linear, to 2.5 cm (1 in) long. Flowers, borne in late spring, variable in colour – pink and shades of red, rarely white – each about 2 cm (¾ in) wide. Satisfactory plant for the rock garden, given moisture-retentive, enriched soil and partial shade. Propagate by division or from fresh seed.

Phuopsis stylosa
RUBIACEAE

The sole species within the genus, originating from Turkey and northwest Iran, and also recorded in the Caucasus. A clump-forming, rhizomatous plant with many prostrate stems and tiny, very narrow, pointed green leaves in whorls, each leaf to about 2 cm (¾ in) long. Small pink flowers in summer and autumn, to 2 cm (¾ in) long, formed into a dense terminal head, having a rather pungent smell. Needs porous soil and sun. Propagate by division in spring.

Phyteuma comosum
CAMPANULACEAE

Syn. *Physoplexis comosa*. A low-tufted, decumbent species with stems to 15 cm (6 in) long, found wild in the southern Alps, growing in rocky limestone areas. It has tufts of kidney-shaped basal leaves, which are deeply toothed, to 5 cm (2 in) long, and lanceolate stem leaves. Flowers appear in summer, somewhat bottle-shaped, to 2 cm (¾ in) long, pinkish-violet, tipped with even deeper colour, on pedicels 5 mm (¼ in) long. Needs sun and a well-drained, alkaline soil. Propagate from newly ripened seed.

Phyteuma orbiculare
CAMPANULACEAE

A rhizomatous rootstock, from which arise erect stems to over 40 cm (16 in) long, found in mountainous areas of southeastern Europe, the Alps, the Apennines and the Carpathians. Has a basal rosette of cordate-oblong leaves with dentate margins, on long stalks, the leaves short-stemmed, lanceolate. Flowers terminal, deep blue, in a dense head, subtended by greenish bracts, throughout summer. Needs sun and an alkaline, open soil. Propagate from freshly harvested seed.

Phyteuma scheuchzeri
CAMPANULACEAE

A small, clump-forming species, originating from the southern Alps and northern Apennines. It has stems to about 45 cm (18 in) long, erect or rather decumbent. Flowers appear during early to mid-summer, deep blue, in rounded heads 3 cm (1¼ in) in diameter, scarcely overtopping the broadly lanceolate, toothed, dark green leaves. A hardy plant, well suited to the rock garden, requiring a sunny site and a well-drained, humus-enriched soil. Propagate from freshly harvested seed.

Pimelea prostrata
THYMELAEACEAE

Syn. *P. coarctata*. A mat-forming plant, native to New Zealand, formed from numerous small stems and leaves in dense formation. Leaves 3 – 6 mm (³⁄₁₆ – ⁵⁄₁₆ in) long, greyish-green, rather ovate to narrowly oblong in shape. Terminal heads of 3 – 10 waxy white, individual miniature flowers, 3 – 4 mm (³⁄₁₆ in) long, appear in spring and summer. Ideal for the rock garden, probably succeeding best in a lime-free soil and full sun. Propagate by division in spring.

Platycodon grandiflorus
CAMPANULACEAE

The sole species of the genus, a small, clump-forming, variable plant from eastern Asia. Stems erect, 15 – 50 cm (6 – 20 in) or more tall. Leaves arranged alternate, usually in whorls, ovate or lanceolate, to 7 cm (2¾ in) long, with toothed margins. Flowers appear in summer, pale purplish-blue, to 7.5 cm (2 ⅞ in) across, widely bell-shaped, borne solitary or in small clusters. A hardy plant suited to rock garden culture, needing a humus-enriched soil and a sunny site. Propagate by division or from seed in spring.

Pleione formosana
ORCHIDACEAE

Syn. *P. bulbocodioides* 'Blush of Dawn'. A semi-epiphytic plant with pseudobulbs, from forest areas on mountains in China. Pseudobulbs last only one season, new ones appearing annually. Short to medium pale green leaves, 3 – 6 cm (1¼ – 2½ in) wide, encircle the flower stem, these varying in length and width. Flowers, 7 – 10 cm (2¾ – 4 in) wide, in early summer, pale lilac-rose with white, often slightly tinged lilac, labellum. Best grown in an alpine house in a peaty soil. Propagate by division.

Pleione formosana alba
ORCHIDACEAE

Syn. *P. bulbocodioides* 'Alba'. In nearly all respects this is similar to the typical form, the principal difference being the unusual colouring of the flowers, which are a brilliant, pure white. Of easy culture, with rewarding results. Propagation can be achieved by careful removal of the pseudo-bulblets, which often form on the parent pseudo-bulb.

Pleione limprichtii
ORCHIDACEAE

Syn. *P. bulbocodioides* 'Limprichtii'. This is native to western China. The pseudobulb is green, producing its foliage after the flowers have developed. Flowers bright reddish-purple, the almost white labellum streaked and freckled crimson, 8 – 10 cm (3 – 4 in) wide, at their best in spring. Fairly hardy if grown in an enriched peat bed in a sheltered position, out of full sun. Propagate by division.

Pleione pogonioides
ORCHIDACEAE

This is one of several species that have caused confusion in botanical circles, and this plant would seem to be identical to *P. speciosa*, a plant native to China. in spring this carries a long-lasting flower of deep magenta-rose, marked with deeper shades on the white throat – the lip is prominently fringed. This terrestrial species arises from a pseudobulb, producing leaves that prove deciduous. Needs a peaty, fibrous compost, enriched by decomposed leaf mould. A slightly shaded location is advantageous. Propagate by division when replanting.

Polygala calcarea
POLYGALACEAE

A tufted, mat-forming plant, originating in parts of western Europe, including Britain. Small, spathulate green leaves to about 2 cm (¾ in) long, densely clustered. Flowering stem has slender, narrow leaves and a terminal raceme of dark blue flowers, each about 6 mm (⁵⁄₁₆ in) long, during summer. A splendid rock garden plant, requiring slight shade and an open, enriched soil. Propagate by division or from cuttings in late spring.

Polygala chamaebuxus
POLYGALACEAE

A perennial, evergreen, low-growing shrubby plant, native to more central parts of Europe. Plants to 10 cm (4 in) tall, with more or less lanceolate leaves 3 cm (1¼ in) long, arranged alternate. Flowers have white wing sepals, usually solitary or in pairs from the upper leaf axils. In the var. *grandiflora* the wings are purple, nearly 2 cm (¾ in) long, borne in spring and summer. Needs an enriched, porous soil in sun. Propagate from seed or cuttings in spring.

Polygonatum hookeri
LILIACEAE

A somewhat prostrate, tuft-forming species from the Himalayas (Sikkim, Tibet and western China), not exceeding 10 cm (4 in) high. Leaves ovate, arranged alternate, dark green, to 2 cm (¾ in) long. The almost stemless flowers appear in late spring or early summer, solitary, but clustered almost at ground level, lilac-pink, about 1.5 cm (⅝ in) long. Needs a partially shaded position and a rich, permeable soil. Propagate from seed, sown in spring.

Polygonatum odoratum
LILIACEAE

Commonly known as Solomon's Seal. A rhizomatous species, with long, arching stems, native to many parts of Europe and through to Japan. Stems rather angled, to 45 cm (18 in) long, with leaves, 5 – 10 cm (2 – 4 in) long, arranged alternate. Flowers, greenish-white, to 2 cm (¾ in) long, fragrant, borne in summer, either solitary or in pairs. Needs a moist, rich soil and partial shade in the rock garden. Propagate by division or from fresh seed.

Polygonum affine 'Donald Lowndes'
POLYGONACEAE

This is a mat-forming, perennial species, from the Himalayas, with ascending stems to about 30 cm (12 in) high. The more or less erect, oblanceolate leaves are up to 10 cm (4 in) long, becoming significantly reddish-brown in autumn. Flowers appear in autumn, in cylindrical spikes of bright rose-pink. A fine rock garden plant, requiring rich soil and sun. Propagate from seed, sown in spring, or by division in late autumn.

Polygonum tenuicaule
POLYGONACEAE

A rhizomatous perennial species, native to Japan, the spreading rhizomes and small leaves forming mats to about 10 cm (4 in) high. Leaves to 6 cm (2½ in) or more long, arranged alternate, more or less oval in shape. Flowers white, in spring, carried in cylindrical racemes about 3 cm (1¼ in) long on slightly longer stems. Suited to the rock garden or an alpine house; sun and very fertile soil are essential. Propagate from seed, sown in spring.

Polygonum vaccinifolium
POLYGONACEAE

A woody-stemmed, prostrate, deciduous species, originating from the Himalayas. The wiry, trailing stems, bearing small, ovate leaves about 1 cm (½ in) long, with pointed tips, form rather loose mats, and before falling become bronze-coloured. Flowers, bright pink, appear in slender spikes in late autumn. An attractive plant for a sloping rock garden; needs good light and an enriched soil. Propagate from cuttings in late spring or summer.

Portulaca grandiflora
PORTULACACEAE

A well-known species, originating from Brazil, Argentina and Uruguay. It is a semi-prostrate, semi-succulent plant, forming tufts to about 15 cm (6 in) high. Leaves cylindrical, fleshy, to 2.5 cm (1 in) long. Flowers appear in summer and early autumn, red, pink, yellow, white or other shades, 2 – 3 cm (¾ – 1¼ in) across when fully open. A useful plant for the rock garden or border, best on sloping ground; needs ordinary garden soil, enriched with decomposed leaf mould, with gritty sand added. Propagate from seed in spring.

Portulaca quadrifida
PORTULACACEAE

A prostrate or decumbent succulent, forming clusters, found growing wild on rocky mountain slopes in West Australia, Saudi Arabia and the Antilles. The flat, fleshy, more or less lance-shaped leaves, are about 3 cm (1¼ in) long, with woolly axillary hairs. Flowers, borne terminally on leafy stems in summer, are cup-shaped, bright yellow, to 1 cm (½ in) across. Requires the protection of the alpine house and an open, fairly rich soil. Propagate from seed, freshly harvested.

Potentilla cinerea
ROSACEAE

A low-growing, somewhat tufted species found at altitudes to 1,600 m (5,300 ft) in the Alps and Pyrenees in rock crevices. Stems partially erect or trailing, bearing digitate, silvery-green leaves in tufts. Flowers bright yellow, about 1.5 cm (⅝ in) across, appear in summer, solitary or in small clusters. Needs a sunny position and well-drained, slightly enriched soil. Propagate from fresh seed, sown in spring.

Potentilla fruticosa
ROSACEAE

A somewhat shrubby species, which forms woody plants but more often tends to be of creeping habit, well known in the Pyrenees and other areas of northern Europe. Leaves are pinnate, with 5 smooth-edged, elliptic leaflets, smooth above but woolly-hairy on the undersurface. Flowers appear in summer, golden-yellow, about 2.5 cm (1 in) in diameter, and are freely produced. Many hybrids are recorded, all worthy alpines. Best in a partially shaded position and a peaty, loamy soil. Propagate from seed in spring.

Potentilla nepalensis
ROSACEAE

A rather tufted species found in the Himalayas, generally 45 cm (18 in) or a little more tall. The dark greenish, hairy leaves are digitate, the leaflets toothed, 3 – 6 cm (1¼ – 2½ in) long. Flowers appear in summer, opening to about 2.5 cm (1 in) across, bright rose-red. Needs a sunny position and a porous soil, enriched with thoroughly decomposed leaf mould. Propagate from stem cuttings after flowering or from seed in spring.

Pratia purpurascens
LOBELIACEAE

A procumbent, glabrous, perennial species, 35 – 50 cm (14 – 20 in) high, found in the wild in moist, shaded areas, mostly near the coast, in New South Wales, Australia. A rather bushy plant, with bright glossy leaves with slightly dentate margins. Flowers appear in summer or autumn, bluish to lilac, borne terminally on slender stems. Essentially a plant for the alpine house; needs slight shade, but warmth, and a moisture-retentive, humus-enriched soil. Propagate from freshly harvested seed, temperature 15°C (59°F).

Primula allionii 'Anna Griffith'
PRIMULACEAE

This is considered to be of hybrid origin, even though it was discovered growing wild in the Alps. A cushion-forming plant, composed of many rosettes of slightly sticky green leaves, 3 – 4.5 cm (1¼ – 1¾ in) long, somewhat lance-shape. Flowers very pale, slightly lilac-pink, with notched petals, emerging on short stems from the toothed foliage in spring. Best treated as an alpine house plant; needs good light and a free-drained, slightly enriched soil. Propagate by division.

Primula allionii 'Crowsley'
PRIMULACEAE

A particularly deep coloured form of the species, which grows wild in the Maritime Alps. Leaves broadly spathulate, slightly sticky but soft and hairy, forming close rosettes. Flowers appear in spring, exceptionally bright, rich pink, about 2.5 cm (1 in) across, carried on very short scapes, almost hiding the foliage below. A beautiful plant for the alpine house; needs partial shade and an open, alkaline soil. Propagate by division in summer.

Primula allionii 'Praecox'
PRIMULACEAE

An early flowering cultivar, possibly the earliest, appearing in early to midwinter, so best given the protection of the alpine house. Leaves dark green, slightly dentate margins, formed into small rosettes. Flowers somewhat variable, bright lilac-pink or pale violet-pink, 2.5 cm (1 in) or little more across, with a neat, quite prominent white eye. Requires bright sun or slight shade, and a rather gritty, alkaline soil. Propagate by division.

Primula allionii 'William Earle'
PRIMULACEAE

A cushion-forming cultivar composed of several rosettes of rather dark green, obovate leaves with very slightly toothed edges. Flowers appear from early spring to early summer, carried singly and terminally on short stems, rich purplish-pink, about 2.5 cm (1 in) in diameter, with a clear, pure white eye, the petals being broadly wavy-edged. Best kept in an alpine house, primarily because it resents wet conditions in winter. Use a gritty soil, enriched with lime and humus. Propagate by division.

Primula auricula 'Haysom'
PRIMULACEAE

One of the comparatively few cultivars of which the petals have greyish edges. Leaves green with serrated margins, finely mealy coated, more or less rounded in shape. Flowers borne terminally on erect stems in spring, 2 cm (¾ in) or more wide, having a black background and densely coated with greyish meal, and a prominent centre 'cup'. Comparatively hardy, but best protected against excessive rain; needs a sunny position and a well-drained soil. Propagate by cuttings in sandy soil in summer.

Primula auricula 'Woodstock'
PRIMULACEAE

This is representative of cultivars of which the flowers are edged in green. Leaves deep green and not mealy coated, about 10 cm (4 in) long, more or less obovate. Flowers carried terminally in spring on thickish stems, somewhat cup-shaped, having a black background colour, with green lobes edged with a paler shade of green, the golden-yellow centre encircled by a thick ring of pure white. Perhaps best suited to alpine house culture. Requires a well-drained, slightly enriched soil, in slight shade. Propagate by cuttings.

Primula auriculata
PRIMULACEAE

A rhizomatous species, widely distributed in the Caucasus and south to Turkey and Iran. Leaves are dark green, more or less tongue-shaped, and slightly crinkled. The flower stems vary considerably in height, bearing compact, terminal clusters of reddish-purple, deep crimson or pale mauve flowers with a distinctive yellow centre. Suited to outdoor culture in a bright, but sheltered position and in an enriched, open soil. Propagate from seed in spring.

Primula x 'Beatrice Wooster'
PRIMULACEAE

A hybrid developed by *P. allionii* x *P.* 'Linda Pope', the latter being a hybrid of *P. marginata*. In many ways similar to *P. allionii*, which is closely and fairly densely cushion-forming. Leaves mid-green, obovate-lanceolate, with slightly jagged edges. Flowers appear during spring on stems about 10 cm (4 in) long, clear pink with a prominent white eye, all flower parts partially farinose. Fairly hardy, but needs protection from rain in winter; needs humus-rich soil. Propagate by division.

Primula elatior
PRIMULACEAE

A fairly tall, hairy-stemmed perennial species, found in woodland clearings (as shown) or grassy areas in central to southern Europe. It has a thick, rhizomatous rootstock and greyish-green, more or less oblong, irregularly dentate leaves, to 15 cm (6 in) or more long. Flowers appear from mid-spring to midsummer, pale to medium yellow with orange throats, to 2.5 cm (1 in) wide, in single-sided clusters. Needs a position in sun or slight shade and an enriched, permeable soil. Propagates readily from seed, sown in early spring.

Primula ellisiae
PRIMULACEAE

A rather fleshy leaved species, found on hill sides in northwest North America. Leaves rather narrow, occasionally slightly farinose, glabrous, formed into loose tufts. Flowers appear in early summer, carried terminally on stems about 15 cm (6 in) or little more long in a rather 1-sided umbel, rich mauve, each lobe having an even deeper purplish-mauve basal blotch. Best suited to alpine house culture; needs sun and a humus-rich soil. Propagate from fresh seed.

Primula farinosa
PRIMULACEAE

A fairly short, herbaceous plant, found in moist grasslands, in peaty soil, on mountain slopes in northern and central Europe at altitudes to 2,500 m (8,200 ft) or more. Has a basal rosette of narrow, oblanceolate leaves, 2 – 10 cm (¾ – 4 in) long, whitish-green above, farinose below, with slightly toothed margins. Flowers appear in summer on mealy stems, in a close terminal cluster, pink or rose-lilac, about 1.5 cm (⅝ in) across, the petals deeply notched. Needs a position in sun and peaty soil. Propagate from seed, sown in spring.

Primula forrestii
PRIMULACEAE

A rather woody-stemmed plant, which originates from western China. Leaves are carried on long stalks, ovate-elliptic, glandular-hairy with a rather coarse surface, 7 – 10 cm (2¾ – 4 in) long. Flowers appear in summer, bright yellow with an orange centre, each about 2 cm (¾ in) across, borne on long stems 30 – 50 cm (12 – 20 in) long. Best suited to the alpine house, needing enriched, peaty, loamy soil and a slightly warm and dry period during winter dormancy. Propagate by division or from seed in spring.

Primula gracilipes
PRIMULACEAE

A rhizomatous plant native to Nepal and Sikkim in the Himalayas and also to Tibet. The toothed, wavy-edged leaves are broadly spathulate and develop into compact tufts. Flowers in winter and spring, so is best kept in an alpine house. The flowers are rich purplish-pink with a whitish ring around the yellow eye, to 3 cm (1¼ in) in diameter, borne singly on very short scapes. Needs good light and a very fertile soil. Propagate by division or from seed in summer.

Primula juliae
PRIMULACEAE

A mat-forming species with rhizomatous root-stock, found wild in the Caucasus. Leaves more or less rounded, with rather crinkled surfaces and coarsely toothed, 2 – 4 cm (¾ – 1½ in) long, on long stalks. Flowers appear in spring, bright red-dish-purple, 2.5 cm (1 in) across, with a yellow centre, borne on short stalks. A position in bright sun or partial shade is recommended and an enriched, porous, but moisture-retentive soil. Propagate from newly harvested seed or by division after flowering.

Primula marginata
PRIMULACEAE

A woody-stemmed species with rhizomatous rootstock, found in rocky regions in the Maritime Alps, usually in calcareous subsoil at altitudes to over 3,000 m (10,000 ft). Rosettes of silvery green, rather fleshy leaves with prominently toothed edges, white mealy on the undersurface, provide a loose basal structure. The erect flower stem carries a dense head of 15 or more pinkish-violet, rarely whitish flowers, 2.5 cm (1 in) across, in early summer. Best suited to the alpine house; needs sun and an enriched, porous soil. Propagate by division.

Primula marginata 'Coerulea'
PRIMULACEAE

This very attractive form of the species has particular charm. A clump-forming plant, often to 15 cm (6 in) high when in bloom, possibly native to the southwest Alps. Leaves lanceolate to obovate, to 9 cm (3½ in) long, the margins toothed and white farinose. Flowers rather funnel-shaped, bright blue, to 2.5 cm (1 in) across, with a white eye, in terminal clusters in spring. Best grown in pots in an alpine house, in a gritty, enriched soil. Propagate by division soon after flowering.

Primula marginata 'Holden Clough'
PRIMULACEAE

This is one of several forms of the species that originates from the Maritime Alps. It has lanceolate to obovate, toothed, greyish-green leaves, heavily powdered, 8 – 10 cm (3 – 4 in) long. Flowers, about 2.5 cm (1 in) wide, appear in spring, bluish, in terminal umbels on rather short stems. An excellent subject for either rock garden or alpine house; needs enriched, permeable soil. Propagate by careful separation of leafy rosettes after flowering.

Primula 'Miniera'
PRIMULACEAE

This is one of the many hybrids of *P. allionii*, the other parent possibly being *P. marginata*. A low-growing plant, forming quite compact cushions of many tiny rosettes composed of greyish-green obovate-lanceolate leaves with toothed edges. Flowers appear in spring, bright rose-pink with whitish throat, the flower petals generally wavy-edged, each flower 2.5 cm (1 in) or more in diameter. Best kept in an alpine house. Needs bright light and a slightly alkaline, porous soil. Propagate by division.

Primula palinuri
PRIMULACEAE

An unusual plant with rhizomatous rootstock, found on limestone hill sides in southern Italy. Leaves narrowly spathulate, bright green, with serrated edges, forming rosette-like tufts. Flowers appear in late spring or early summer, deep yellow, in 1-sided umbels, on stems 20 cm (8 in) long. A desirable plant for the alpine house; needs a sunny position and a calcareous soil. Propagate from seed.

Primula x pubescens alba
PRIMULACEAE

Syn. *P. helvetica* 'Alba'. One of several hybrid plants, in many colours, developed from crosses between *P. auricula* and *P. rubra*. Leaves are usually farinose, more or less lance-shaped. The quite large white flowers of this hybrid, which appear in late spring, are possibly the most unusual of all: they are borne in clusters, each flower 2 – 2.5 cm (¾ – 1 in) wide. Best suited to the alpine house. Propagate from freshly harvested seed.

Primula x pubescens 'Joan Gibbs'
PRIMULACEAE

A cultivar of the hybrid between *P. auricula* and *P. rubra*, exemplifying its parentage and most probably an improved form. Plants, 10 – 15 cm (4 – 6 in) high, develop clumps to about 20 cm (8 in) in diameter. Leaves pale green with dentate, often in-rolled, margins. Flowers deep purplish-red with a gold centre, appearing in spring. Needs a free-draining soil, enriched with humus, and a reasonably sunny position. Propagate by stem cuttings in sandy soil in summer.

Primula rosea
PRIMULACEAE

A large-flowered species, its origin uncertain but possibly found wild in the Himalayas. The toothed leaves are about 20 cm (8 in) long, obovate to oblanceolate. Length of flower scapes from 5 –15 cm (2 – 6 in). Flowers appear in early summer, about 2 cm (¾ in) wide, rose-pink with a yellow throat. Best kept in an alpine house; needs full sun and a porous, enriched soil. Propagate from fresh seed.

Primula scotica
PRIMULACEAE

A tiny, tuft-forming species of considerable rarity, native to more northern parts of Scotland. It has linear, rather spoon-shaped leaves to 5 cm (2 in) long. Flowers appear in summer, borne on stems to 10 cm (4 in) long, dark purple with a yellow or whitish throat, to 8 mm (⁷⁄₁₆ in) across, usually in small, terminal heads. Plants tend to die after 2 – 3 years but can be propagated from seed sown in spring. Benefits from bright light and an enriched, open soil.

Primula sieboldii 'Snowflake'
PRIMULACEAE

The type species is of Japanese origin. Leaves oblong-cordate, about 7 cm (2¾ in) long, the edges finely crenate. Flowers, pure white, almost 3 cm (1¼ in) in diameter, appear in early summer on scapes about 20 cm (8 in) tall – deserving of its title. Thrives in sun or slight shade; needs an enriched, open soil. Propagate by division after flowering, or from seed if hand-pollination of the flowers has been undertaken.

Primula veris
PRIMULACEAE

The cowslip. A well-known plant, found wild in many parts of Europe, including Britain, and also in western Asia. Leaves 5 – 15 cm (2 – 6 in) long, often pubescent on the upper surface, grey or whitish below, ovate-oblong in shape. Stems vary in length, often 15 cm (6 in) or more, bearing bright yellow flowers with orange-yellow dots at the base of the lobes, always sweetly scented, in spring. Well suited to the rock garden or general garden use. Best planted in rich, porous but moisture-retentive soil, in sun or partial shade. Propagate by division or from seed.

Primula verticillata
PRIMULACEAE

A rather tender species, early flowering, a native of Arabia. It has plain green, lanceolate leaves, 6 cm (2½ in) or more long, the margins irregularly toothed. Terminal whorls of many bright golden-yellow and fragrant flowers on leafy, elongating stems in early spring. Plants form clumps about 20 cm (8 in) in diameter and to 30 cm (12 in) high. Best kept in an alpine house and given the best light possible. Use a free-draining soil, such as John Innes No. 2. Propagate by division or from seed.

Primula 'Viscountess Byng'
PRIMULACEAE

One of the several hybrids of *P. allionii*. It has rosettes of broadly spathulate, slightly sticky leaves with toothed margins, which gradually form fairly compact cushions. Flowers, about 2.5 cm (1 in) across, appear in early spring, borne singly on short stems, rich purplish-pink with a white eye, contrasting with the attractive greyish-green foliage. Fairly hardy, but alpine house culture is, nevertheless, recommended. Needs a gritty soil with lime and leaf mould added, and a fairly sunny site. Propagate by division.

Prunella hyssopifolia
LABIATAE

A stiffly erect, hairy or hairless species found in central and eastern parts of Spain and southern France, principally in rocky limestone regions. Leaves linear-lanceolate to elliptic-lanceolate, totally stalkless. Flowers are borne in summer in quite dense clusters at the tips of the stems, violet or pinkish-violet, rarely white, each 1.5 – 2 cm (⅝ – ¾ in) long, 12 – 20 or more, providing an attractive cluster, each cluster subtended by leaves. Needs sun and an alkaline soil. Propagate by division in spring or autumn.

Pseudogaltonia clavata
LILIACEAE

A bulbous species, often 15 cm (6 in) or more in diameter, found wild in southwestern Africa and Angola. Leaves lanceolate, to about 10 in number, to 30 cm (12 in) or more long, 6 – 9 cm (2½ – 3½ in) wide. Flowers are borne in autumn on an inflorescence 45 cm (18 in) or more long, in a terminal raceme, white, funnel-shaped, slightly pendent, on pedicels about 3 cm (1¼ in) long. Needs protection, so is best kept in an alpine house in a fairly rich, permeable soil. Propagate from fresh seed, temperature 15°C (59°F).

Psoralea bituminosa
LEGUMINOSAE

A low-growing, leafy plant, found in many parts of the Mediterranean region, particularly Portugal and Spain. Leaves are dark green, trifoliate, and when crushed have a strong smell of tar. Rounded heads of bluish-violet flowers, 1 – 2 cm (½ – ¾ in) in diameter, are terminally borne on leafy stems, in summer. Suitable for a sunny but protected site outside or for alpine house culture. Best grown in a permeable, rather rich soil. Propagate from seed sown in early spring, temperature 12°C (54°F).

Pteridophyllum racemosum
PAPAVERACEAE

The sole species of the genus. A tufted, rosette-forming plant from woodlands in Japan. The rosette is composed of deeply cut, pinnate, almost fern-like leaves. Flowers are white, very small, 4-petalled, somewhat cup-shaped, freely borne in summer on stems 15 cm (6 in) or more long, in racemes. Plants require a shady position in humus-rich soil. Suited to alpine house culture. Propagate from seed, sown immediately it is harvested.

Pterocephalus perennis
DIPSACEAE

Syn. *P. parnassi*. Low-growing, mat-forming plants found in mountainous and rocky regions of Greece and Albania. It has short, prostrate stems with velvety-grey, hairy, club-shaped leaves, 2 – 5 cm (¾ – 2 in) long, usually with crenate margins. Flower heads are similar to *Scabious*, 3 – 4 cm (1¼ – 1½ in) wide, with small pink or purplish-mauve tubular florets, borne in summer on short stalks, just topping the foliage. Needs sun and well-drained, rich soil. Propagate from seed, freshly harvested.

Pterocephalus pinnardii
DIPSACEAE

Low, mat-forming plants originating from rocky mountain slopes of Anatolia, Turkey. Similar in many ways to *P. perennis* but differing principally because of the very attractive, silvery grey-greenish leaves, which form a quite dense cluster at almost ground level. Flowers pink to pale purple, united in a compact, dense head about 3 cm (1¼ in) in diameter, in late summer. Needs sun and well-drained soil. Propagate from seed or by careful division in spring.

Pterodiscus speciosus
PEDALIACEAE

A low-growing, semi-succulent plant, to about 15 cm (6 in) high, found at fairly high altitudes in mountains of southwest Africa (Angola) and Transvaal, South Africa. The caudex, to about 6 cm (2½ in) in diameter, is partly subterranean. Usually a solitary stem bears several linear-oblong, dark green leaves with dentate edges, to 6 cm (2½ in) long, 1 cm (½ in) wide. In summer pinkish-red flowers, about 4 cm (1½ in) long, appear. Needs alpine house culture; keep dry in winter. Propagate from seed.

Pterostylis nutans
ORCHIDACEAE

Known in Australia as the nodding greenhood. A rather dainty orchid, 23 – 30 cm (9–12 in) high, found wild throughout most of the eastern regions of Australia. It develops a small rosette of 3 – 4 more or less short lanceolate leaves. Flowers appear during summer, borne singly at the apex of the stem, prominently bent and curved over, the hood pale green, the lower sepals narrow, sometimes bulging, the lip brownish and curved. For alpine house or orchid house culture; grow in an orchid compost. Propagate from seed.

Pulicaria dysenterica
COMPOSITAE

The common fleabane. A softly hairy, stoloniferous perennial species, with erect, branching stems, found wild in many parts of the Mediterranean region, mostly in moist areas. It has oblong basal leaves, which quickly wither before flowering. Stem leaves are more arrow-shaped, clasping the stem, all green above, grey-downy on the underside. Flowers, golden-yellow, appear in late summer and autumn, borne terminally in flower heads up to 3 cm (1¼ in) wide, in clusters, the flower bracts downy. For rock garden culture in ordinary garden soil. Propagate from seed.

Pulmonaria officinalis
BORAGINACEAE

A low-growing plant, rarely exceeding 15 cm (6 in) in height, found wild in many parts of Europe, including Britain. Leaves broadly ovate, green with whitish blotches and bristly hairs, to 15 cm (6 in) or a little more long. Flowers in early summer, reddish to pale purple, about 2 cm (¾ in) long, borne in terminal, branched clusters. Can be used to advantage in the garden, especially the rock garden, in a shady position, in ordinary garden soil. Propagate from seed in spring.

Pulsatilla alpina
RANUNCULACEAE

A most beautiful, free-flowering, anemone-like species from mountainous regions of Europe, from Spain to the Caucasus. The rather fern-like, stiff, hairy leaves surround the sturdy base of the plant and are also apparent in whorls on each flower stem. Flowers appear from early summer, solitary, pure white, 5 cm (2 in) or more in diameter, followed invariably by masses of feathery, fluffy, silver seeds. Plants require a rather calcareous, open soil, enriched with humus, and sun. Propagate from seed, sown when ripe, but flowering may take several years.

Pulsatilla vulgaris
RANUNCULACEAE

Commonly known as the pasque flower, this popular species is found in many parts of Europe, including southern England, on chalk hill sides. Leaves are rather fern-like and encourage the formation of attractive tufted plants. Flowers are mainly purple, but other colours are known, each 5 – 8 cm (2 – 3 in) long, at their best during spring, then followed by prominent, silky seed heads. An alkaline soil is recommended, and a fairly bright position where they are likely to be undisturbed, for this is resented! Propagate from seed, freshly harvested.

Pulsatilla vulgaris ssp. grandis
RANUNCULACEAE

The pasque plant. A tufted species, widely distributed throughout much of Europe, including Britain, more frequently in calcareous regions. leaves rough, hairy, pinnate, the leaflets generally bipinnate. Scapes erect, about 30 cm (12 in) tall, bearing deep rich violet flowers, larger than those of the species in late spring or early summer. A rich, well-drained soil and sun are essential. Propagate from newly ripened seed.

Puschkinia scilloides
LILIACEAE

Syn. *P. libanotica*. Commonly known as the striped squill. A small, bulbous species, originating from western Asia. The rather slender, channelled leaves, up to 15 cm (6 in) long, are all basal. Flowers open in early spring, borne in racemes on scapes about 15 cm (6 in) tall, pale to deep blue or white, about 1.5 cm (⅝ in) wide when fully open, each petal with a deeper coloured median line. Needs slightly moist, permeable soil and sun. Propagate from seed.

Rubus arcticus

R

Raffenaldia primuloides
CRUCIFERAE

A tuft-forming plant, originating from north Africa (Morocco and Algeria), the main centre being the Atlas Mountains. Leaves slender, dark green with dentate margins, arranged in a somewhat ragged cluster. Flowers appear in summer, bright yellow, borne on stems to about 8 cm (3 in) long, continuing over quite a long period. Needs sun and a very porous soil – best in a mixture of equal parts loam, decomposed leaf mould and sharp, gritty sand. Propagate from seed sown in late spring.

Ramonda myconi
GESNERIACEAE

A stemless perennial plant, found in rocky terrain in wooded mountainous areas of northeastern Spain, including much of the Pyrenees, at altitudes to 1,800 m (6,000 ft). Forms a flat rosette of hairy, wrinkled leaves about 5 cm (2 in) long, these being somewhat rounded with prominent, crenate margins, borne on short stalks – the lower surface has orange-coloured hair, while the upper surface has short white hairs. Flowers appear in summer, in violet shades, to 4 cm (1½ in) across. Needs a calcareous soil, in semi-shade. Propagate from seed.

Ranunculus ficaria
RANUNCULACEAE

This is a tuberous-rooted, rather tufted perennial species, generally found in moist meadows in many parts of Europe, including Britain, and also in north Africa. Leaves cordate, dark green, fleshy, bluntly angled. The cultivar shown, 'Collarette', has deep yellow flowers, about 3 cm (1¼ in) in diameter, in late spring or early summer. Very suitable for the rock garden, in ordinary garden soil enriched with decomposed leaf mould. Propagate from seed in spring or by division.

Ranunculus gramineus
RANUNCULACEAE

Sometimes known as the grass-leafed buttercup. A clump-forming species, found growing wild on hills and mountains in rocky and grassy areas of southwest Europe. Its common name derives from the grass-like basal leaves, 30 cm (12 in) or a little more long. Flowers yellow, 2 – 3 cm (¾ – 1¼ in) across, produced terminally during summer. Suitable for the garden, and can be an added attraction in a rockery area. Succeeds in ordinary garden soil, especially if gritty sand and humus are added. Propagate from seed in spring.

Raoulia australis
COMPOSITAE

A flat, mat-forming species, originating from New Zealand, which spreads very freely to cover quite substantial areas. Spoon-shaped leaves with silvery grey tips, 2 mm (¹⁄₁₆ in) long, densely clustering together. Flowers in summer, yellow, in heads 4 – 5 mm (³⁄₁₆ – ¼ in) wide. Needs a moisture-retentive but open, enriched soil plus full sun for successful culture, and is best kept in an alpine house. Propagate by division or from seed in spring.

Reichardia tingitana
COMPOSITAE

An annual, low-growing species found growing in rocky areas (as shown) in many parts of southern Europe and north Africa. (Although considered an annual, it does sometimes prove to be perennial.) Green, oblong, pinnately lobed leaves, wide-spreading, almost rosette-like, with long stalks arising from the base, bear solitary, terminal, bright yellow flowers, to 2.5 cm (1 in) across in late spring. Needs sun and an open soil, which is slightly alkaline. Propagate from seed in spring.

Reseda alba
RESEDACEAE

Sometimes called white mignonette. A species whose value in an alpine garden is often overlooked. It is found in both high and fairly low rocky areas of southern and eastern regions of Spain. Usually of medium height, with deeply lobed feathery leaves. Flowers, pure white, 6 – 8 mm (5/16 – 7/16 in) across, the petals 3-lobed, appear from late winter, often through to early summer, several densely arranged on a conical spike. Needs sun, and a partially alkaline soil is advisable. Easily propagated from seed.

Rhododendron pemakoense
ERICACEAE

A hummock-forming species, originating from the Himalayas (Tibet), reaching 30 – 40 cm (12 – 16 in) or more in height. Leaves more or less oblong in shape, dark green on upper surface, glaucous and brown scaly below. Flowers, from late spring to early summer, pinkish-purple, solitary or 2 together, each to about 5 cm (2 in) across, widely funnel-shaped. A reasonably hardy plant, providing a pleasing addition to the rock garden. Needs a moisture-retentive, porous, somewhat acid soil. Propagate from seed, sown freshly harvested, temperature 15 °C (59 °F).

Rhodohypoxis baurii
HYPOXIDACEAE

This has proved to be a half-hardy, bulbous plant. It originates from high altitudes in South Africa and will, with due care, accept the changeable climate of Britain. The leaves are small, short and hairy, linear in shape, forming tufts. Flowers, 2 cm (3/4 in) wide, are borne on short stems from late spring to well into summer, generally reddish-pink, though a white form is also known. Needs a bright position, protected from excessive cold and rain during dormancy. A sandy, peaty soil is recommended. Propagate by division of the rootstock in spring.

Rhodohypoxis baurii 'Fred Broome'
HYPOXIDACEAE

This is one of several splendid cultivars, and in all respects is identical in growth and general requirements to the species. Flowers occur throughout much of the summer, creamy pink. Best in the alpine house in partial shade. When the leaves wither, it is advisable to keep the soil completely dry. Propagate only by division of the rootstock in spring.

Rhodohypoxis baurii var. platypetala
HYPOXIDACEAE

A peculiarly attractive variety of the species, originating from the same habitat. In general characteristics it is similar to the type, differing mainly in its flowers, which appear in summer to autumn, are pure white, occasionally suffused pale pink. May prove hardy if planted in a sheltered, sunny position and in enriched, very porous soil. Propagate by division of the rootstock in spring.

Rhodohypoxis rubella
HYPOXIDACEAE

A plant with a corm-like rootstock, originating from mountainous regions of South Africa, in particular the Drakensberg Mountains. Leaves more or less cylindrical, narrow and slightly hairy. Flowers appear in early summer, bright pink, about 1 cm (1/2 in) across, carried on a long tube. It has proved totally hardy and can therefore be used for rock garden purposes, as long as it is sheltered from excessive cold. A soil of equal parts peat, sand and leaf mould is satisfactory. Propagate from seed, sown in spring.

Richea dracophylla
EPACRIDACEAE

A small, branching, shrub-like plant, found only
in Tasmania, in forests on mountain sides. Leaves
very slender, lanceolate and pointed, many
sheathing, in a crowded display, at the end of the
branches, which can be 45 cm (18 cm) or more in
length. Flowers appear in summer or early
autumn, the white inflorescence subtended by
pink or brownish bracts, which fall as the flowers
develop. Half-hardy, so best kept in an alpine
house atmosphere, set in rich, slightly acid soil.
Propagate from freshly harvested seed.

Rigidella orthantha
IRIDACEAE

An unusual cormous plant, found at altitudes over
2,500 m (8,200 ft) in Oaxaca and Chiapas, Mexico.
Leaves are 30 cm (12 in) or more long, glabrous,
plicate, narrowing at the base and tip. Stem about
45 cm (18 in) long, bearing orange-scarlet or deep
orange flowers in summer, the outer segments
3 – 4 cm (1¼ – 1½ in) long, almost oblong in
shape, with broad claws forming a cup 1 cm (½ in)
deep, the inner segments 2.5 cm (1 in) long, rich
deep scarlet. Grow in the alpine house, in a
permeable, humus-rich soil. Propagate from
freshly harvested seed, temperature 15°C (59°F).

Romulea atandra var. lewisae
IRIDACEAE

An attractive cormous plant, suitable for alpine
house culture, found in the wild in many areas of
Cape Province, South Africa. Leaves are scarcely
more than 1 mm (1/16 in) wide, and distinctly
grooved. Flowers appear in summer, borne on
rather short stems, pale lilac to whitish with
prominent purplish-brown throat, the outer
segments with dark longitudinal lines externally.
Needs sun or slight shade and a well-drained,
humus-enriched soil. Propagate from seed,
freshly gathered.

Romulea bulbocodium
IRIDACEAE

A cormous species, found widespread in the
Mediterranean region. It has narrow, rush-like
leaves, to about 10 cm (4 in) long, all basal.
Flowers appear in spring, on stems 2 – 3 cm
(¾ – 1¼ in) long, varying in colour, purple or
bluish-lilac with an orange throat, more rarely
yellow or white. Two unsheathing bracts subtend
the flower. Flowers funnel-shaped, about 3 cm
(1¼ in) in diameter, with a hairy throat. A plant
for the alpine house; needs a peaty, sandy soil
enriched with humus. Propagate from freshly
harvested seed.

Romulea leipoldtii
IRIDACEAE

An erect-stemmed, cormous species found in
rather a restricted area of Cape Province (Calvinia
to Malmesbury), South Africa. Usually 2 slender,
erect, narrowly grooved, dull green leaves to
45 cm (18 in) or more long. Flowers in early
summer, 4 – 6 to a spike, cream or white, with
yellow veins in upper part of segments, golden-
yellow or orange in lower part, throat yellow or
orange. Essentially an alpine house subject; needs
a fairly sunny site and a rather rich, porous soil.
Propagate from seed sown in spring.

Romulea obscura var. campestris
IRIDACEAE

A cormous plant found wild in an area between
Clanwilliam and Malmesbury, Cape Province,
South Africa. The stem is generally almost hidden
by leaf bases. Leaves erect, all basal. Flowers
appear during spring or summer, yellow to
apricot or pale rose-pink, sometimes with dark
blotches towards the base, throat yellow with thin,
dark lines, the segments 3.5 cm (1⅜ in) or more
long, 1 cm (½ in) wide, the inner longer than the
outer. Needs alpine house culture, in a sunny site
and a rich, open soil. Propagate from seed in
spring.

Rosularia pallida
CRASSULACEAE

Syn. *Sedum chrysanthum*. A hardy rock garden plant of Asian origin. Leaves elliptic to spathulate, to 1.5 cm (⅝ in) long, 5 mm (¼ in) wide, the tips short triangular, pale green, fine hairy and ciliate, formed into a rosette. Flowers whitish-yellow, tubular in shape, appearing on short spikes in spring and early summer. Suited also to the alpine house; needs good light and a very open, rich soil. Propagate by division in spring.

Rosularia sempervivoides
CRASSULACEAE

Syn. *Sedum sempervivum*; in recent times this has also been placed in both *Pseudorosularia* and *Promethium*. A rosette-forming plant, native to the Caucasus, with grey or glaucous, purple-mottled, pubescent leaves to about 2.5 cm (1 in) long. The terminal inflorescence is branched, many flowered, bright carmine red, each about 1 cm (½ in) wide, star-like, appearing in early summer. Needs sun and a porous soil. Propagate from fresh seed.

Rubus arcticus
ROSACEAE

A low-growing, creeping species with rhizomatous rootstock, well distributed in the northern hemisphere, including the Arctic regions. Grows to about 20 cm (8 in) tall, with trifoliate leaves, the leaflets finely toothed, 2 – 5 cm (¾ – 2 in) long. Flowers appear in midsummer, rich rose-pink, about 2 cm (¾ in) wide, borne solitary on short stems; the fruits that follow are dark red. Needs sun or partial shade, and a fertile soil. Propagate by division or from ripened seed.

Rupicapnos africana
PAPAVERACEAE

A tufted species, to 15 cm (6 in) high, forming large clumps of numerous glaucous-grey, very finely cut, almost fern-like leaves, native to north-western parts of Africa. Flowers appear during summer, narrowly spurred, pinkish-white, carried terminally on slender stems, hardly exceeding the foliage. Generally considered a short-lived plant, so best kept in the alpine house for longer life! Needs a sunny position, and a porous, slightly acid soil. Propagate from freshly harvested seed.

Sempervivum giuseppii

S

Salvia argentea
LABIATAE

The silver sage. A semi-erect, herbaceous, perennial plant, found in many parts of southern Europe and the Balkans. Leaves ovate to oblong, slightly lobed or toothed, to 20 cm (8 in) long, coated with silvery hairs, basal, almost rosulate. Flowers white or pale pinkish, to 5 cm (2 in) long, borne on a branching inflorescence in summer. Sun and porous soil are essential. Propagate by cuttings in summer or from seed in spring.

Salvia caespitosa
LABIATAE

A short, woody-based species, 10 – 15 cm (4 – 6 in) high, originating from Europe, in the Pyrenees to Turkey. Stems arise from the base of the plant, bearing aromatic green, silvery hairy leaves, which are either entire or pinnate. Flowers, lilac-pink, carried in summer in short-stemmed clusters. Prefers alpine house culture; needs full sun and an enriched, open soil. Propagate from newly harvested seed.

Sandersonia aurantiaca
LILIACEAE

A tuberous-rooted, slender-stemmed species, to about 45 cm (18 in) high, from low hills in Natal, South Africa. The oval-lanceolate, pointed leaves, 5 – 8 cm (2 – 3 in) long, are borne along the stem. Tendrils protrude from the leaves, providing support for the stems. Flowers, in summer, are orange, urn-shaped, 2.5 – 3 cm (1 – 1¼ in) long, pendent on long pedicels. Foliage withers after flowering and the tubers become dormant. Suited to alpine house culture in rich, open soil. Propagate from seed, freshly ripened.

Sanguinaria canadensis 'Flore Plena'
PAPAVERACEAE

This form is also known as 'Multiplex'. The sole species within the genus, a rhizomatous plant originating from more northerly parts of the USA and Canada. It has large, long-stalked, rounded, somewhat cordate shiny green leaves with scalloped margins, prominently veined. Flowers double, white, borne solitary, 4 – 5 cm (1½ – 2 in) in diameter, in summer. All parts of the plant exude a red sap. Best suited to alpine house culture, in a shaded position and in a humus-enriched, moisture-retentive soil. Propagate from seed, freshly harvested.

Santolina rosmarinifolia
COMPOSITAE

An evergreen, shrubby plant, freely encountered in southern Europe in stony places on hill sides and mountains, about 40 cm (15 in) high when in bloom. Leaves pale green or greyish-green, narrowly linear and aromatic, 2 – 5 cm (¾ – 2 in) long, slightly toothed. Flowers solitary and terminal on long stems, bright golden-yellow in button-like heads, subtended by papery bracts, in summer. A fairly hardy species, which can be grown in the rock garden, in a sunny site but sheltered from excessive cold winds. Propagate from fresh seed.

Saponaria x 'Bressingham'
CARYOPHYLLACEAE

An attractive hybrid between S. ocymoides and S. x olivana, developed at Bressingham Nursery in the UK. A mat-forming plant, composed of short reddish stems and small, greenish, softly hairy leaves. Flowers bright pink, 1 – 2 cm (½ – ¾ in) across, borne in clusters, terminally, on short stems in summer. Needs a fairly fertile soil and a bright, sunny position; suited to outdoor culture. Propagate by division or non-flowering stems in spring.

Saponaria x olivana
CARYOPHYLLACEAE

An attractive hybrid between *S. pumillo* and
S. caespitosa. A cushion-forming plant, similar in
many ways to both its parents. The small, slender
green leaves, to 2.5 cm (1 in) long, and the
greenish stems tend to form a dense, compact
mass. Flowers are 1.5 cm (⅝ in) or more wide, rich
pink, carried on short, spreading stems in summer.
An ideal plant for the rock garden, needing sun
and a rich, fertile, porous soil. Propagate by
division in late summer.

Sarracenia minor
SARRACENIACEAE

Syn. *S. variolaris*. Commonly known as the hooded
pitcher plant. Originating from North Carolina to
Florida, USA, this has bright green, tubular,
hollow leaves, occasionally purplish, with white
translucent spots near the rather yellowish, cap-
like top, the lid arching over the mouth, purple-
netted on the inner surface. Flowers are carried on
a leafless stem to 60 cm (24 in) tall, pale yellow,
slightly nodding, in spring or summer. Needs to
be grown in an alpine house. Plant in a mix of
peat and sphagnum moss, with a little loam and
sand added. Propagate by division in spring.

Sarracenia purpurea
SARRACENIACEAE

The sweet pitcher plant. A species growing to
about 15 cm (6 in) tall and found wild in more
northern parts of the USA (Labrador to Maryland
and the Rocky Mountains). The prostrate, pitcher-
like leaves are formed into a low rosette, the
pitchers broadly winged, the throat and lid rather
hairy, attractively veined crimson or purple.
Flowers appear in summer, in purple shades, and
nodding. A fairly hardy plant that can be grown in
peat and moss in a moist rock garden, but needs
protection in winter. Propagate by division.

Saxifraga bryoides
SAXIFRAGACEAE

Syn. *S. aspera* var. *bryoides*. Commonly known as
moss saxifrage. A densely hummock-forming
species, found wild in moist, rocky areas of the
Pyrenees in central southern France. Hummocks
5 – 8 cm (2 – 3 in) high. Leaves narrow, bristly and
pointed, closely set on the short stems. Flowers,
in late spring and early summer, borne singly and
terminally, pale yellowish with orange-red
markings. A moisture-retentive soil is essential,
and a bright but sheltered position. Propagate by
division or from seed.

Saxifraga caesia
SAXIFRAGACEAE

A variable, widespread species found in the
Pyrenees to the eastern Alps. It forms cushions of
rather small rosettes of tiny, dark or bluish-green
recurved leaves, each leaf 3 – 6 mm (³⁄₁₆ – ⁵⁄₁₆ in)
long. Flowers, to 1.5 cm (⅝ in) across, are borne on
very short, slender stems in early summer –
generally white or slightly suffused pale pink. Best
grown in a slightly calcareous soil, which must be
porous, and preferably on slightly sloping ground.
Propagate from seed or by division in early
autumn.

Saxifraga cochlearis
SAXIFRAGACEAE

A densely cushion-forming species, somewhat
dome-shaped, found in the Maritime Alps on the
French-Italian border. The silver grey, narrowly
spathulate leaves, with reflexed tips, are 1 – 4 cm
(½ – 1½ in) long, arranged in tufted rosettes.
Stems 15 cm (6 in) or more long, somewhat
reddish in colour, bear white flowers in panicles,
usually dotted with red, in spring and summer.
Needs a bright, sunny location and a well-drained
soil. Propagate from seed when ripe.

Saxifraga exarata
SAXIFRAGACEAE

A more or less tufted perennial, which forms loose, but dense, cushions. It is native to mountainous regions of southern Europe, the Caucasus and the Balkans. Leaves usually 3-lobed, to 1.5 cm (⅝ in) long, arranged in basal rosettes. Leafy stems are erect, bearing 3 – 10 white or cream-coloured flowers in summer, usually with a reddish dot on each petal. Needs a bright, sunny position and a slightly alkaline, well-drained soil. Best suited to the alpine house. Propagate from seed when ripe.

Saxifraga globulifera
SAXIFRAGACEAE

A rather loosely cushion-forming species found wild on rocky mountain slopes in southern Spain. Leaves more or less circular, deeply lobed, the lobes acute. Flowers appear in late spring and early summer, white, 8 mm (⁷⁄₁₆ in) across, borne terminally on stems 7 – 12 cm (2¾ – 5 in) long, 3 – 7 flowers to a stem. An excellent rock garden plant; needs an open, fairly rich soil, and a bright, sunny setting – best on sloping ground. Propagate by division or from freshly ripened seed.

Saxifraga grisebachii 'Wisley'
SAXIFRAGACEAE

The parent plant originates from the Balkan Peninsula, and it has more recently been found in Albania, identical to the Wisley plant. Both species and variety are hummock-forming, with oblanceolate to spathulate leaves of silvery grey, to 3 cm (1¼ in) long. The inflorescence, to 18 cm (7½ in) long, is coated with red glandular hairs, topped with pale purple or pink flowers, 4 – 5 mm (³⁄₁₆ – ¼ in) wide, in late spring. Bright light is essential, and a rich, porous soil. Propagate by division after flowering.

Saxifraga x 'Haagii'
SAXIFRAGACEAE

A hybrid plant, apparently of unknown parentage, growing to about 10 cm (4 in) high. Mat-forming, composed of clusters of dark green, pointed leaves arranged on short stalks. Flowers appear in late spring and early summer, bright yellow, in small clusters, borne terminally on short stems. A hardy plant, ideally suited for inclusion in a rock garden where it can be set in crevices. Needs a slightly calcareous, porous soil. Propagate by division.

Saxifraga x 'Irvingii' and
S. x 'Jenkinsiae'
SAXIFRAGACEAE

Two almost identical hybrids derived from *S. burseriana* x *S. lilacina*, the former being native to the Alps, the latter to the Himalayas. Forms quite dense cushions, 5 – 7 cm (2 – 2¾ in) high, of small, bluish-grey leaves. Short stems bear solitary, pale pink flowers during the spring; generally very free-flowering. Needs a sunny position and a rich, porous soil, top-dressed with limestone chippings. Propagate by division after flowering.

Saxifraga juniperifolia
SAXIFRAGACEAE

A hummock-forming species, found in the Caucasus and Bulgaria, which smells of juniper when crushed. The leaves are dark green, very small and spiny, only 1 cm (½ in) or little more long. Stems, 2 – 4 cm (¾ – 1½ in) long, bear terminal clusters of 6 – 11 bright yellow flowers, each up to 1.5 cm (⅝ in) wide, with very pronounced stamens, during summer. Needs as sunny a location as possible, and a fairly porous soil, enriched with humus. Propagate by division.

Saxifraga juniperifolia 'Macedonica'
SAXIFRAGACEAE

Syn. *S. santa-macedonica*. The parent plant of this form is of Greek origin and forms small hummocks of small, green, spiny leaves, little more than 1 cm (½ in) long. Flowers appear in late spring and early summer, on stems to about 4 cm (1½ in) long, deep yellow, in terminal clusters. Needs a bright, sunny position and a slightly calcareous soil, which must be well-drained. Propagate by division in autumn.

Saxifraga longifolia
SAXIFRAGACEAE

A particularly attractive rosette-forming plant, found in eastern Spain and the Pyrenees. The rosette is composed of narrow, lime-encrusted, greyish leaves, to 8 cm (3 in) long. The inflorescence is to 60 cm (24 in) long, with a narrow, pyramidal, branched display of white, often red-dotted, flowers in summer. Needs a bright, sunny position and a porous, slightly alkaline soil. Suited to the rock garden or alpine house.

Saxifraga marginata
SAXIFRAGACEAE

A cushion-forming plant, originating from the Balkan region, central and southern Italy and the Carpathians. The small green leaves, to about 1 cm (½ in) long, linear-oblong, fleshy and encrusted, form basal rosettes. Flowers, each to 2.5 cm (1 in) wide, appear in summer, in terminal pink clusters on stems 5 – 9 cm (2 – 3½ in) long. Needs sun or partial shade. A very porous but enriched soil is essential; ideally suited to the rock garden. Propagate by division after flowering or from freshly harvested seed.

Saxifraga marginata 'Popelka'
SAXIFRAGACEAE

Very similar in most respects to the species, which is found wild in central and southern Italy, as well as in the Carpathians and the Balkan Peninsula. A mat-forming plant, with deep green, more or less oblong, pointed leaves, formed into very dense rosettes. Pure white terminal flowers, to 2.5 cm (1 in) across, borne on stems 5 – 7 cm (2 – 2¾ in) long, in summer. Well suited to rock garden culture if given a sunny, sheltered position and enriched, well-drained soil; otherwise grow as a potted plant in the alpine house. Propagate by division.

Saxifraga media
SAXIFRAGACEAE

A low-growing perennial forming somewhat rosette-like tufts of leaves, from the Pyrenees and eastern mountain ranges of Spain. Leaves greyish-green, broad and sharply pointed, to 2 cm (¾ in) long. Flowers appear in summer, pink or pinkish-purple, in dense panicles, on stems 8 – 10 cm (3 – 4 in) high, covered with fine reddish hairs – the flowers only just visible as they emerge from the bell-shaped calyces. A useful plant for the rock garden, needing sun and an open, calcareous soil. Propagate by division.

Saxifraga oppositifolia
SAXIFRAGACEAE

A loosely mat-forming species with creeping, trailing stems found in many parts of Europe, including Britain, also in North America and the Himalayas. A variable species, with leaves to 6 mm (⁵⁄₁₆ in) long, obovate to rounded, ciliate, arranged in opposite pairs, dark green, with thickened tips and lime glands. Flowers almost stalkless, solitary, purple-red or pink, appearing early to midsummer, to 2.5 cm (1 in) wide. Needs sun and an enriched, porous soil. Propagate by division after flowering or from seed.

Saxifraga oppositifolia 'Splendens'
SAXIFRAGACEAE

This is, in general, an improved form of the species and the one usually available for planting in the rock garden. A selected hybrid, chosen primarily because of the remarkably attractive, bright red-purple flowers, which are at their best in late spring and early summer. Needs a very sunny position, and a very permeable, enriched soil will encourage good flowering. Propagate by division or from seed in early spring.

Saxifraga paniculata
SAXIFRAGACEAE

Syn. *S. aizoon*. A mat-forming plant, native to the mountains of Europe, from south to north, even semi-Arctic regions. A most variable species, with greyish, lime-edged leaves to 4 cm (1½ in) or more long, forming rosettes with runners, which develop low clumps. Flower stems slender, bearing in summer a pyramidal panicle of white or cream flowers 1.5 cm (⅝ in) wide, sometimes with red dots on the petals. Needs sun and a rich, permeable soil. Propagate by division or from seed in early spring.

Saxifraga x 'Winifred'
SAXIFRAGACEAE

A fairly modern hybrid, of which *S. lilacina* is considered one of the parents. It has dark greyish-green leaves formed into close, compact rosettes, which multiply to form low-set cushions, 5 – 7 cm (2 – 2¾ in) high. Flowers appear in late spring, borne on very short stems, deep rich crimson, the petals edged fresh pink. Possibly best treated as an alpine house plant; needs a very sunny position and a permeable, humus-rich soil. Propagate by division in autumn.

Scabiosa caucasia
DIPSACEAE

A perennial species found widespread in the Caucasus, northern Iran and neighbouring regions. Leaves are variable – the lower more lanceolate, the upper pinnately divided, glaucous green. Flowers, bright lavender blue, are carried solitary in summer on long, slender stems in a loose head 6 cm (2½ in) or more across. An attractive, hardy plant for the rock garden; needs a sunny position and well-drained, fairly rich, slightly calcareous soil. Propagate by division of the rootstock.

Scabiosa graminifolia
DIPSACEAE

A somewhat tufted perennial species, fairly widely distributed in southern Europe, not exceeding 30 cm (12 in) or so high. Leaves, grey-green, are densely arranged, basal, generally bipinnate, the leaflets being slenderly lanceolate. Flowers appear from the tips of the stems in summer, solitary or few together, mauve or pink, each about 3 cm (1¼ in) across. Needs sun and a fertile soil. Propagate by division or from seed in spring.

Schizostylis coccinea
IRIDACEAE

The kaffir lily. A short, rhizomatous-rooted species, found in the wild near streams in South Africa and mountainous regions of central Africa. It has several basal leaves, to 50 cm (20 in) or more long, and a very erect stem bearing in early summer bright red or pink flowers, singly or in clusters, each flower to about 4 cm (1½ in) in diameter. Suited to rock garden culture; needs an almost constantly moisture-retentive soil, especially during the growing season. Propagate by division or from seed.

Scilla autumnalis
LILIACEAE

A rather low-growing, short-stemmed plant, native to many parts of Europe, including Britain. Leaves are usually not seen before the flowers appear, and are very narrow, barely 3 mm (³⁄₁₆ in) wide, generally up to 12 in number. Flowers appear in late summer and early autumn, each about 7 mm (³⁄₈ in) across, borne in a many flowered raceme of blue, pinkish-purple and other shades, including white. Thrives in sun or shade; needs an enriched, gritty soil and moisture during the growing season. Propagate from seed, freshly harvested.

Scilla bifolia
LILIACEAE

A rather dwarf plant, found in several locations – meadows, woods and low hill sides in southern Europe and through to Palestine. It has 2 very shiny, channelled, green leaves, 2 – 6 mm (⅛ – ⁵⁄₁₆ in) wide, the bases encircling the flower stem. Flowers vary in colour from blue to pale violet, appearing in a spreading, terminal head, generally in late spring and early summer. Bulbs easily naturalize in a sunny position or partial shade; they need ordinary garden soil.

Scilla cilicica
LILIACEAE

A rather short perennial bulbous plant, native to much of the eastern Mediterranean region, growing on rocky limestone hill sides. Leaves bright green, basal, very slender and channelled, 2 – 4 in number. Flowers appear in early spring in a few-flowered raceme, purplish-blue, each about 2.5 cm (1 in) long with spreading petals, borne terminally on a purplish scape. Needs sun and a slightly alkaline soil. Propagate from newly ripened seed.

Scilla litardierei
LILIACEAE

Syn. *S. amethystina*. Commonly known as the meadow squill. A handsome species, native to the Balkan region, where it is found in grassy meadows in somewhat limestone areas. It has 8 – 10 erect, fleshy, green leaves 3 – 8 mm (³⁄₁₆ – ⁷⁄₁₆ in) wide, tapering to a pointed tip. Flowers in early summer, blue, white or lilac-pink, each 5 – 7 mm (¼ – ³⁄₈ in) long, in a fairly loose but dense raceme. Requires an open, slightly alkaline soil and as sunny a position as possible. Propagate from seed, freshly harvested.

Scilla peruviana
LILIACEAE

A bulbous species found in many parts of southern Europe and north Africa. Flower stems, 20 – 50 cm (8 – 20 in) long, arising from a very large bulb. Leaves glossy green, soft, often with hairy margins, mostly recurving, 4 – 6 cm (1½ – 2½ in) wide. Flowers borne in late spring to early summer in a dense cluster, generally blue, but frequently white, up to 100 to a raceme, each 1 – 2 cm (½ – ¾ in) on long stalks. Needs a moist, fairly bright position in normal garden soil, with a small amount of peat and sand placed around the rootstock. Propagate from seed, freshly harvested.

Scilla pratensis
LILIACEAE

A fairly short plant, rarely exceeding 30 cm (12 in) high, native to quite high altitudes in the Balkan region. Leaves dark green, soft, somewhat elongated, generally only few in number, to 8 mm (⁷⁄₁₆ in) wide at best, tapering to a pointed tip. Flowers appear in late spring and early summer, the stem bearing a rather dense raceme of blue or pinkish-violet flowers about 6 mm (⁵⁄₁₆ in) across. Needs a bright, fairly sunny position and an enriched, porous soil. Propagate from seed, freshly harvested.

Scilla scilloides
LILIACEAE

Syn. *S. chinensis*. A hardy, attractive, bulbous plant, originating from rocky hill sides in China and Japan. It has stems to about 8 cm (3 in) long, arising from a cluster of slender basal leaves, 3 – 4 cm (1¼ – 1½ in) long. Flowers, in late summer, are bright pink, each about 5 mm (¼ in) wide, borne in a dense terminal raceme. Can be grown in the rock garden, on a raised sloping bed, or in an alpine house. Needs a sunny site and a porous, humus-rich soil. Propagate by division or from seed.

Scilla sibirica ssp. armena
LILIACEAE

A bulbous plant to 15 cm (6 in) tall, found wild in northwestern Turkey and the southern Caucasus, in mountain meadows near the snow-line. Leaves 1 – 3, broad linear-oblanceolate, to 2 cm (¾ in) wide. Flowers appear in early summer, pale blue, each petal with a deeper blue median line, borne terminally and solitary on fleshy stems. Needs a very well-drained soil, enriched with humus, in sun or partial shade – ideal for the rock garden. Propagate from seed sown soon after harvesting.

Scilla tubergeniana
LILIACEAE

Syn. *S. mischtschenkoana*. A late winter-flowering, bulbous species, native to northern Iran and the southern Caucasus. Leaves glossy green, strap-shaped, 10 – 15 cm (4 – 6 in) long, all basal. Flowers appear in late winter or early spring, very pale blue with a deeper blue median line, opening almost as soon as the buds emerge from the soil, on stalks eventually to 15 cm (6 in) long. Needs well-drained soil, in sun or shade. Propagate from offsets in the dormant season.

Scilla violacea
LILIACEAE

Syn. *Ledebouria socialis*. A bulbous plant, found wild in South Africa. A clustering plant, the bulbs being planted almost at soil level, or even totally exposed. Leaves ovate-lanceolate to 8 cm (3 in), dark purple-green, flower bell-shaped, rather small, appearing in late summer and early autumn. A plant for the alpine house; needs a very rich, porous soil. Propagate by division in spring.

Scopiopus bigelovii
LILIACEAE

An unusual, low-growing plant, 30 – 40 cm (12 – 16 in) tall, found on shaded hill sides in Humboldt County to Santa Cruz County, California, USA. Leaves very broad, with purplish dots and mottling, more or less lanceolate and forming a close rosette, from which appears a slender stem bearing greenish-lilac flowers with reddish veining in summer. Best kept in an alpine house in a reasonably bright location. Needs a well-drained, humus-enriched, gritty soil. Propagate from newly ripened seed, in temperature 15°C (59°F).

Scutellaria alpina
LABIATAE

A low, mat-forming species found in the wild in central and southern Europe, also in Russia. The greenish leaves are oval and invariably toothed, arranged in opposite pairs. Flowers are borne on short, erect stems, in dense quadrangular clusters, bluish-violet with cream lips, about 2 cm (¾ in) long, in summer. Plants rarely exceed 15 cm (6 in) high. Needs a sunny position, and normal garden soil with a little added lime. Best suited to the rock garden. Propagate from seed in spring.

Scutellaria indica var. japonica
LABIATAE

A somewhat dwarf, bushy plant, originating from Japan. It has many small, greyish-green, slightly toothed leaves carried on stems about 15 cm (6 in) long. Flowers are borne in racemes, bluish or lavender purple, somewhat hooded, about 2 cm (¾ in) long, in summer. A useful species for the alpine garden, which adapts to ordinary garden soil; needs a really bright, sunny position.

Scutellaria orientalis
LABIATAE

A low-growing, spreading or prostrate plant, found in southern Spain, also in the Balkans and Turkey. A perennial species, with a woody base and generally hairy. The greyish-green leaves, more or less oval in shape, are prominently toothed. Flowers appear in early summer, rather variable in colour, but usually yellow, the lower lip being reddish, 1.5 – 3 cm (⅝ – 1¼ in) long. Suited to the rock garden; needs an open, alkaline soil. Propagate from seed in spring.

Sedum acre
CRASSULACEAE

A vigorous, evergreen, stoloniferous, low-growing perennial species, native to many parts of Europe, Asia and north Africa, not exceeding 5 cm (2 in) high. It can form large carpets by means of its pinkish stolons, which produce green, fleshy, leafy stems with succulent leaves about 3 mm (³⁄₁₆ in) long, densely arranged alternate along their length. Flowers, bright yellow, 1 cm (½ in) wide, appear in summer, loosely arranged along the stems. Needs sun and well-drained soil. Propagate by division.

Sedum aizoon
CRASSULACEAE

Currently known as *Aizopsis aizoon*. A perennial, loose-clustering species native to Siberia, China and Japan, to about 30 cm (12 in) high. The tuberous, fleshy rootstock produces annual, leafy stems, erect, brownish at the base, with recurving, oblanceolate, greenish, marginally dentate leaves arranged alternate, to 5 cm (2 in) long. In summer a many flowered cyme of pale yellow flowers, terminally borne, each 1 cm (½ in) wide, appears. Needs sun and well-drained soil. Propagate by division or from seed in spring.

Sedum bellum
CRASSULACEAE

A fascinating caespitose species of succulent growth, which is native to Durango in Mexico, where it is found among rocks on low mountain slopes. Tufts are composed of pale green, mealy white, spathulate leaves to about 3 cm (1¼ in) long, formed into loose rosettes. Flowers appear in late winter, many, pure white, carried in a 'false', flattish umbel on fleshy stalks to 15 cm (6 in) long. One of the most beautiful of this genus. Best grown in an alpine house in well-drained soil. Propagate by division in summer.

Sedum coeruleum
CRASSULACEAE

Syn. *Oreosedum coeruleum*. A rather bushy annual species, originating from many of the more easterly Mediterranean islands and north Africa. The pale green, later reddish, leaves, about 8 mm (⁷⁄₁₆ in) long, cluster freely. Inflorescence much branched, with few-flowered cymes of pale blue flowers in midsummer, each flower 5 mm (¼ in) wide. Needs sun or slight shade. Propagate from seed, sown in gritty soil in spring or autumn, temperature 10°C (50°F).

Sedum cupressoides
CRASSULACEAE

A low-growing, semi-prostrate species, found wild in Oaxaca, Mexico. It has very succulent branches spreading dichotomously, the sterile shoots forming tufts, with side shoots very cypress-looking. Leaves more or less ovate, wider towards the base, densely arranged, about 1.5 mm (¹⁄₁₆ in) long, those on the stems much looser. Flowers appear in early summer, borne solitary or 2 – 3 together, star-like, bright yellow, about 1 cm (½ in) across. Needs alpine house culture, in sun and an open, humus-enriched soil. Propagate by division in spring.

Sedum dasyphyllum
CRASSULACEAE

Now included within *Oreosedum*. An evergreen, perennial, low-growing, cushion-forming species from right around the Mediterranean region, rarely more than 4 cm (1½ in) high. Pinkish-grey stems arise from the ground-level stolons crowded with greyish-green oval, fleshy leaves about 4 mm (³⁄₁₆ in) long, arranged opposite or alternate. The few-flowered terminal inflorescence has white flowers, 5 mm (¼ in) wide, in summer. Needs rich, open soil and a position in sun. Propagate by division in spring.

Sedum dasyphyllum var. glanduliferum
CRASSULACEAE

Like the species, this is now included within *Oreosedum*. It is in almost all respects similar to the species: low-growing, leafy stems forming dense cushions, found in the same areas. The principal difference is in the most conspicuously hairy, egg-shaped leaves, arranged opposite along the fleshy stems in dense formation. Flowers terminal, white with pinkish streaks in summer. Propagate by division in autumn.

Sedum hispanicum var. minus
CRASSULACEAE

An annual or perennial plant, which forms loose clusters, originating from west of the Balkans to the Caucasus. It tends to die down as winter approaches, with a few small leaves remaining on the stem tips. As spring arrives, new growth usually appears and, subsequently, flowers similar to those of the species – 6-partite, star-like, about 8 mm (⁷⁄₁₆ in) in diameter, white, veined pinkish, with a pale green keel. Needs rich, gritty soil and a position in sun. Propagate by division or from seed in spring.

Sedum humifusum
CRASSULACEAE

A low-growing, mat-forming perennial not exceeding 8 mm (⁷⁄₁₆ in) high, native to Queretaro, Mexico. It has creeping, brownish stems, which root at the nodes. Leaves greyish-green, about 4 mm (³⁄₁₆ in) long, the edges smooth and ciliate, forming very compact basal rosettes. Flowers, bright yellow, appear in early summer, about 8 mm (⁷⁄₁₆ in) across, just protruding above the foliage. Needs a position in sun. Propagates easily from division in early spring, using an open, gritty soil.

Sedum kamtschaticum variegatum
CRASSULACEAE

Now classified within the genus *Aizopsis*. A particularly attractive variety from the Far East, Korea to Siberia, China, Japan, especially Kamchatka. A clustering plant to about 12 cm (5 in) tall, the stems arising annually from lower parts of the old growth. Leaves more or less oblanceolate, with partially dentate margins, to 4 cm (1½ in) long, fresh green, white-margined. Flowers terminal, in summer, orange-yellow, 1.2 cm (⁹⁄₁₆ in) wide. Requires a position in sun and rich, porous soil. Propagate from seed or by division.

Sedum moranense
CRASSULACEAE

A low, bushy species with many slender, mostly erect stems with aerial rootlets, found on limestone rocks on mountains in central Mexico. Stems have leafy branches; the fresh green, red-tipped leaves, about 3 mm (³⁄₁₆ in) long, are set alternate and very crowded. Flowers white, tipped red dorsally, star-like, about 8 mm (⁷⁄₁₆ in) wide, borne in midsummer on a simple, terminal, few-flowered inflorescence. A position in sun and enriched, permeable garden soil are essential. Propagate by stem cuttings in spring.

Sedum multiceps
CRASSULACEAE

A fascinating, mat-forming, perennial species, native to north Africa. Leaves are formed in a series of small, elongating rosettes of dark green, each leaf about 6 mm (⁵⁄₁₆ in) long; these, however, die back during the dormant season. Small, bright yellow flowers appear in early summer, borne in a somewhat flattened 2 – 4 branched cyme. Being a low mountain plant, it is best grown in a very porous, gritty soil, preferably with humus added; needs a position in full sun or partial shade. Propagate by division.

Sedum praealtum ssp. dendroideum
CRASSULACEAE

A fairly tall, evergreen perennial, succulent plant, native to high mountainous country in Mexico and Central America, usually at altitudes of 2,500 m (8,200 ft) or more. A semi-shrubby species, 30 cm (12 in) or more high, with several branching stems. Leaves are alternate, fleshy, to 2.5 cm (1 in) long and glossy pale green. Flowers, bright yellow, are borne in a fairly dense, terminal cluster, each flower about 1.3 cm (⁹⁄₁₆ in) across. Propagate from cuttings or from seed.

Sedum sexangulare
CRASSULACEAE

A mat-forming species distributed over much of Europe and southwest Asia. Plants stoloniferous, bearing reddish-brown stems, which are much branched. Leaves bright green, to 6 mm (⁵⁄₁₆ in) long, fleshy, cylindrical with blunt tips, arranged in 6 spiralling ranks. Flowers about 1 cm (½ in) across, bright yellow, in a few-flowered, flat, terminal inflorescence in summer. Tends to become invasive and thrives in a rock garden in ordinary garden soil. Propagate by division in spring.

Sedum spathulifolium
CRASSULACEAE

A vigorous, perennial, mat-forming species originating in hills and mountains at altitudes to 1,700 m (5,600 ft) in California, USA, and British Columbia, Canada. Plants to 10 cm (4 in) tall, with stem-clasping, spathulate, glaucous leaves arranged alternate and forming rosettes, the leaves to 2 cm (¾ in) long. Flowers appear in early summer, yellow, about 1.5 cm (⅝ in) wide, in a terminal, flat, leafy inflorescence. Needs a peaty, sandy soil in shade or sun. Propagate by division in autumn.

Sedum spathulifolium
ssp. pruinosum var. purpureum
CRASSULACEAE

This plant is recorded from Orcas Island, in the Gulf of Georgia, British Columbia, Canada, and it is a very low-growing variety, with quite wide-open rosettes. Leaves are dull green but become purplish during the summer period, when the flowering season arrives. Flowers bright yellow, similar in size to those of the species, borne on short, fleshy stems. Needs a peaty, loamy mix and a position in sun or shade. The dense clusters of rosettes may be divided in early spring or autumn.

Sedum spurium tricolor
CRASSULACEAE

A low-growing, cushion-forming species introduced from the Caucasus. Forms dense clusters of tangled shoots set with oval, dark green leaves, 2 – 3 cm (¾ – 1¼ in) long, with slightly serrated edges, which are prominently coloured yellow. Flowers appear in summer, small, star-shaped, purplish-pink, red or white, carried in slightly rounded heads. A totally hardy plant for rock garden or general garden use; grows well in any ordinary garden soil.

Sedum tatarinowii
CRASSULACEAE

A low hummock-forming, herbaceous perennial species with a tuberous rootstock, originating from northern China in high mountainous areas. Purplish stems rise annually, to 15 cm (6 in) long, with glaucous green, flat, lanceolate leaves about 1.5 cm (⅝ in) long, the margins sharply dentate, arranged alternate along their length. Flowers appear in midsummer, pinkish-white, about 1 cm (½ in) wide, in a many flowered terminal cluster. Plant in a sunny position in a peaty, loamy mix. Propagate by division or from seed in spring.

Selaginella denticulata
SELAGINELLACEAE

A low-growing, totally prostrate, creeping plant, found in many parts of the Mediterranean region, principally in shaded, moist, rocky areas. A moss-like species with very flat stems bearing minute leaves, about 2.5 mm (⅛ in) long, arranged in 4 rows, closely pressed to the stem. Being non-flowering, it produces spores in very small, inconspicuous 'cones' at the tips of the lateral branches. Useful in every area of the garden, preferably on broken rocks or in a bog garden. Propagate by division.

Sempervivum arachnoideum
CRASSULACEAE

The cobweb houseleek. A species that originates from the Pyrenees, the Alps, the Apennines and the Carpathians. It has small rosettes, no more than 2 cm (¾ in) across, composed of crowded green and pink leaves, the tips united by a dense spread of cobweb-like, white hairs. Flowers are carried on stems about 12 cm (5 in) tall, bright red, borne terminally in small clusters, in summer. Prefers a humus-rich soil in a bright setting. Propagate by division in spring.

Sempervivum arachnoideum ssp. tomentosum
CRASSULACEAE

A widely spreading, low-growing plant, found growing in profusion in the mountains of Spain. In common with most of the varieties of this very pleasing species, the apical hairs of the numerous leaves that form the rosette are very long and flexible, and they interweave to form something of a spider's web across the rosette. The rosettes are compressed to being almost globose, multiplying to form cushions. Flowers dark red on longish stem in summer. Ideal plants for the rock garden. Propagate by division in spring.

Sempervivum atlanticum
CRASSULACEAE

Syn. *S. tectorum* var. *atlanticum*. A rosette-forming plant, found in mountainous regions of Morocco, particularly the Atlas Mountains. It is the only known species from the area. It has a rosette 7 – 10 cm (2¾ – 4 in) in diameter, composed of green leaves, often reddish near the apex, minutely glandular when young, becoming glabrous with age. Flowers in summer are borne on inflorescence to 20 cm (8 in) high, each large, pink flower 3 – 4 cm (1¼ – 1½ in) in diameter. Best kept in an alpine house in a rich, gritty soil; needs warmth in winter. Propagate by division in spring.

Sempervivum ballsii
CRASSULACEAE

A rosette-forming species found in a limited area of northwest Greece. The rosettes, 2.5 – 3.5 cm (1 – 1⅜ in) in diameter, cluster freely, composed of uniformly bright green leaves tinged with yellow, to about 1.8 cm (¹¹⁄₁₆ in) long, more or less obovate in shape, slight ciliate towards the base. Inflorescence about 10 cm (4 in) high with a compact, dome-shaped apex of dull rose-pink flowers to about 2 cm (¾ in) across, appearing in summer. Considered by some to be rather uninteresting! Needs very gritty soil and slight shade. Propagate by division in spring.

Sempervivum 'Commander Hay'
CRASSULACEAE

This appears to be identical to a red-rosetted plant named 'Hayling', a hybrid of *S. tectorum giganteum* x *S. tectorum* x *S. marmareum rubrifolium*. The large rosettes, 12 cm (5 in) or more wide, are composed of dark red leaves with slightly greenish tips. Flowers, in summer, are said to be pinkish or pale purplish in colour, borne on reddish, leafy stems. Just one of the many hybrids occurring within this genus. Suited to rock garden culture in full sun or slight shade, in a gritty soil. Propagate by division.

Sempervivum giuseppii
CRASSULACEAE

A rosette-forming succulent plant found wild in mountains in northwest Spain. The rosettes measure 2.5 – 5 cm (1 – 2 in) across, composed of many densely downy, stiffly ciliate, pale green leaves with brownish tips. The leafy inflorescence, 12 – 15 cm (5 – 6 in) or more long, bears in summer a terminal cluster of bright rose-red flowers with yellow centres. A hardy species, suited to the rock garden in a slightly shaded position. Needs a very gritty, enriched soil. Propagate by division in spring, before flowering.

Sempervivum globuliferum
CRASSULACEAE

Syn. *S. armenum*. A large-rosetted species, found in the Caucasus and neighbouring areas. The very open rosettes, 2 – 10 cm (¾ – 4 in) wide, are composed of obovate-cuneate, yellowish-green leaves, with short pointed tips and both surfaces bearing glandular hairs. The inflorescence bears a cluster of greenish-yellow flowers, each with rather indistinct lines at the base of each petal, in summer. A very hardy plant, requiring only partial shade, gritty, enriched soil, but infrequent watering. Propagate by division in spring.

Sempervivum heuffelii
CRASSULACEAE

A plant widely distributed in southern Europe and even more so in the Balkans. A variable species, with rosettes having a slightly swollen caudex and inclined not to develop offsets. Each rosette 6 – 12 cm (2½ – 5 in) in diameter, composed of dark green, obovate-lanceolate leaves, narrowing towards the base but with a bristly apex, about 5 cm (2 in) long, 1.5 cm (⅝ in) wide and generally hairy. Bell-shaped yellowish flowers, to 1.5 cm (⅝ in) long, appear in summer. Needs bright sun and a very porous soil. Propagate by division in late summer.

Sempervivum heuffelii
var. reginae-amaliae
CRASSULACEAE

Originally this enjoyed specific status. Found in the wild in several areas of southern Europe, particularly the mountains of Greece. A glabrous variety, with dull green leaves, tipped red on occasion, forming a dense rosette, to 12 cm (5 in) across. The inflorescence is erect, bearing many red flowers, the petals edged white and with a central crimson band, in summer. Suited to the rock garden, requiring a slightly alkaline soil and bright light. Propagate from seed, freshly harvested.

Sempervivum marmoreum 'Rubrifolium'
CRASSULACEAE

A rosette-forming plant, the parent of which was found in the Balkan region and areas of eastern Europe. It forms quite large rosettes, to 18 cm (7½ in) wide, of dull green, pointed, wide-obovate leaves, the lower half being reddish-brown or red. Flowers are purplish-pink, borne terminally on leafy stems in late spring and early summer. Suited to the rock garden, in a sunny site. Needs a porous, humus-enriched soil. Propagate by division in autumn or spring, before flowering.

Sempervivum montanum ssp. burnatii
CRASSULACEAE

One of the several forms of *S. montanum*, probably the most robust, native to the Alps and Pyrenees, mostly in rather sparse grassland. Rosette large, to about 15 cm (6 in) in diameter, composed of dark green, cuneate to oblanceolate leaves. Robust inflorescence, with flowers of reddish-purple or varying shades of violet, carried on short stems, appearing in summer – the rosettes die after flowering. Thrives in a coarse, gritty, slightly enriched compost in sun or slight shade. Propagate by division or from seed.

Sempervivum montanum ssp. montanum
CRASSULACEAE

A rosette-forming species, found widespread at high and low altitudes in the Alps, the Pyrenees and the Balkans on rocky hill sides. The globose rosettes, 2 – 4.5 cm (¾ – 1¾ in) in diameter, are pale green, hairy, composed of more or less oblanceolate leaves. Flowers in summer, 2 – 8 together, pale purplish-violet, each petal about 1 cm (½ in) long, with a prominent median line. Has proved to be hardy, so is very useful for the rock garden. Needs fairly rich, porous soil. Propagate by division.

Sempervivum montanum ssp. stiriacum
CRASSULACEAE

Syn. *S. funckii*. A large-rosette variety, found in rocky crevices in the Austrian Alps. It has the unusual feature of the leaves tending to elongate and encourage the rosette to expand during the summer. Generally, the rosette is inclined to be loose, the pale green leaves, with a reddish-brown tip, often covered with short glandular hairs. The inflorescence bears 3 – 11 deep violet flowers, about 2 cm (¾ in) long, in summer. Needs full sun and a very open, enriched soil. Propagate by division in autumn.

Sempervivum pittonii
CRASSULACEAE

A rosette-forming species, found only in rocky areas in the valley of the Mur, Austria, on serpentine rocks. Leaves to about 2 cm (¾ in) long, 8 mm (⁷⁄₁₆ in) wide, scarcely acuminate, with glandular hairs, and ciliate, form a rosette about 5 cm (2 in) across. Flowers appear in late spring, pale greenish-yellow, 1 – 3 cm (½ – 1¼ in) across, in a terminal cluster. Fully hardy, so can be grown in a rock garden, in partial shade and well-drained, slightly enriched soil. Propagate by division.

Sempervivum soboliferum
CRASSULACEAE

Syn. *Jovibarba sobolifera*. A rosette-forming species, found mostly in eastern Europe and Russia. It develops very globular rosettes, 2 – 3 cm (¾ – 1¼ in) in diameter, of bright green, often tinted with reddish-brown, incurving leaves. Offsets are borne on stolons and readily become detached. The greenish-yellow flowers are only rarely produced, in summer, and are carried on stems to 20 cm (8 in) tall. A very suitable plant for the rock garden, given an open, fairly rich soil. Propagate by division in summer.

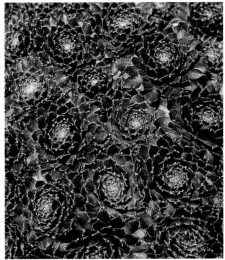

Sempervivum tectorum ssp. alpinum
CRASSULACEAE

Syn. *S. alpinum*, *S. fuscum*. A high-altitude variety of this variable species, found in the Alps and the Pyrenees. A plant with large rosettes, 2 – 6 cm (¾ – 2½ in) in diameter, the bluish-green leaves always red at the base, the tips, often the whole leaves, becoming reddish-brown, forming a semi-open rosette with the leaf margins ciliate. Flowers appear in summer, borne on a fairly medium sized stem, bright pink. Best planted outside, in sun, in sandy, enriched soil. Propagate from freshly ripened seed.

Sempervivum tectorum x 'Beta'
CRASSULACEAE

One of several cultivars of this popular roof houseleek. The exceptionally attractive rosette gradually changes from deep green to bronze-red before the flowering period. The rosette elongates to form a leafy stem, 30 cm (12 in) or more long, which bears terminal pinkish flowers in late spring to midsummer. Very useful for the rock garden or for crevices in other parts of the garden or as a pot plant; needs rich, gritty soil. Propagates best by division.

Sempervivum tectorum ssp. calcareum monstrosum
CRASSULACEAE

Syn. *S. calcareum*. A variety found at sub-alpine levels in the French and Italian Alps, mostly on limestone. The rosettes, 4 – 6 cm (1½ – 2½ in) in diameter, are composed of linear-elongated leaves of pale greyish-green, reddish at the tips and generally ciliate, with minute white hairs. Infrequently, the leaves develop a monstrose form (as shown). Flowers are pale pink, having quite narrow petals, blooming in summer. Ideal for indoor or outdoor cultivation; needs enriched, gritty soil. Propagate by division in autumn.

Sempervivum zelebori 'Alpha'
CRASSULACEAE

A very pleasing, succulent, rosette-forming cultivar of a rather unusual species, native to Bulgaria and Romania. In a comparatively short time it forms dense cushions to about 30 cm (12 in) in diameter. The rosettes are composed of greyish-green leaves, about 3 cm (1¼ in) or little more across. When these become flower-bearing in summer, the leaves turn reddish and elongate to provide a stem with pink flowers at the tips. Hardy, so is useful for the rock garden, in a very porous garden soil. Propagate by division.

Senecio doronicum
COMPOSITAE

A hairy leaved plant, to about 45 cm (18 in) tall, found in the wild in rocky places in the Alps and Pyrenees at altitudes to 3,000 m (10,000 ft). Leaves elliptical to oval and slightly toothed. Flowers, borne in summer, are bright yellow, 3 – 5 cm (1¼ – 2 in) across, usually solitary, occasionally few together, borne on slender, hairy stems. Suited to rock garden culture, in slightly calcareous, gritty soil. Propagate from seed.

Senecio gallicus
COMPOSITAE

A rather short, annual species, freely branched from the base, found wild from low to medium stony hill sides in southern Europe. Dark green leaves, thick, pinnately lobed into very slender leaflets. Flowers appear throughout summer, yellow, borne in few-flowered terminal clusters, with deep orange centres, each about 2 cm (¾ in) across. Suited to rock garden culture in ordinary garden soil. Propagate from seed in spring.

Serapias lingua
ORCHIDACEAE

A short perennial orchid, widely distributed in southern Europe and northwest Africa. Plants to 25 cm (10 in) tall, the basal leaves glaucous, narrow-lanceolate, the sheathing leaves fresh green. Bracts suffused purple, about 2 cm (¾ in) long. Spike 6 – 9 cm (2½ – 3½ in) long, appearing in late spring and early summer, usually bearing 2 – 6 flowers, each 1 – 3 cm (½ – 1¼ in) long, sepals purplish, green speckled and forming a hood, the lip 3-lobed, purplish, with a black 'hump' at the base of the lip. Best suited to the alpine house in a peaty, loamy mix. Propagate from seed.

Sessilanthera citrina
IRIDACEAE

A bulbous species found wild in pine wood areas at over 2,000 m (6,600 ft) in Guerrero, Mexico. It has one basal leaf, to about 45 cm (18 in) long, and one slightly shorter cauline leaf. The inflorescence has 8 flowers, appearing in succession in early summer. Flowers lemon yellow, 5 – 6 cm (2 – 2½ in) across, the inner petals purple-flecked on the margins, with reddish-yellow spots at the base. A plant for alpine house culture, in a rich, free-draining soil. Propagate from newly harvested seed.

Sessilanthera latifolia ssp. heliantha
IRIDACEAE

A rare bulbous species, found wild in Mexico (Chiapas Guerrero), to altitudes of about 1,800 m (6,000 ft), and in Guatemala. Basal leaves, to 50 cm (20 in) or more long, and 1 – 2, much shorter cauline leaves. In late summer inflorescence bears about 9 flowers, bright yellow, purple-spotted at base of segments, which are 2 – 3 cm (¾ – 1¼ in) long. Essentially a subject for alpine house culture; set deep in well-drained, enriched soil. Propagate from freshly ripened seed.

Silene acaulis
CARYOPHYLLACEAE

A variable, densely mat-forming plant, found in many parts of Europe, from the north, including Britain, to much of the south. It has many glossy green, narrow, pointed leaves about 1 cm (½ in) long, forming cushions. Flowers bright pink, varying to paler shades, even white, appearing in summer, almost stemless. A sunny position is necessary, otherwise a reluctant flowerer, and needs ordinary garden soil. Propagate by division or from seed in spring.

Silene californica
CARYOPHYLLACEAE

A taller growing perennial plant, found in the wild in more northerly parts of California and Oregon, USA. Leafy stems to 30 cm (12 in) or slightly more bear quite large, rich scarlet flowers in summer, the petals being deeply cleft. Needs a rather sheltered, warm place, so is best kept in an alpine house, otherwise it may die back completely as cooler weather arrives. An enriched, well-drained soil is important. Propagate from newly ripened seed.

Silene vulgaris
CARYOPHYLLACEAE

Syn. *S. cucubalus*. Known as the bladder campion because of its veined, bladder-like calyx. A variable species as far as size is concerned, found in coastal regions to fairly high alpine areas of Europe and Asia. Leaves narrowly lance-shaped, somewhat fleshy, greyish-green, 2 – 3 cm (¾ – 1¼ in) long. Flowers are borne on stems about 10 cm (4 in) high during summer, white, about 2 cm (¾ in) wide, with notched petals. Needs full sun and an enriched, peaty, loamy, porous soil. Propagate from newly ripened seed.

Sisyrinchium albidum
IRIDACEAE

Syn. *S. niveum*. A species closely allied to *S. angustifolium*, found in the wild in the USA (Carolina and eastern Mississippi). Leaves pale bluish-green, 15 cm (6 in) or more long. Stems 30 cm (12 in) or more long, carrying a terminal whitish flower about 1.5 cm (⅝ in) in diameter, with a brownish eye, in early summer. A clump-forming plant suited to the rock garden; needs a fairly sunny position, an enriched, slightly acid soil, and careful watering, especially during cooler weather. Propagate from seed, freshly harvested.

Sisyrinchium angustifolium
IRIDACEAE

Syn. *S. bermudiana*. Commonly known as the blue-eyed grass. A tufted plant, found wild in Carolina to Florida, USA, Canada and Bermuda, and naturalized in parts of Europe and Australasia. It has slender, grass-like leaves and a 10 – 50 cm (4 – 20 in) tall stem, which is generally branched. Spathe has 2 – 3 flowers, in varying shades of blue, rarely white, with a yellow eye, flowering in summer. Needs a sheltered position in bright light and a rich, open soil. Propagate from seed sown in spring.

Sisyrinchium arenarium
IRIDACEAE

Syn. *S. cuspidatum*. A variable, tufted species, introduced from the Andes at Mendoza, Chile. Leaves glabrous, flaccid or linear, striated, 30 – 40 cm (12 – 16 in) long. Stems simple or branched, with leaf-like bracts, ovate, 2.5 cm (1 in) long, about 1.2 mm (⁹⁄₁₆ in) wide, the cauline leaves only 18 cm (7½ in) in length. Spikes have 6 – 9 flowers in early summer, yellow, with a brownish throat and petal striate. It has proved hardy, so can be recommended for the rock garden; needs a rich, moisture-retentive soil. Propagate by division or from seed.

Sisyrinchium bellum
IRIDACEAE

A clustering species with spreading, fibrous root-stock, found wild on moist hill sides in the USA (California to Texas). Leaves almost grass-like, to about 30 cm (12 in) long. Stem erect, 2-winged, often branching, to 45 cm (18 in) long. The terminal spathes bear 4 – 7 flowers in early summer; flowers pubescent, amethyst-violet and veined purple with yellow centre. Suited to rock garden culture in full sun, in humus-rich soil. Propagate from seed.

Sisyrinchium californicum
IRIDACEAE

Commonly known as golden-eye grass. A plant with slender, almost grass-like leaves, found wild in North America (southern California to Vancouver Island). Leaves very erect, bright green, 15 – 20 cm (6 – 8 in) long. Stem erect, simple, broadly winged, 30 – 45 cm (12 – 18 in) or more long, bearing bright golden-yellow flowers, about 2 cm (¾ in) across in early summer. Needs a rather moist position, preferably in an alpine house; a peaty, humus-enriched soil is recommended and a bright location. Propagate from seed, freshly harvested.

Sisyrinchium campestre var. kansanum
IRIDACEAE

A tufted species with stiff, erect, striated, slender green leaves, originating from Kansas and Oklahoma, USA, in open prairies. Stems to about 30 cm (12 in) tall, 1 – 2 mm (¹⁄₁₆ – ⅛ in) wide, with purplish-tinged bracts. Flowers pure white, about 2 cm (¾ in) across, with an orange-yellowish eye, appearing in late spring and early summer. Needs a sunny position and a well-drained, humus-enriched soil. Probably best kept in an alpine house. Careful watering is necessary at all times. Propagate from seed, freshly harvested.

Sisyrinchium douglasii
IRIDACEAE

An erect, rather elegant species, 15 – 30 cm (6 – 12 in) tall, native to North America (British Columbia, Canada, to Utah and northern California, USA) in fairly moist areas. Leaves firm, erect, rather rush-like, to 30 cm (12 in) long. Stems slightly longer when in flower, having 1 – 4 spathes in terminal clusters. Flowers bell-shaped, pendent, reddish-rose or purplish, about 1.5 cm (⅝ in) in diameter, in early summer. Needs a partially shaded, moist position, and a rich, permeable, peaty soil. Best suited to an alpine house. Propagate from seed, freshly harvested.

Sisyrinchium fasciculatum
IRIDACEAE

Densely tufted plants to 30 cm (12 in) tall, with a slender, fibrous rootstock, native to Argentina, Paraguay and Uruguay. Leaves basal, narrowly linear, shorter than the stem. Stems rigid, leafless, 30 – 50 cm (12 – 20 in) or more long, bearing terminal clusters of flowers. Spathes of 2 – 8 flowers, whitish-yellow with prominent brown veining, about 1.5 cm (⅝ in) across, in summer. Best suited to the alpine house; needs a moisture-retentive soil, and as sunny position as possible. Propagate from seed, freshly harvested.

Sisyrinchium idahoense var. macounii
IRIDACEAE

A fibrous-rooted plant 30 – 45 cm (12 – 18 in) tall, native to Idaho, USA, and British Columbia, Canada, in fairly moist regions. Stems simple or branched, with elongated, slender bracts, which taper to an acute tip. Inflorescence purple, with 2 – 4 flowers, the segments to 2 cm (¾ in) long, seen at its best in midsummer. Hardy if set in a sheltered position, otherwise best kept in an alpine house; needs fairly rich, porous soil. Propagate by division or from seed, freshly harvested.

Sisyrinchium idahoense var. segetum
IRIDACEAE

Syn. *S. macounii* var. *album*. A tufted species, with pale glaucous leaves, native to Washington State, USA, in moist ground. Stem simple or branched, bearing pale blue to deep violet or white (as shown) flowers in early summer, the segments to 1.8 cm (¹¹⁄₁₆ in) long. A useful plant for either rock garden or alpine house, given the sunniest possible position and a peaty, loamy soil mix with added sand. Propagate by division or from seed.

Sisyrinchium macrocarpum
IRIDACEAE

An attractive species, native to the Patagonian region of Argentina. A somewhat tufted plant, arising from a rhizome. The deep green leaves are slenderly sword-shaped, varying considerably in length. Flowers, deep yellow, 1.5 – 2.5 cm (⅝ – 1 in) in diameter, appear in summer, borne terminally on a stem compressed with sheathing leaves. Needs a bright position, preferably sheltered from extreme cold weather conditions, and an enriched garden soil. Propagate from seed, freshly harvested.

Sisyrinchium pringlei
IRIDACEAE

A plant found in a rather restricted habitat in Guadalajara, Mexico. It has a rootstock of short, thickened fibres, and leaves 15 – 20 cm (6 – 8 in) long, slender, pointed, with short, broad, sheathing, persistent bases. Stem simple, to 60 cm (24 in) long, with a terminal inflorescence 2.5 cm (1 in) or more long. Spathes have 3 – 5 flowers in late summer, yellow, enclosed by lanceolate bracts, the petals 1 cm (½ in) or more long. Needs sun or partial shade and a rich, moisture-retentive soil. Best suited to alpine house culture. Propagate from seed, freshly harvested.

Smilax aspera
SMILACACEAE

A climbing or scrambling plant, usually encountered at medium altitudes on mountain sides in southern Europe. Stems are angled, often with prickles, and can reach lengths of several metres. Leaves tough, shiny, deep green, mostly rather triangular in shape, with tendrils at their base. Flowers, in late summer, are greenish-white, very small, about 5 mm (¼ in), borne in clusters. Needs rich, open soil and protection in winter. Propagate from fresh seed.

Soldanella minima
PRIMULACEAE

A small clustering plant, found in the eastern Alps and the Apennines. The small, almost circular, bright green leaves, to 1 cm (½ in) in diameter, sometimes slightly heart-shaped, are carried on wiry petioles. The scapes, to 10 cm (4 in) tall, bear solitary, bell-shaped flowers, pale blue or violet, rarely white, each to about 1.5 cm (⅝ in) long, in spring. Best suited to alpine house culture; needs good sunlight or partial shade and an enriched, gritty soil. Propagate from newly harvested seed.

Sparaxis pillansii
IRIDACEAE

A cormous species, with stems 45 cm (18 in) or more tall, found in rocky country in Cape Province, South Africa. Leaves slender, lightly ribbed, 30 cm (12 in) or more long, forming basal tufts. Flowers appear in late spring and early summer, several flowers borne on a spike, deep rose-pink, each petal with a yellow, heart-shaped marking at the base. Only half-hardy in cultivation, so if planted outside must be lifted before winter. Perhaps best kept in an alpine house; needs a rich, porous soil and slight shade. Propagate from seed in spring.

Sprekelia formosissima
AMARYLLIDACEAE

The Aztec lily. A clump-forming, bulbous species, originating from southern Mexico and Guatemala, often in scrub or grassland. It has strap-shaped, semi-erect leaves, all basal, often before the flowers, about 30 cm (12 in) long. Flowers appear in spring, borne on a stem 30 cm (12 in) or more long, deep red, the petals having green-lined bases. An alpine house plant; needs to be planted in a porous, humus-enriched soil, the tip of the bulb protruding above the soil. Propagate by division or from seed.

Stachys corsica
LABIATAE

A mat-forming species, originating from Corsica and Sardinia. A quickly spreading plant with bright, almost glossy green, oval leaves, which very soon develop into dense mats. Flowers are borne in summer on stems barely 5 cm (2 in) tall, creamy pink in colour and massed in small clusters. A sun-loving plant; very useful for the rock garden. Needs a well-drained, humus-rich soil. Propagate by division after summer flowering.

Stachys lavandulifolia
LABIATAE

A fairly low-growing species with creeping, rooting stems, native to the Caucasus and Armenia, hardly exceeding 15 cm (6 in) in height. Leaves greyish-green and quite velvety. Flowers during summer on stems to 15 cm (6 in) long, purplish-red, arranged in whorls along almost their full length. Needs a position in full sun and a well-drained, peaty, loamy soil, preferably in a rock garden. Propagate by division at planting time in spring or autumn.

Staehlina dubia
COMPOSITAE

The tassel flower. A perennial, woody-based, bushy plant with white-felted, erect or semi-erect branches, widespread in the Mediterranean region, invariably on dry, stony ground. Leaves very slender, deep green, minutely hairy on the underside, the margins mostly serrated, 3 – 5 mm (³⁄₁₆ – ¼ in) wide. Flowers terminal in summer, in an almost cylindrical head, about 3 cm (1¼ in) long, 5 mm (¼ in) wide, of purplish-pink flowers and apical tufts of whitish, slightly bristly hairs. Needs alpine house culture and an open, rich soil. Propagate from seed in spring.

Stapelia desmetiana var. pallida
ASCLEPIADACEAE

A succulent species, found widespread in hilly country in southeastern regions of Cape Province, South Africa. Stems 20 – 25 cm (8 – 10 in) long, semi-erect, about 3 cm (1¼ in) thick, with 4 dentate angles. Flowers, solitary or several together, are borne in summer; the corolla about 1.5 cm (⅝ in) across with lance-shaped, tapering lobes to 7 cm (2¾ in) long, 3 cm (1¼ in) wide, yellowish with brownish transverse lines, reddish-brown ciliate margins. For alpine house cultivation; needs an open soil. Propagate from cuttings.

Stenomesson humile
AMARYLLIDACEAE

A small bulbous plant of particularly dwarf growth, originating from the Peruvian Andes, at altitudes to about 3,000 m (10,000 ft). It has 3 – 4 very slender, dark green leaves, which scarcely remain erect, all basal. Flowers usually appear in early summer, borne on a very short stem about 10 cm (4 in) long, singly and terminally, red and sulphur yellow. Needs alpine house culture in a permeable soil, enriched with leaf mould. Propagate only from freshly harvested seed, temperature 15°C (59°F).

Stenomesson variegatum
AMARYLLIDACEAE

Syn. *S. coccineum*, *S. incarnatum*. A clump-forming, bulbous species, found wild in the Peruvian Andes at altitudes over 3,200 m (10,500 ft). Grows to about 45 cm (18 in) high when in bloom, the leaves, slender and strap-like, most often produced after the flowers, occasionally at the same time. Flowers usually appear in spring, and are variably coloured – reddish-yellow, pink, yellow or white – somewhat tubular, with 6 green-tipped lobes. For alpine house culture, in an enriched soil. Propagate by division or from seed.

Sternbergia sicula
AMARYLLIDACEAE

Syn. *Sternbergia lutea* var. *angustifolia*. A fairly low-growing, bulbous plant, found in hills and low mountainous regions of southern Italy, southern Greece and the Aegean Islands. Leaves deep green, strap-shaped, to 1.5 cm (⅝ in) wide, appearing with or before the flowers. Flowers bright yellow, about 5 cm (2 in) long, borne solitary on slender scapes in late summer. Best suited to the alpine house; needs a slightly calcareous, open soil. Propagate by division of bulbs when dormant or from freshly harvested seed.

Strumaria salteri
AMARYLLIDACEAE

A bulbous species, introduced from the slopes of the Pakhuis Mountains in the Clanwilliam district of South Africa. Leaves, slender, lance-shaped, appear after the flowers. Flowers appear in summer, terminally on a rather decumbent scape, to about 40 cm (16 in) long, rose-pink with a darker central keel on the petals, the white stamens protruding. A plant for alpine house culture; needs a well-drained soil enriched with leaf mould. Propagate from seed, freshly harvested.

Strumaria truncata
AMARYLLIDACEAE

A bulbous species, found wild in the Clanwilliam district (west Karoo, Namaqualand), South Africa, in stony or sandy sites. Leaves strap-shaped, erect, 20 cm (8 in) or more long, appearing with the flowers. Flowers in summer, white or pale pink, borne terminally on stems to 35 cm (14 in) long, 4 – 5 in a loose cluster, always pendulous. Alpine house culture very necessary; needs an enriched, open soil, in sun. Propagates best from freshly harvested seed, temperature about 15℃ (59℉).

Stylidium graminifolium
STYLIDIACEAE

A widespread, perennial species, found wild in Tasmania and eastern Australia. The slender, grass-like leaves, to 15 cm (6 in) long, form a fairly dense, tuft-like, basal cluster. Flowers, about 1 cm (½ in) long, appear in early to midsummer, pink to magenta, several borne on a long, glandular spike. A fascinating plant for alpine house culture; needs a very rich, permeable soil and a sunny site, away from any cool draughts. Propagation can be achieved only by careful pollination of the tiny flowers and the seed sown immediately it is harvested.

Sutherlandia montana
LEGUMINOSAE

A species closely resembling the better known *S. frutescens*, but of shorter growth, found wild in mountainous areas in Cape Province, South Africa, and in Namibia. A shrub, to about 60 cm (24 in) high, with leaves divided into 13 – 17 leaflets set opposite, each about 1.8 cm (¹¹/₁₆ in) long, greyish-green. Flowers bright red, to about 5 cm (2 in) long, carried in loose clusters towards the tips of the stems, flowering in summer. It may prove hardy in southern Britain, but is generally best kept in an alpine house. Needs a rich, permeable soil. Propagate from fresh seed.

Symphyandra wanneri
CAMPANULACEAE

A campanula-like, herbaceous, perennial species, originating from the Balkan region. The broad, lanceolate, deeply toothed leaves form a many-leaved rosette, these being dark green, hairy on the upper surface. Stems 20 – 45 cm (8 – 18 in) long, bearing many rich violet, bell-shaped flowers to 3.5 cm (1⅜ in) long, the petals outward-spreading at the tips, during summer. Needs a rich, sandy loam and a position in slight shade. Propagate from seed sown in spring.

Synnotia parviflora
IRIDACEAE

A rather short, cormous plant, found in sandy soil on low mountain sides in Cape Province (Malmesbury), South Africa. Stems, to 30 cm (12 in) high, occasionally have a single branch from base. Leaves, 7 – 9 in number, 3 – 18 cm (1¼ – 7½ in) long, very slender and pointed. Flowers, borne in late spring, are cream, about 2.5 cm (1 in) across, the lower segments bright yellow with brown dots at the base. For alpine house culture; needs an enriched, sandy soil. Propagate from seed, freshly harvested.

Synnotia variegata
IRIDACEAE

Syn. *Sparaxis wattii*. A cormous species, found in the low hills around Paarl and Clanwilliam in Cape Province, South Africa. Stems vary considerably in length, 8 – 30 cm (3 – 12 in) or more tall, simple or 1 – 3 branched. Leaves to 15 cm (6 in) long, 2 cm (¾ in) wide, with a prominent midrib, arranged in a rosette. Flowers in midsummer, pale mauve and yellow cream, to dark purple and yellow, 2 – 7 on a spike. For the alpine house; needs sun and a well-drained, enriched soil, and a completely dry dormancy. Propagate from seed, freshly harvested.

Synthyris missurica
SCROPHULARIACEAE

A clump-forming, low-growing species, to about 15 cm (6 in) tall, introduced from North America. It has fairly deep green, kidney-shaped leaves, which are tough and quite leathery, the edges minutely toothed. Flowers appear in early summer, many, small, clear blue, bell-shaped, in compact, cylindrical racemes on stems just over-topping the leafy cushion. Alpine house culture is essential; needs a lime-free, gritty soil mix, which includes decomposed leaf mould. Propagate by division or from newly ripened seed.

Synthyris reniformis
SCROPHULARIACEAE

A clump-forming plant, but only low-growing, to 10 cm (4 in) high, found wild in North America. Leaves dark green, evergreen, basal, 2 – 5 cm (¾ – 2 in) wide, somewhat kidney-shaped, with crenate margins and frequently hairy. Flowers purple-blue, slender, bell-shaped, in racemes, appearing in late spring and early summer. Best grown in an alpine house, in a rather rich soil, which must be porous. Propagate by careful division or from fresh seed.

Syringodea unifolia
IRIDACEAE

A cormous species, native to Cape Province, South Africa, primarily in the Worcester and Calvinia areas in hilly country. It produces a solitary, rather succulent leaf, which is very slender, scarcely 12 cm (5 in) long. Flowers during summer, solitary or 1 – 4 together, pale bluish-pink with darker purplish marking at the base of each segment, the throat yellowish-orange, 5 – 6 cm (2 – 2½ in) wide when fully open. Suited to alpine house culture, in a very sandy, humus-enriched soil. Propagate from seed in spring.

Trillium sessile

Talinum okanoganense
PORTULACACEAE

A totally prostrate succulent species from Washington State, USA. It has very fleshy stems with narrow-pointed, grey-green, fleshy leaves forming mats. Flowers appear in spring, creamy white, almost stemless, to 2.5 cm (1 in) across, with somewhat dense clusters of stamens protruding. Best suited to alpine house culture, needing protection from chilly conditions. Needs a rich, porous soil. Propagate from seed, soon after harvesting.

Tecophilaea cyanocrocus
AMARYLLIDACEAE

A cormous-rooted species, originating from Chile. Leaves basal, linear-lanceolate, to 12 cm (5 in) long, usually only 2 – 3 in number. Flowers appear in spring, solitary, on stems to 15 cm (6 in) long, crocus-like, 3 – 4 cm (1¼ – 1½ in) deep, intense blue with whitish throat. Best in an alpine house. Plant in autumn in an enriched, fertile soil, in a bright but sheltered position. Keep moist until growth is evident, then water freely until leaves fade; keep dry thereafter. Propagate from offsets.

Tecophilaea cyanocrocus var. leichtlinii
AMARYLLIDACEAE

A botanical variety, very similar in all respects to the species and from similar habitats. The principal difference is in the flowers, which are a paler shade of blue and have a more prominent, large white eye, borne solitary, occasionally 2 – 3 to a stem. Cultural requirements are the same as for the species. Propagate from offsets or from seed sown in spring, temperature 21 °C (70 °F).

Tephrocactus articulatus var. syringacanthus
CACTACEAE

A low-growing, spreading species, found wild on very high ground in more westerly areas of Argentina (around Catamarca). Stems, greyish-green, are about 5 cm (2 in) thick and to 10 cm (4 in) high. Flowers, in early summer, are whitish, with very pale pink suffusion. Spines are very prominent, brownish-green, 5 cm (2 in) or more long. Best kept in an alpine house in a normal cactus compost. Propagate from stem cuttings in summer.

Teucrium aroanium
LABIATAE

A semi-prostrate, twiggy-stemmed species, from mountainous regions of southern Greece, forming hummocks to 30 cm (12 in) in diameter. Leaves obovate, silvery green, white-woolly on under-surface, 8 – 15 mm (⁷⁄₁₆ – ⅝ in) long, are set in opposite pairs along the short flowering stems. Flowers, soft bluish-purple, to 2 cm (¾ in) long, appear in summer. A plant ideal for a trough garden, in a bright sunny position and in a well-drained soil. Propagate by cuttings in summer.

Teucrium marum
LABIATAE

Syn. *Micromeria corsica*. An aromatic, shrubby plant, found on many islands in the Mediterranean and Adriatic, to about 30 cm (12 in) tall. Stems slightly white-woolly, bearing white-felted, somewhat lanceolate leaves, 1 cm (½ in) long. Flowers appear in summer, pinkish-purple, about 1 cm (½ in) or a little more long, in a somewhat cylindrical inflorescence. Needs a very porous, gritty but rich soil, and a position in bright light. Propagate by cuttings in summer or from seed in spring.

Teucrium pyrenaicum
LABIATAE

A spreading, somewhat prostrate, shrubby plant, found in northern Spain and southwestern France. It has stems about 20 cm (8 in) long, bedecked with rounded, crenate, softly hairy, green leaves, to 2.5 cm (1 in) long. Flowers appear in summer and early autumn, cream or purple and white, 2 cm (¾ in) long, in terminal heads. Needs a very porous, slightly enriched soil and sun. Propagate from seed or by division in spring.

Thlaspi rotundifolium
CRUCIFERAE

A tufted, stoloniferous species, found in mountainous regions of eastern France and Italy. Growth arises from a deep taproot, the stolons spreading to form rosette-like tufts to 10 cm (4 in) or more high. Leaves waxy, dark green, broadly ovate, about 1 cm (½ in) wide. Flowers scented, rose-lilac to purple, about 8 mm (⁷⁄₁₆ in) across, in spring. Needs a porous soil and sun. Propagate from seed in spring.

Thymelaea tartonraira
THYMELAEACEAE

A small, branching, more or less erect shrub to about 45 cm (18 in) high, coated with numerous silvery, silky hairs, found principally in southern Spain and northwestern Africa. Leaves narrowly oblong and silky, spreading, 1 – 2 cm (½ – ¾ in) long. Flowers appear in summer, yellowish, but inconspicuous, 3 – 4 mm (³⁄₁₆ in) long, in small clusters among the upper leaves; these, too, are silky. Plants are male or female, so both must be obtained if seed is to be produced. Perhaps best grown in an alpine house in a very open soil. Propagate from seed in spring.

Thymus cilicicus
LABIATAE

A small, bush-like plant to 18 cm (7½ in) high, sometimes more prostrate, forming mats, which is native to Turkey. Its linear, ciliate leaves are about 1 cm (½ in) long, pale green, arranged in opposite pairs. Flowers appear in summer, borne on short stems in clusters of pinkish-lilac to mauve, individual flowers 7 mm (⅜ in) long. Best suited to alpine house culture; needs bright light and a well-drained soil. Propagate by division or from seed in spring.

Thymus comosus
LABIATAE

A low-growing, spreading plant, to about 15 cm (6 in) high, originating from eastern Europe and Asia Minor. An aromatic plant, with more or less ovate, hairy, green leaves set opposite in pairs along the trailing stems. Flowers appear in summer, bright pink, in wide clusters, carried on short stems. There are forms of the species, some of which have exceptionally hairy leaves. Suitable for rock garden culture, preferably on sloping ground; needs sun and a porous soil.

Thymus x 'Doone Valley'
LABIATAE

An attractive hybrid of unknown parentage. A mat-forming plant suitable for the rock garden, the rather pale, olive green leaves invariably lined and dotted with bright yellow. Flowers appear in summer, pale to deep lavender, carried in rounded clusters on stems about 12 cm (5 in) long. Needs a position in sunlight and a gritty, but enriched soil. Propagate by cuttings in summer.

Thymus serpyllum 'Elfin'
LABIATAE

The species is a widely distributed plant in Europe, and this is a tightly dome-forming form. The very slender, almost thread-like stems carry small, ovate leaves to about 8 mm ($^{7}/_{16}$ in) long, distinctly aromatic and closely compacted together. Flowers appear in summer, variable in colour, 4 – 6 mm ($^{3}/_{16}$ – $^{5}/_{16}$ in) long, borne in terminal heads. A plant for the rock garden; needs sun and a permeable soil. Propagate by cuttings in summer.

Thymus zygis
LABIATAE

An erect, perennial herb, native to the Iberian Peninsula, often used for culinary purposes. The woody stems, to 22 cm (8$^{3}/_{4}$ in) tall, are hairy, as are the linear to elliptic, greyish-green leaves, fringed with hairs at their base. Flowers white or pale pinkish, each about 5 mm ($^{1}/_{4}$ in) long, appear in clusters in early summer. Probably best suited to the alpine house; needs warmth, sun and a rich, porous soil. Propagate by cuttings in summer.

Thysanotus patersonii
LILIACEAE

A tuberous-rooted fringe lily, found wild in Victoria, South Australia. It has leafless, creeping or climbing stems – its very slender radical leaves appear, then wither very early. Flowers borne in summer on lateral branches, solitary, about 1 cm ($^{1}/_{2}$ in) wide, with 3 sepals and 3 petals, violet, very hairy edges and centre line. Needs to be grown in an alpine house, in a gritty, humus-rich soil and in the brightest possible position. Can be propagated by division, but best from seed sown in spring.

Tigridia cristata
IRIDACEAE

A rare bulbous species, which originates from the high Andes (Peru), at altitudes of 3,500 m (11,500 ft) or more. Leaves, lance-shaped, are all basal, 30 cm (12 in) or more long. Flowers, borne in spring on an inflorescence shorter than the foliage, are whitish with pale lilac-pink feathering, 2 – 4 cm ($^{3}/_{4}$ – 1$^{1}/_{2}$ in) across. Can be used in the rock garden, set in well-drained, rich soil; bulbs should be planted 15 cm (6 in) deep. Propagate from fresh seed.

Tigridia dugesii
IRIDACEAE

Syn. *Nemastylis dugesii*. A bulbous plant, rarely exceeding 12 cm (5 in) high, found wild in wooded areas in Durango and Jalisco, Mexico, on mountain slopes at altitudes of about 2,000 m (6,600 ft). Leaves rather slender, soon withering. Flowers in mid- to late summer, bright yellow on erect stems, each 3 – 4.5 cm (1$^{1}/_{4}$ – 1$^{3}/_{4}$ in) in diameter, the outer segments having reddish-brown spots on the blade. Can be grown in a rock garden, but must be lifted when the flowers have died down; otherwise keep in an alpine house. Needs a rich, porous soil. Propagate from seed.

Tigridia durangensis
IRIDACEAE

A short-stemmed, bulbous species, found at altitudes of over 2,500 m (8,200 ft) in moist areas in Durango, Mexico. It has a few slender basal leaves to about 12 cm (5 in) long. Flowers in summer, erect, to 4.5 cm (1$^{3}/_{4}$ in) in diameter, outer segments to 2 cm ($^{3}/_{4}$ in) long, lavender-coloured with white spots and feathering, inner segments bright purple-dotted. Semi-hardy, so better kept in an alpine house; needs a very rich but gritty soil. Propagate from seed, sown when newly ripened, temperature 15 °C (59 °F).

Titanopsis calcarea
AIZOACEAE

A plant from high altitudes in west Griqualand, Cape Province, South Africa, which forms dense clusters. The spathulate, greenish-blue, succulent leaves – usually about 2.5 cm (1 in) long, 1.2 cm (⁹⁄₁₆ in) wide at the tips, 8 mm (⁷⁄₁₆ in) wide at the base – have many greyish tubercles on the surface. Flowers, in summer, are bright golden-yellow, about 2 cm (¾ in) in diameter. Best kept in the alpine house; needs an open, humus-rich soil. Propagate from seed, newly ripened.

Townsendia exscapa
COMPOSITAE

A mat-forming species with aster-like flowers, originating from western areas of the USA. It has greyish, rather silky, slightly erect, linear leaves, about 5 cm (2 in) long. Flowers in summer, borne almost sessile, hardly exceeding the foliage, pure white or very pale pink, 2 cm (¾ in) or little more in diameter, with a prominent, bright orange-yellow disc. Needs a sunny, free-draining position and a humus-enriched soil. Propagate from freshly harvested seed.

Townsendia formosa
COMPOSITAE

A tuft-forming, hardy, low-growing species, found in New Mexico, USA. Tufts of about 10 cm (4 in) in diameter are formed of narrow, thin-textured, lanceolate leaves. Aster-like flowers appear in summer, lilac to violet-blue, carried singly on very short stalks scarcely topping the foliage. A bright, sunny position is recommended, preferably on slightly sloping ground, in an enriched, well-drained soil. Propagate from newly ripened seed.

Trachelium asperuloides
CAMPANULACEAE

Syn. *Diosphaera asperuloides*. A cushion-forming perennial plant, with stems about 5 cm (2 in) long, found in rock crevices in southern Greece. It has short, shiny green leaves, more or less rounded and stalkless. Flowers in spring and summer, pink or pale bluish, with a tubular corolla to 6 mm (⁵⁄₁₆ in) long and 5 shorter lobes. Needs sun and gritty soil. Propagate from seed sown in spring or from basal cuttings in summer.

Trachelium caeruleum
CAMPANULACEAE

A fairly hardy perennial species, widely distributed throughout much of southern Spain and southern Portugal, mainly on low hill sides or among rocks. When in flower, plants can be 45 cm (18 in) or more tall. Leaves oval, with toothed margins, to 8 cm (3 in) long. Flowers are terminally borne in spring and summer, in dense, flat-topped clusters, small, about 6 mm (⁵⁄₁₆ in) long, with minute spreading lobes of lavender blue or lilac shades. Needs a bright position and a porous, enriched soil. Propagate from seed or basal shoot cuttings.

Trachelium jacquinii rumelianum
CAMPANULACEAE

A woody-based perennial plant, found in Greece and Bulgaria. Fairly low-growing, forming tufts of green, oval-shaped, serrated leaves, 2 – 5 cm (¾ – 2 in) long, carried on rather sprawling stems. Flowers appear in late summer, about 5 mm (¼ in) long, lilac to deep blue, in dense heads. Best grown in an alpine house; needs a bright, sheltered position and a fertile, slightly alkaline soil. Propagate by basal cuttings or from seed in spring.

Tradescantia sillamontana
COMMELINACEAE

A cushion-forming, semi-succulent species, found at low altitudes on mountains in northeast Mexico. The stems and leaves form quite thick cushions to about 15 cm (6 in) across. Stems, 5 – 6 cm (2 – 2½ in) long, are coated with thick, white hairs, and bear many green leaves, distichously arranged, more or less oblong with pointed tips, to 2 cm (¾ in) long, 2 mm (⅛ in) thick and densely covered with white hairs. Flowers, in summer, are pinkish-mauve, 1.5 cm (⅝ in) or more wide. Requires alpine house culture. Propagate by division or from seed.

Trichodiadema bulbosum
AIZOACEAE

A low-growing, spreading plant, native to hill sides in Cape Province, South Africa. This succulent species has a tuberous rootstock, producing a stem up to 20 cm (8 in) high. Leaves grey-green from papillae, more or less cylindrical, 3 – 8 mm (³⁄₁₆ –⁷⁄₁₆ in) long, to 4 mm (³⁄₁₆ in) thick, with minute white bristles. Flowers appear during summer, each about 2 cm (¾ in) in diameter and deep red in colour. Ideally suited for the alpine house; needs an open, enriched compost and a position in full sun. Water freely in summer; keep dry in winter.

Tridentea dinteri
ASCLEPIADACEAE

Syn. *Stapelia dinteri*. A low-growing, succulent species, found on high ground in many northern areas of southwest Africa, especially Namibia. Stems to 12 cm (5 in) high, 1 – 1.5 cm (½ – ⅝ in) thick, 4-angled, greyish-green with brown dots and blotches. The corolla, about 3 cm (1¼ in) across, has greenish-yellow lobes, densely coated with reddish-brown dots, the margins edged with reddish-brown cilia. For alpine house culture. Propagate from stem cuttings.

Tridentea longipes
ASCLEPIADACEAE

Syn. *Stapelia longipes*. A compact, clump-forming species, native to high ground in southwest Africa and Namibia. Clumps often to 30 cm (12 in) or more in diameter. Stems, to 12 cm (5 in) long, 1.5 cm (⅝ in) thick, and 4-angled and greyish-green. The corolla, about 6 cm (2½ in) across, with lobes about 2 cm (¾ in) long, tapering towards the tips; the upper part deep purplish, with white blotches, dots and lines below. Alpine house culture is essential for midsummer flowering. Propagate from stem cuttings.

Trillium sessile
LILIACEAE

A short, rhizomatous species, originating from more easterly parts of North America. It has ovate or elliptic leaves, with pale and dark green mottling, about 10 cm (4 in) long. Flowers more or less stalkless, to about 4 cm (1½ in) long, generally maroon, though yellowish-green flowers are also known. Fairly hardy, useful for the rock garden. Needs a moisture-retentive, well-drained soil, enriched with leaf mould, and a position in partial shade. Propagate by division or from fresh ripe seed.

Trimezia martinicensis
IRIDACEAE

A cormous species found wild throughout much of South America (Brazil to Mexico), also on many of the West Indian islands, at altitudes to 1,700 m (5,600 ft). Leaves very narrow, flattened, distichously arranged, to 30 cm (12 in) long. Stems erect, terete, glabrous, bearing several flowers in succession in summer, each to 2.5 cm (1 in) across, bright yellow, sometimes tinged greyish-blue. Best kept in an alpine house, in a humus-rich, porous soil. Propagate from seed, sown soon after harvesting.

Triteleia bridgesii
LILIACEAE

Syn. *Brodiaea bridgesii*. A cormous species, native to northwestern areas of the USA, which forms basal tufts of long, slender, fleshy leaves. Flowers appear in early summer, in clusters of up to 20, funnel-shaped, lilac or blue, starry, borne terminally on stems to 45 cm (18 in) long. A reasonably hardy species; plant about 15 cm (6 in) deep in spring or autumn, in full sun, in a well-drained, humus-enriched soil. Propagate from seed or from offsets in autumn.

Tritonia crocata
IRIDACEAE

A cormous plant, originating from Cape Province to Natal, South Africa. Leaves basal, lanceolate, distichously arranged, 12 – 15 cm (5 – 6 in) long. Stem somewhat wiry, about 30 cm (12 in) long, rarely branching. Flowers mostly orange, some-times pinkish, appearing in succession in summer from a spike bearing several flowers, each about 3 cm (1¼ in) in diameter when fully open. Needs to be grown in an alpine house for best results, in a rich, light soil. Propagates easily from seed, sown in spring, temperature 15 °C (59 °F).

Tritonia deusta ssp. miniata
IRIDACEAE

A rare plant with cormous rootstock, found wild on high ground in Cape Province, South Africa. It has 4 – 8 more or less erect leaves, distichously arranged, lanceolate and striated, to 20 cm (8 in) long, about 1 cm (½ in) wide. Flowers, which appear in summer, are bright reddish-orange, usually solitary or up to 3 on a spike, often with a deeper coloured median line to the petals. Essentially a plant for the alpine house; needs a rich, open, fertile soil. Propagate from freshly harvested seed.

Tritonia lancea
IRIDACEAE

A cormous-rooted species originating from Picketberg, Cape Province, South Africa. It has 4 – 5 lanceolate leaves to about 20 cm (8 in) long, the margins in-rolled. The stem, to 25 cm (10 in) long, has 1 – 2 cauline leaves, to 7 cm (2¾ in) long, and a spike with 1 – 7 flowers overtopping the leaves. Flowers are white with short, reddish lines on the upper segments, about 3 – 4 cm (1¼ – 1½ in) across, appearing in summer. Not thoroughly hardy, so best grown in an alpine house, in a well-drained, humus-enriched soil. Propagate from fresh seed.

Tritoniopsis ramosa
IRIDACEAE

A cormous species, widespread in southwestern districts of Cape Province, South Africa, at altitudes of about 1,500 m (5,000 ft). Leaves, which usually appear after the flowers have developed, are slender, about 25 cm (10 in) long. The sweetly scented flowers are pinkish-mauve, the lower segments having a reddish median line between 2 white lines, on a spike 15 cm (6 in) long, borne on a stem 45 cm (18 in) or more in length. Grow in an alpine house, in a humus-rich, well-drained soil. Propagate from the fresh, winged seed, temperature 15 °C (59 °F).

Tropaeolum polyphyllum
TROPACOLACEAE

A tuberous-rooted, mat-forming, perennial species, found on mountain slopes in Chile. Stems vary in length, widely spreading, with digitate leaves divided into 5 – 7 oval leaflets of deep green. Flowers are borne terminally in summer in dense, leafy clusters, each about 3 cm (1¼ in) across, bright yellow or orange, the petals prominently notched. Reasonably hardy if planted in a warm, sheltered, sunny position in a rock garden, in a humus-rich, very porous soil. Propagate from freshly ripened seed, temperature 12 °C (54 °F).

Tulbaghia fragrans
LILIACEAE

A bulbous plant found wild in rocky areas of Transvaal, South Africa. Leaves greyish-green, somewhat fleshy, 30 – 45 cm (12 – 18 in) long and to 2 cm (¾ in) wide. Terminal umbels, about 8 cm (3 in) in diameter, of small, deep lilac, scented flowers, on stems about 35 cm (14 in) long, appear in summer. Only half-hardy, so best kept in an alpine house, in a good, rich, well-drained soil. Propagate from bulbils or seed.

Tulipa humilis
LILIACEAE

Syn. *T. pulchella* var. *humilis*. A low-growing, bulbous plant, only about 10 cm (4 in) high, originating from Iran. The very slender leaves are more or less erect, dark green in colour. Flowers appear in spring, about 3.5 cm (1⅜ in) long, greenish-red on the outer surface of the segments, yellow and purple on the inner surface. Very well suited to a rock garden or alpine house; needs sun and an open, enriched soil. Propagates easily from seed.

Tulipa polychroma
LILIACEAE

Syn. *I. biflora* A small bulbous species, originating from mountainous regions of Iran, Turkey and the Caucasus. Usually 2 lanceolate leaves embrace the branched, fleshy stem. Flowers appear in late winter and early spring, often up to 5, whitish, with distinct yellow centres, on stems up to 15 cm (6 in) long. Best kept in an alpine house; needs cool conditions and a well-drained soil. Bulbs are best lifted during dormancy. Propagate from seed, freshly harvested.

Tulipa tarda
LILIACEAE

A very short-stemmed species, native to eastern Turkestan, rarely exceeding 15 cm (6 in) high. Leaves usually basal, bright green, linear to lanceolate, about 20 cm (8 in) or a little more in length. Flowers appear on short stems about 5 cm (2 in) long, 5 – 7 to a stem, star-like, golden-yellow, tipped with white, each to 4 cm (1½ in) long, at their best in late spring. A freely spreading plant, requiring bright light and an enriched, free-draining soil. Propagate from freshly ripened seed.

Tulipa violacea
LILIACEAE

Syn. *T. pulchella* var. *violacea*. This is very similar in most respects to *T. humilis* as far as foliage is concerned, but with flowers in varying shades of violet-purple. The general growth and flowering pattern is the same. A good plant for the rock garden; it thrives in a bright, sunny position and needs an enriched, permeable soil to flower at its best. Propagate from freshly ripened seed.

Tulipa vvedenskyi
LILIACEAE

One of the most attractive species; a large bulbous plant, found wild in central Asia, especially in the Tien Shan region. Leaves are narrow, greyish-green. Flowers appear in midsummer, carried on a fleshy stem 35 – 45 cm (14 – 18 in) long, brilliant red or orange-red with either a black or yellow centre, and when fully open may reach 20 cm (8 in) in diameter. Needs a warm position in the rock garden (so flourishes in a hot summer) and a well-drained soil. Best lifted before winter. Propagate from seed, freshly harvested.

Verbena peruviana

U-Z

Ulex minor
LEGUMINOSAE

A low-growing, evergreen shrub, the stems of which are all spine-tipped, found wild in much of the Mediterranean region on exposed limestone rock-faces. Leaves gradually reduced to scales as growth matures, the spine tips becoming more pronounced. Flowers in summer, golden-yellow, about 1.5 cm (⅝ in) long, slightly fragrant, clustering along the length of the shoots to the very tips. Succeeds in a sunny rock garden in calcareous soil; otherwise best kept in an alpine house. Propagate from seed in spring.

Umbilicus rupestris
CRASSULACEAE

A rather variable, perennial, semi-succulent species, native to rocky hill sides (as shown) in many parts of Europe and North Africa. It has a tuberous rootstock and large, smooth, green, orbicular leaves, with prominently scalloped edges, varying from 8 mm (⁷⁄₁₆ in) to 6 cm (2½ in) across, narrowing from the base to the upper part of the stem. Flowers tubular, whitish-pinkish, to 1 cm (½ in), in early summer. Needs a fairly rich, gritty soil and a position in slight shade. Propagate by division in autumn.

Urceolina peruviana
AMARYLLIDACEAE

A bulbous plant, originating from Peru and Bolivia. It is more or less leafless at flowering time, those that are produced remaining almost prostrate. Stems about 24 cm (9½ in) long bear 2 – 6 bright red, tubular flowers, each on a short pedicel, scented, about 4 cm (1½ in) long, always pendent, in early summer. Needs humus-rich, slightly sandy soil; best kept in pots in an alpine house. Keep dry when the leaves and flowers have withered. Propagate from seed in spring.

Urospermum picroides
COMPOSITAE

A medium sized perennial species found wild in southern Europe, in grasslands and rocky places. The basal leaves are oblong-spathulate, pinnately lobed, the stem leaves more lanceolate, often toothed. Flowers appear in early summer, bright yellow, about 4 cm (1½ in) across with a small, brownish centre, the rays numerous and pointed. Can be grown in a rock garden in a sheltered, sunny position and in a permeable, slightly enriched soil. Propagate from seed sown soon after ripening.

Veltheimia bracteata
LILIACEAE

A winter-flowering, bulbous species, native to South Africa, mainly in forest areas. Leaves shiny green, basal, about 7 cm (2¾ in) wide, with crinkled edges. Stems 30 cm (12 in) or more high, bearing a short raceme of reddish-pink, tubular, pendent flowers. The cultivar 'Rosalba' is similar in growth habit, but with yellowish flowers tinted red (as shown), each flower 3 – 5 cm (1¼ – 2 in) long. An excellent plant for the alpine house; needs a sunny position and a rich soil mix of loam, leaf mould and manure. Propagate from freshly ripened seed.

Veltheimia capensis
LILIACEAE

A large, bulbous, early spring-flowering species from eastern regions of Cape Province, South Africa. Leaves short and slightly fleshy, with undulate margins, forming a basal rosette. Flowers variable in colour – yellow, pinkish or pale reddish – tubular in shape, borne terminally and tending to be widely spreading, 3 – 5 cm (1¼ – 2 in) long, and long-lasting. Needs to be grown in an alpine house, in a fairly sunny position, and in a soil composed of equal parts of loam, peat and manure. Propagate from freshly ripened seed, minimum temperature 15 ℃ (59 ℉).

Veratrum album var. flavum
LILIACEAE

A robust, perennial species, found wild in mountain pastures in more northerly parts of Spain and Portugal and France. It has basal, slender leaves, about 30 cm (12 in) long, and more obovate, pleated stem leaves arranged in whorls, somewhat hairy on the underside. Yellowish flowers are borne in summer in a terminal, branched panicle, to 30 cm (12 in) long. Ideally suited to the rock garden, in sun or partial shade; needs a humus-rich, moisture-retentive, but slightly gritty soil. Propagate from seed in spring.

Verbascum x 'Letitia'
SCROPHULARIACEAE

A hybrid of *V. dumulosum* and *V. spinosum*. This is a small, shrubby plant, to about 25 cm (10 in) in diameter. The bright, silvery white leaves, about 5 cm (2 in) long, are woolly, oblong-lanceolate, arranged in fairly dense formation along the stems. Flowers appear in summer, terminally in short racemes, bright yellow, each 2.5 cm (1 in) wide, each petal with a basal brown blotch. Needs sun and a very porous soil. Propagate from seed in spring.

Verbascum thapsus
SCROPHULARIACEAE

A tall species, to 1 m (3ft) or more, which is, nevertheless, an attractive, elegant background plant for the rock garden. Found at low and high altitudes in much of southern Europe. Stems soft, greyish-woolly, with more or less blunt, oblong leaves at the base, and smaller stem leaves. Flowers, in summer, yellow, about 3 cm (1¼ in) wide, are borne in long, many flowered racemes. Needs a very open, slightly enriched soil. Propagate from seed, freshly harvested.

Verbena peruviana
VERBENACEAE

A half-hardy, prostrate plant originating from South America (Argentina to southern Brazil). The stems, normally prostrate, tend to become fairly erect, to 10 cm (4 in) tall. Leaves more or less oval, to 5 cm (2 in) long. Rich scarlet flowers, about 1 cm (½ in) across, are produced terminally in low spikes in summer and early autumn. Best kept in an alpine house, where it can be grown success-fully in full sun and fertile soil. Propagate from seed in spring.

Verbena supina
VERBENACEAE

A low-growing, almost prostrate species, native to moist areas on low hill sides in southern Europe. Leaves, 1 – 2 pinnately divided, are carried opposite on somewhat woody branches. Flowers, pinkish-lilac, very small, borne in dense, often branched spikes, about 6 cm (2½ in) long, appear in early summer. Best treated as an annual; needs moisture-retentive soil and a position in partial shade. Propagate from seed sown immediately after ripening.

Veronica cinerea
SCROPHULARIACEAE

A mat-forming species found in Turkey, perennial, eventually to 15 cm (6 in) tall. Leaves linear to lanceolate, evergreen with in-rolled edges, greyish and downy. Spikes of pale blue flowers, each about 6 mm (⁵⁄₁₆ in) wide, appear in summer. Suited to either rock garden or alpine house; needs bright sun and an enriched, permeable soil. Propagate by division in spring or cuttings in summer.

Veronica prostrata
SCROPHULARIACEAE

Syn. *V. rupestris*. A mat-forming plant, not exceeding 10 cm (4 in) high, found in many parts of Europe, from Spain to northern central Russia. The leaves are downy, more or less oblong, 2 cm (¾ in) or a little more long. Flowers appear in early summer, pale blue, about 8 mm (⁷⁄₁₆ in) wide, in racemes, near the tips of the stems. A good rock garden plant; needs sun and a very fertile, porous soil. Propagate by division in spring.

Veronica prostrata 'Rosea'
SCROPHULARIACEAE

A most attractive cultivar, very similar to the species in growth, foliage and flowering. The bright pink flowers are a most distinctive feature and are borne in fairly compact spikes throughout much of the summer. Well suited to the rock garden, and can also be grown in an alpine house. Propagate by division or from seed sown in spring.

Vinca minor
APOCYNACEAE

A trailing plant, native to the Mediterranean region of Europe. The stems root at the nodes, subsequently forming large mats. Leaves elliptic, glossy green, to 4 cm (1½ in) long, borne on stems to 60 cm (24 in) in length. Flowers appear in spring and early summer, bluish-purple, mauve or white, to 3 cm (1¼ in) across, with blunt petals. Suited to the rock garden, but has a preference for partial shade. Succeeds in ordinary garden soil. Propagate by division in autumn.

Viola calcarata
VIOLACEAE

A miniature pansy, 5 – 8 cm (2 – 3 in) high, found wild in the Alps of central Europe. Leaves are small, somewhat heart-shaped, dark green, often slightly hairy. Flowers appear in summer and vary in colour from white to rich deep violet, always solitary. In the wild it flourishes best if set in rock crevices (as shown), so it is obviously suited to the rock garden. Needs a moderately rich soil, preferably with plenty of small grit added. Propagate from seed in spring.

Viola cornuta var. minor
VIOLACEAE

A small, clump-forming plant, which forms a dense mat of bright green leaves. Like the species, it is found wild in the Pyrenees. The ovate green leaves hardly exceed 3 – 4 cm (1¼ – 1½ in) in length and become tufted. The clear blue flowers appear in midsummer, scarcely more than 3 cm (1¼ in) in diameter, and borne on stems 5 – 7 cm (2 – 2¾ in) long. Prefers partially calcareous soil and seems to produce the best results if given slight shade. Propagate by division or from seed.

Viola cretica
VIOLACEAE

A low-growing, slightly hairy leaved, perennial species, found only in wooded areas and rocky places on the mountains of Crete. Leaves, dark green, more or less oval, form a basal tuft. Flowers, pale to deep mauve, about 2 cm (¾ in) across, fragrant, appear in early spring. Can be successfully grown in a rock garden in a somewhat sheltered position. Propagates easily from seed, freshly harvested.

Viola labradorica var. purpurea
VIOLACEAE

A mat-forming, low-growing species from northerly parts of North America and Greenland. Plants are not likely to exceed 10 cm (4 in) high. The typical viola-like, orbicular, cordate leaves are to 3 cm (1¼ in) long, green and almost totally suffused with deep purple. Flowers generally appear in spring, pale purplish-blue to about 1.5 cm (⅝ in) wide. A bright position is advisable and a slightly moisture-retentive soil. Propagate by division or from seed.

Viola odorata
VIOLACEAE

The sweet violet. A species native to many parts of Europe, including Britain, also Asia and north Africa. A stoloniferous plant, which multiplies freely to form dense mats. The heart-shaped, orbicular green leaves are to 7 cm (2 in) long, forming loose tufts, borne on runners, which root at the tips. The fragrant violet-purple or white flowers are about 1.5 cm (⅝ in) across, appearing in early spring and extending well into summer. Needs enriched garden soil and a position in sun or partial shade. Propagate by division or from seed in spring or autumn.

Watsonia aletoides
IRIDACEAE

A deciduous, cormous plant, native to coastal hill sides in Cape Province, South Africa. Leaves, 4 – 6 in number, are basal, erect, narrow and to about 30 cm (12 in) long. The flowering stem, to 60 cm (24 in) high, has a many flowered terminal spike of salmon pink flowers, each about 5 cm (2 in) long. Suitable for the rock garden; needs good light, an enriched, permeable soil and protection from excessive moisture in winter. Propagate from cormlets or from seed in early spring.

Watsonia meriana
IRIDACEAE

A deciduous, cormous plant, varying in height from 30 cm (12 in) upwards, found in the wild at altitudes to 1,750 m (5,700 ft) in many parts of Cape Province and Natal, South Africa, often in marshy areas. Leaves erect, slender, arranged in a fan-shape. Flowers 6 – 8 cm (2½ – 3 in) long, in a variety of colours – from white, pinkish, red to mauve – borne in early summer on a many flowered spike. Can be grown in the rock garden if planted deep in rich soil. Propagate from cormlets or from seed.

Weldenia candida
COMMELINACEAE

The sole species of this genus, originating from Mexico and central America, where it is reputed to be confined to extinct volcanic country. It has a fleshy rootstock, which each year produces tufts of strap-shaped, dark green, pointed leaves, to 15 cm (6 in) tall, which remain in the form of a basal rosette. Flowers throughout much of summer, white, cup-shaped, continuing in succession for weeks on end. A plant for the alpine house; needs a peaty, loamy mix. Keep dry during dormancy. Propagate from root cuttings in autumn.

Whiteheadea bifolia
LILIACEAE

A perennial bulbous plant originating from north-western Cape Province, South Africa, and south-western Namibia, in shady, rocky areas on hill sides. The leaves are in opposite pairs, to 30 cm (12 in) long, broadly ovate. Individual white flowers in summer, cup-shaped, about 1 cm (½ in) wide, on a dense spike with longer greenish bracts. Essentially a plant for the alpine house; needs a sunny site and very porous, slightly calcareous soil with added leaf mould. Propagates best from seed sown soon after harvesting, temperature 15 °C (59 °F).

Witsenia maura
IRIDACEAE

The sole species of the genus, found in moist areas at high altitudes in southwestern Cape Province, South Africa. It has a caudex-like rootstock. Leaves distichous, ribbed, clustered at the tips of the branches of this rather woody plant. Flowers appear in summer, on stems to 50 cm (20 in) or more long, tubular perianth tube 5 cm (2 in) long, yellow below, dark blue above, the petals about 1.5 cm (⅝in) long, covered with yellowish hairs. A rare species for the alpine house; needs a moisture-retentive, rich soil. Propagate from seed, freshly harvested.

Zephyranthes candida
AMARYLLIDACEAE

A bulbous species growing up to about 20 cm (8 in) high, introduced from Uruguay and Argentina, where it is found in moist grassland. Leaves evergreen, somewhat grass-like, 20 – 30 cm (8 – 12 in) long, bright, shiny green. Flowers funnel-shaped, white, tinged greenish in the centre, to about 4 cm (1½ in) across, borne terminally. Generally considered hardy, useful for the rock garden; needs a porous, fertile soil. After flowering in autumn allow the soil to partially dry out for a while. Propagate from offsets or seed.

Zephyranthes grandiflora
AMARYLLIDACEAE

A small bulbous species found wild in parts of Central America, including southern Mexico. The long, slender leaves, recurve freely, 6 – 8 mm (⁵⁄₁₆ – ⁷⁄₁₆in) wide, often 30 cm (12 in) or more long. The scapes are more or less erect, to about 20 cm (8 in) tall, bearing large, pinkish-reddish, white-striped flowers to 10 cm (4 in) long, the petals widely spreading, in early autumn. It can only be considered half-hardy, so is best kept in an alpine house; needs a fairly rich, peaty soil. Propagate by division of offsets or from seed in spring.

Zigadenus fremontii
LILIACEAE

A tall-growing, bulbous species, found growing wild in northern California and southern Oregon, USA, in scrub on low hill sides. Leaves slender, strap-shaped, to 35 cm (14 in) or more long, 1 – 3 cm (½ – 1¼ in) wide. Flowers appear in early summer, creamy greenish-yellow with a green nectary, and 2 cm (¾ in) wide, in racemes. After flowering plants should be allowed to become dormant while the flowers and leaves wither. Needs a porous, gritty, enriched soil, in sun. The var. *minor* is similar but shorter. Propagate from seed in spring, temperature 15 °C (59 °F).

Zygophyllum simplex
ZYGOPHYLLACEAE

A mat-forming, prostrate, succulent species, branching from the base, native to high ground in Saudi Arabia. Leaves are cylindrical, fleshy, obtuse, to about 1 cm (½ in) long. Flowers, very small, yellow, appear in early summer and are followed by a seed capsule only 2 mm (⅛ in) in diameter. Best suited to alpine house culture; needs a very porous, mineral-based, enriched soil and a position in full sun. Propagate by division or from seed, freshly harvested.

GLOSSARY

alternate Leaves that are arranged alternately up a stem, rather than being opposite or arranged in a whorl.

appressed Pressed close to, or flat against, a surface.

areole A cushion-like growing point of a cactus.

basal Leaves that rise directly from the bulb or rootstock rather than being borne on the stem.

bilabiate Divided into two lips, as in the antirrhinum.

bract A modified or reduced leaf that is adjacent to the stalk of a flower or the flower itself.

bulbil A small bulb produced on the stem or in a leaf axil, or in the inflorescence.

bulblet A small bulb produced around the parent bulb.

calcareous Containing or resembling calcium carbonate; chalky.

caudex The fleshy or woody section that develops at or below ground level and that possess terminal growing points.

cauline Of or growing on a stem.

cilia Small, fine hairs.

corm A globular stem base, swollen with food and surrounded by papery scale leaves; as in the crocus.

corymb An inflorescence in the form of a flat-topped flower cluster, with the oldest flowers at the periphery.

cyme An inflorescence in which the first flower is the terminal bud of the main stem, with subsequent flowers developing as terminal buds of lateral stems.

decumbent A stem, lying flat, with the tip growing upwards.

dentate Toothed.

distichous Arranged in two vertical rows.

ensiform Sword-shaped.

entire Used to describe leaves with smooth margins.

farinose Having a mealy appearance.

glabrous Smooth; with a covering of wool or hair.

glaucous Covered with greyish, wax-like bloom.

involucre A series of bracts surrounding an inflorescence, forming an envelope.

labellum The lip, or lowest of the three petals, forming the corolla of an orchid.

labiate Having a lip.

lanceolate Tapered towards each end, with the widest point below the centre.

monocarpic A plant that produces fruit once only before dying.

opposite Leaves that are borne as a pair, one on each side of a stem.

panicle An inflorescence with several flowers.

pilose Covered with fine, soft hairs.

pinnate A compound leaf with the leaflets growing opposite each other in pairs on either side of the stem.

plicate Pleated; folded in a fan-like fashion.

procumbent Trailing or resting on the ground.

pruinose Covered with a wax-like bloom.

pubescent Densely covered with minute, fine hairs or down.

raceme A number of individual flowers forming an inflorescence, each flower on its own stalk or pedicel.

rhizome A stem formation at or below ground level.

rosulate Rosette-like.

sessile Having no stalk; attached directly by the base.

spadix The thick, fleshy, pencil-like organ of the arum 'flower'.

spathe A large bract, often subtending a bud.

spathulate or **spatulate** Spoon-shaped in outline.

stolon A horizontal stem above or below ground, which roots and produces new plants.

subtended A bract, stem and so forth with a bud or similar growing in its axil.

terete Cylindrical and tapering.

tomentose Densely covered in fine hairs.

trifid Divided into three parts or lobes.

villous Covered with hairs.

zygomorphic Having a single plane of symmetry so that the two halves are mirror images.

INDEX OF SYNONYMS
AND ALTERNATIVE NAMES

Synonym	Main Entry
Acidanthera murieliae	Gladiolus callianthus
Aizopsis aizoon	Sedum aizoon
Aizopsis kamtschaticum variegatum	Sedum kamtschaticum variegatum
Albuca major	Albuca canadensis
Allium albopilosum	Allium christophii
Alium ostrowskianum	Allium oreophilum
Allium senescens ssp. montanum	Allium montanum
Alyssum maritima	Lobularia maritima
Amaryllis hallii	Lycoris squamigera
Androsace imbricata	Androsace vandellii
Androsace primuloides watkinsii	Androsace limprichtii
Androsace sarmentosa watkinsii	Androsace limprichtii
Arenaria nevadensis	Arenaria tetraquetra 'Granatensis'
Arenaria tetraquetra amabilis	Arenaria tetraquetra 'Granatensis'
Arenaria verna	Minuartia verna
Argyranthemum frutescens	Chrysanthemum frutescens
Astericus maritimus	Odontospermum maritimum
Bolax glebaria	Azorella trifurcata
Brodiaea bridgesii	Triteleia bridgesii
Campanula allionii	Campanula alpestris
Campanula hercegovina	Campanula herzegovinensis
Campanula pusilla	Campanula cochleariifolia
Caralluma lutea ssp. *lutea*	Orbeopsis lutea ssp. lutea
Caralluma lutea ssp. *vaga*	Orbeopsis lutea ssp. vaga
Centaurea conifera	Leuzia conifera
Cistus ladanifer latifolius	Cistus palhinhae
Cleretum bellidiformis	Dorotheanthus bellidiformis
Convolvulus altheoides ssp. tenuissimus	Convolvulus elegantissimus
Convolvulus mauritanicus	Convolvulus sabatius
Corydalis malkensis	Corydalis caucasica var. alba
Cotyledon oppositifolia	Chiastophyllum oppositifolium
Crocus zonatus	Crocus kotschyanus
Cyanotis somaliensis	Cyanotis lanata
Cyclamen intaminatum	Cyclamen cilicium var. intaminatum
Cyclamen neopolitanum	Cyclamen hederifolium
Cyclamen orbiculatum	Cyclamen coum
Cyclamen vernum	Cyclamen coum
Cypella hauthalii	Herbertia hauthalii

Synonym	Main Entry
Cytisus scoparius var. prostratus	Cytisus scoparius var. maritimus
Daphne candida	Daphne alpina
Dianthus alpinus	Dianthus brachyanthus var. alpinus
Diosphaera asperuloides	Trachelium asperuloides
Diplocyatha ciliata	Orbea ciliata
Dracocephalum argunense	Dracocephalum ruyschiana var. speciosum
Echium lycopsis	Echium plantagineum
Edraianthus caudatus	Edraianthus dalmaticus
Erica carnea	Erica herbacea
Erigeron alpinus	Erigeron borealis
Erigeron multifidus	Erigeron compositus
Erinacea pungens	Erinacea anthyllis
Euryops evansii	Euryops acraeus
Evansia tectorum	Iris tectorum
Fritillaria carduchorum	Fritillaria minuta
Fritillaria imperialis var. chitralensis	Fritillaria chitralensis
Fritillaria minor	Fritillaria ruthenica
Fritillaria montana	Fritillaria orientalis
Fritillaria severtozovii	Fritillaria sewerzowii
Fritillaria tenella	Fritillaria orientalis
Genista sagittalis var. minor	Genista sagittalis var. delphinensis
Genistella delphinensis	Genista delphinensis
Gentiana kochiana	Gentiana acaulis
Geum coccineum	Geum chiloense
Geum quellyon	Geum chiloense
Globularia bellidifolia	Globularia meridionalis
Gypsophila prostrata var. fratensis	Gypsophila repens
Helianthemum oelandicum ssp. alpestre	Helianthemum alpestre
Helichrysum virgineum	Helichrysum sibthorpii
Hepatica triloba	Hepatica nobilis
Herbertia brasiliensis	Kelissa brasiliensis
Herbertia unguiculata	Onira unguiculata
Homeria collina	Homeria breyniana var. aurantiaca
Hyacinthella hispida var. glabrescens	Hyacinthella glabrescens
Hyacinthus amethystinus	Brimeura amethystina
Hyacinthus comosus var. plumosum	Leopoldia comosa var. plumosum
Impatiens congolensis	Impatiens niamniamensis
Iris chamaeiris	Iris lutescens
Iris fimbriata	Iris japonica
Iris nepalensis	Iris decora

Synonym	Main Entry	Synonym	Main Entry
Iris orchioides	Iris bucharica	*Sarracenia variolaris*	Sarracenia minor
Iris pumila ssp. *attica*	Iris attica	*Saxifraga aizoon*	Saxifraga paniculta
Iris rubromarginata	Iris suaveolens	*Saxifraga aspera*	Saxifraga bryoides
Iris tuberosa	Hermodactylus tuberosus	var. *bryoides*	
Ixiolirion montanum	Ixiolirion ledebourii	*Saxifraga*	Saxifraga juniperifolia
Jovibarba heuffelii	Sempervivum heuffelii	*santa-macedonica*	'Macedonica'
Jovibarba sobolifera	Sempervivum	*Scilla adlamii*	Ledebouria cooperi
	soboliferum	*Scilla amethystina*	Scilla litardieri
Juno orchidioides	Iris orchidioides	*Scilla chinensis*	Scilla scilloides
		Scilla mischtschenkoana	Scilla tubergeniana
Lachenalia tricolor	Lachenalia aloides	*Sedum album*	Oreosedum album
Ledebouria socialis	Scilla violacea	*Sedum chrysanthum*	Rosularia pallida
Leucanthemum vulgare	Chrysanthemum	*Sedum sempervivam*	Rosularia sempervivoides
	leucanthemum	*Sedum sediforme*	Petrosedum sediforme
Lewisia bernardina	Lewisia nevadensis	*Sedum spectabile*	Hylotelephium spectabile
Linaria cymbalaria	Cymbalaria muralis	*Sempervivum alpinum*	Sempervivum tectorum
Lithospermum fruticosum	Lithodora fruticosa		ssp. alpinum
Lycoris africana	Lycoris aurea	*Sempervivum armenum*	Sempervivum
			globuliferum
Mazus rugosus	Mazus reptans	*Sempervivum calcareum*	Sempervivum tectorum
Merendera caucasia	Merendera trigyna		ssp. calcareum
Merendera montana	Merendera pyrenaica		monstrosum
Merendera nivalis	Merendera trigyna	*Sempervivum funckii*	Semperivium montanum
Mesembryanthemum	Dorotheanthus		ssp. stiriacum
criniflorum	bellidiformis	*Sempervivum fuscum*	Sempervivum tectorum
Micromeria corsica	Teucrium marum		ssp. alpinum
Muscari comosum	Leopoldia comosa	*Sempervivum* 'Hayling'	Sempervivum
Muscari comosum	Leopoldia comosa		'Commander Hay'
var. *plumosum*	var. plumosum	*Sempervivum hirtum*	Jovibarba hirta
Muscari moschatum	Muscarimia	*Sempervivum tectorum*	Sempervivum
var. *flavum*	macrocarpum	var. *atlanticum*	atlanticum
		Silene cucubalus	Silene vulgaris
Narcissus juncifolius	Narcissus assoanus	*Sisyrinchium bermudiana*	Sisyrinchium
Nemastylis dugesii	Tigridia dugesii		angustifolium
Nierembergia rivularis	Nierembergia repens	*Sisyrinchium cuspidatum*	Sisyrinchium arenarium
		Sisyrinchium macounii	Sisyrinchium idahoense
Oenothera taraxacifolia	Oenothera acaulis	var. *album*	var. segetum
Oreosedum coeruleum	Sedum coeruleum	*Sisyrinchium niveum*	Sisyrinchium albidum
Oreosedum dasyphyllum	Sedum dasyphyllum	*Sisyrinchium*	Orthrosanthes
Oreosedum dasyphyllum	Sedum dasyphyllum	*polystachyum*	polystachus
var. *glanduliferum*	var. glanduliferum	*Sisyrinchium striatum*	Phaiophleps nigricans
Oxalis cernua	Oxalis pes-caprae	*Sparaxis wattii*	Synnotia variegata
		Spiraea hendersonii	Petrophytum hendersonii
Pelargonium tricolor	Pelargonium violarium	*Spraguea multiceps*	Calyptridium umbellatum
Penstemon crassifolius	Penstemon fruticosus	*Spraguea umbellata*	Calyptridium umbellatum
Penstemon gordonii	Penstemon glaber	*Stapelia dinteri*	Tridentea dinteri
Penstemon menziesii	Penstemon davidsonii	*Stapelia longipes*	Tridentea longipes
Physoplexis comosa	Phyteuma comosum	*Stenomesson coccineum*	Stenomesson variegatum
Pimelea coarctata	Pimelea prostrata	*Stenomesson incarnatum*	Stenomesson variegatum
Pleione bulbocodioides	Pleione formosana	*Sternbergia lutea*	Sternbergia sicula
'Alba'	alba	var. *angustifolia*	
Pleione bulbocodioides	Pleione formosana		
'Blush of Dawn'		*Tanacetum argenteum*	Achillea argentea
Pleione bulbocodioides	Pleione limprichtii	*Tanacetum coccineum*	Chrysanthemum
'Limprichtii'		'Kelway's Glorious'	coccineum
Primula helvetica 'Alba'	Primula x pubescens alba		'Kelway's Glorious'
Pterocephalus părnassi	Pterocephalus perennis	*Tulipa biflora*	Tulipa polychroma
Ptilotrichum spinosum	Alyssum spinosum	*Tulipa pulchella*	Tulipa humilis
Puschkinia libanotica	Puschkinia scilloides	var. *humilis*	
Pyrethrum roseum	Chrysanthemum	*Tulipa pulchella*	Tulipa violacea
'Kelway's Glorious'	coccineum	var. *violacea*	
	'Kelway's Glorious'		
Rhodanthemum	Chrysanthemum	*Veronica rupestris*	Veronica prostrata
hosmariense	hosmariense		

BIBLIOGRAPHY

Alpine Flora
    by H. Correvon and P.H. Robert
Alpine Flowers
    by Gudio Moggi, London, Macdonald, 1985
Alpine Flowers of Britain and Europe
    by Christopher Grey-Wilson and Marjorie Blamey,
    London, Collins, 1979
Alpine Flowers of New Zealand
    by A.F. Marks and Nancy M. Adams
Asiatic Primulas
    by Roy Green, Woking,
    Alpine Garden Society, 1976
The Bulb Book
    by Martyn Rix and Roger Phillips,
    London, Pan,1981
The Bulb Book
    by P. Schauenberg, London, Warne, 1965
Bulbs
    by Christopher Grey-Wilson and Brian Mathew,
    London, Collins, 1981
Cacti
    by J. Borg, Poole, Dorset, Blandford, 1976
Cactus Lexicon
    by Curt Backeberg, Poole, Dorset, Blandford, 1977
Campanulas
    by Clifford Crook, London, Country Life, 1951
Collins Guide to Bulbs
    by Patrick M. Synge, London, Collins, 1961
Color Dictionary of Garden Plants
    New York. McGraw-Hill
Dwarf Bulbs
    by Brian Mathew, London, Batsford, 1973
The Encyclopedia of Cacti
    by Cullman, Götz and Gröner,
    Sherborne, Dorset, Alphabooks, 1986
Flora Europea
    by T.G. Tutin and others, Cambridge,
    Cambridge University Press, 1964–76
Flowers of Europe
    by O. Polunin, London,
    Oxford University Press, 1969

Flora of Japan
    by Jisaburo Ohwi, Washington, DC, 1965
Flora of South Africa
    by R. Marloth, Cape Town, 1913–32
Flora of the British Isles
    by A.R. Clapham, T.G. Tutin and E.F. Warburg,
    Cambridge, Cambridge University Press, 1962
Flowers of the Mediterranean
    by Anthony Huxley and Oleg Polunin, London,
    Chatto & Windus, 1965
Handbook of Crocus and Colchicum
    by E.A. Bowles, London, Bodley Head, 1952
Handbook of Cultivated Sedums
    by R.L. Evans, Northwood, Middlesex,
    Science Reviews, 1983
The Illustrated Encyclopedia of Cacti
    by C. Innes and C. Glass, London, Headline, 1991
Illustrated Flora of the Pacific States
    by Leroy Abrams, Stanford, CA,
    Stanford University Press, 1952
Lexicon of Succulent Plants
    by H. Jacobsen, Poole, Dorset, Blandford, 1974
Manual of Alpine Plants
    by Will Ingwersen, London, Cassell, 1991
Mountain Flowers
    by Anthony Huxley, Poole, Dorset, Blandford, 1986
Orchideen Europas
    by E. and 0. Danesch, Hallwag, 1969
Plant Jewels of the High Country
    by H.E. Payne, Columbia, CA, Pine Cone, 1972
Sedums of North America North of the Mexican Plateau
    by R.T. Clausen, Ithaca, NY,
    Cornell University Press, 1976
The Subgenus Tephrocactus
    by G. Leighton-Boyce and J. Iliff, London,
    Succulent Plant Trust, 1973
Wild Flowers of the United States
    by H.W. Rickett, New York, McGraw-Hill, 1966–75
The World of Iridaceae
    by Clive Innes, Ashington, West Sussex,
    Holly Gate International, 1985

PICTURE ACKNOWLEDGEMENTS

Key: *T* top, *C* centre, *B* bottom, *L* left, *R* right.

All photographs © Clive Innes except for the following, which are © Peter Stiles, who would like to thank the Royal Botanic Gardens, Kew, and the Royal Horticultural Society's Wisley Gardens for their help in facilitating the photography of cultivated plants.

13TL, 13TC, 13TR, 13BC, 13BR, 14TL, 14TR, 15TC, 15TR, 15BR, 16TL, 16TC, 16BR, 17TC, 18BL, 20TC, 20TR, 20BC, 21TL, 21TR, 21BC, 21BR, 22TL, 22TC, 22TR, 22BL, 22BC, 23BL, 23BC, 23BR, 23TL, 23TC, 23TR, 24BL, 24BR, 24TL, 24TC, 24TR, 25TL, 26TR, 27TC, 27TR, 27BL, 27BR, 28TL, 28TR, 28BC, 29TC, 29TR, 29BL, 29BC, 29BR, 30TL, 30TC, 30TR, 30BR, 31BL, 33TR, 33BR, 34TL, 34TC, 34BL, 35TL, 35TC, 35TR, 35BC, 37TL, 37TC, 37BC, 37BR, 38TL, 38TC, 38TR, 38BL, 38BC, 38BR, 39TL, 39TC, 39BC, 40TL, 40TC, 40BC, 40BR, 41TC, 42TL, 42BC, 43BC, 43BR, 44TC, 44BR, 46TL, 46BR, 48TR, 48BL, 48BC, 48BR, 49TC, 49TR, 49BL, 49BC, 49BR, 50TC, 50TR, 51TL, 51TC, 51BL, 51BC, 51BR, 52TC, 53TC, 53BL, 53BC, 53BR, 54BL, 54TL, 54TR, 55BC, 55BR, 57BL, 57BC, 57TR, 58BL, 58BR, 59BL, 59TL, 59TC, 59TR, 60TL, 60TR, 60BL, 60BC, 60BR, 61TC, 61TR, 61BL, 61BC, 61BR, 62TL, 62TC, 62TR, 62BL, 62BC, 64BR, 65TL, 65BL, 65BC, 65BR, 66BL, 66BC, 66BR, 66TC, 66TR, 67TL, 67TC, 67TR, 67BL, 67BC, 67BR, 68BL, 68BC, 69TR, 70BC, 72BR, 73BL, 73BC, 73TL, 73TC, 73TR, 74BL, 74BC, 74BR, 74TL, 74TC, 74TR, 75BC, 75TL, 75TC, 75TR, 77TC, 77TR, 77BL, 77BC, 77BR, 78TC, 78TR, 78BL, 78BC, 79BC, 79BR, 79TC, 80TC, 82TC, 82TR, 83BL, 83BC, 85TL, 85TC, 85TR, 86BL, 86BC, 86BR, 86TC, 86TR, 87BL, 87BC, 87TC, 87TR, 88TL, 88TC, 89TL, 90TL, 90TR, 90BR, 91BL, 91BC, 92TC, 92TR, 92BC, 92BR, 94TL, 94TC, 94BL, 94BC, 94BR, 95TL, 95TC, 95TR, 96BC, 96TC, 97TC, 98TL, 98TR, 98BC, 98BR, 99TL, 99TC, 99BC, 100TR, 100BL, 101TR, 103TL, 103TC, 104BL, 104BC, 105BB,

105TL, 105TC, 106TL, 106TC, 106TR, 106BL, 106BC, 106BR, 107TL, 107TC, 107TR, 107BL, 107BC, 107BR, 108BR, 109TL, 109TC, 109BC, 110BC, 111TL, 111TC, 114BL, 114BC, 114BR, 115TL, 115BL, 115BC, 115BR, 116BL, 116BC, 116BR, 116TL, 116TR, 117BC, 117BR, 118TL, 118TR, 118BL, 118BC, 118BR, 119BC, 119TL, 119TC, 120TR, 120BR, 121TC, 123TC, 123TR, 124TL, 127TC, 127TR, 127BL, 127BC, 128TC, 128BL, 129TL, 129TC, 129BC, 129BR, 130TL, 130TC, 130BL, 130BC, 132BR, 133BL, 133BC, 133BR, 134TL, 134TC, 134TR, 134BL, 134BC, 135BC, 135BR, 136TL, 136TR, 136BL, 136BR, 137TL, 137TR, 137BL, 137BC, 137BR, 138TL, 138TC, 138TR, 138BL, 138BC, 139TL, 139BL, 139BR, 140TL, 140TC, 140TR, 140BL, 140BC, 140BR, 141TL, 141TC, 141TR, 141BC, 142BL, 142BC, 142BR, 142TL, 142TC, 143TL, 143TC, 143TR, 143BL, 143BC, 143BR, 144TL, 144TR, 144BL, 145TC, 145TR, 145BL, 145BR, 146BC, 146BR, 148TL, 148TC, 148TR, 149BL, 149BC, 149BR, 150TL, 150BL, 151TL, 151TC, 151TR, 151BL, 153TL, 153TC, 153BL, 154BR, 154TL, 154TC, 154TR, 155BL, 155BC, 155BR, 155TL, 155TR, 156TL, 156TC, 156BL, 156BR, 157TL, 157TC, 157TR, 157BL, 157BC, 158TL, 158TR, 158BR, 159TC, 159TR, 159BR, 160TL, 160TC, 160TR, 160BL, 160BR, 161TC, 161TR, 161BL, 161BC, 161BR, 162TL, 162BL, 162BC, 162BR, 163TL, 163TC, 163TR, 163BC, 163BR, 164TL, 164TC, 164TR, 164BL, 164BC, 164BR, 165TL, 165TR, 165BL, 165BC, 165BR, 166TL, 166TC, 166TR, 166BL, 167BL, 167BC, 167BR, 168TC, 169TR, 170TC, 170BC, 170BR, 172TC, 172TR, 173TL, 173TR, 175TL, 175TC, 175TR, 175BC, 175BR, 176TL, 176TC, 176BL, 176BC, 176BR, 177TL, 177TC, 178TC, 178TR, 178BL, 178BC, 179BR, 180TL, 180BR, 181TC, 181TR, 181BL, 181BC, 181BR, 184TC, 184BL, 185BC, 184BR, 185TL, 185TC,